Marx and Teilhard

MARX AND TEILHARD

Two Ways to the New Humanity

Richard Lischer

ORBIS BOOKS
Maryknoll, New York 10545

The Catholic Foreign Mission Society of America (Maryknoll) recruits and trains people for overseas missionary service. Through Orbis Books Maryknoll aims to foster the international dialogue that is essential to mission. The books published, however, reflect the opinions of their authors and are not meant to represent the official position of the Society.

Library of Congress Cataloging in Publication Data

Lischer, Richard.
  Marx and Teilhard.

  Includes bibliographical references.
  1. Man (Christian theology) 2. Marx, Karl, 1818-
1883. 3. Teilhard de Chardin, Pierre. I. Title.
BT701.2.L54 233 79-4438
ISBN 0-88344-303-1

To
Tracy Kenyon Lischer

CONTENTS

ABBREVIATIONS

(All primary sources and other works cited appear in the notes at the end of the book.)

KARL MARX AND FREDERICK ENGELS

Collected Works: Marx and Engels

Werke   *Werke,* 41 vols.

Collections: Marx and Engels

Brit.	*On Britain*
Corres.	*Selected Correspondence*
Relig.	*On Religion*
Sel. Wks. I, II	*Selected Works,* vols. I, II

Individual Works: Marx and Engels

Germ.	*The German Ideology,* Pts. I & III
Germ. II	*The German Ideology,* Pt. II
Holy	*The Holy Family*
Manif.	*Manifesto of the Communist Party*

Collections: Marx

Essays	*Selected Essays*
Letters	*Letters to Dr. Kugelmann*

Individual Works: Marx

Capt. I, II, III	*Capital,* vols. I, II, III
Grund.	*Grundrisse*
MSS.	*Economic and Philosophical Manuscripts* (Paris Manuscripts)
Pov. Phil.	*The Poverty of Philosophy*
Pre-Capt.	*Pre-Capitalist Economic Formations*

PIERRE TEILHARD DE CHARDIN

Collections: Teilhard and Blondel

B-T	*Correspondence*

Collections

AE	*Activation of Energy*
AM	*The Appearance of Man*
BE	*Building the Earth*
CE	*Christianity and Evolution*
FM	*The Future of Man*
HE	*Human Energy*
HU	*Hymn of the Universe*
LLZ	*Letters to Leontine Zanta*
LT	*Letters from a Traveller*
LTF	*Letters to Two Friends*
MM	*The Making of a Mind: Letters from a Soldier-Priest 1914–1919*
SC	*Science and Christ*
VP	*The Vision of the Past*
WTW	*Writings in Time of War*

Individual Works

MD	*Le milieu divin*
MPN	*Man's Place in Nature*
PM	*The Phenomenon of Man*

PREFACE

This book appears as a token of a long-held interest in Christianity's intersection with philosophy. Christian theology has never seemed so fascinating to me as when it is conversing or colliding with other disciplines or worldviews. For then theology does its job, not only of expounding catholic doctrine for the church, but also of road testing the strength and resiliency of those doctrines in the world where the church, after all, still lives and works. The roots of this book lie in the European Christian-Marxist dialogue of the 1960s, a dialogue which, even after the news media tired of it and the Vietnamese War chilled it, today continues on academic, political, and neighborhood levels. The present study is also nourished by my interest in the philosophy and theology of history, especially the overwhelming influence of Christian thought in the formation of western, including Marxist and evolutionary, theories of history. So pervasive is this influence that in dialogue with what are usually considered rival systems of thought, Christian theology meets itself coming and going, often in the ill-fitting disguise of anti-idolatries, self-redemptive processes, open futures, and the like. Sorting out the presence and contribution of Christianity in this complex of ideas, it seems to me, remains an exciting and useful project.

Luther and Lutheran ideas surface in every chapter of the book. Whether the Luther/Marx motif reflects only my own sectarian way of looking at things, or an authentic and heretofore recessed accent in Marx studies must be left for the reader to decide.

The book is about what was once known as the doctrine of man. So central is this organizing point and so inadequately does our language allow for alternative usage that much of the language of this book, despite conscientious revision, remains sexist. For this defect, along with its other, graver companions, I bear sole responsibility.

I want publicly to acknowledge and thank Prof. Robert Bertram who, at Concordia Seminary, introduced me to the philosophy of history and encouraged me to continue in that field. The research for this study was made possible by a grant from the Lutheran World Federation. My thanks are due Prof. E. L. Mascall of King's College, the University of London, who guided the development of this study in its original form to a successful conclusion. Mme. René Croose-Parry of the Teilhard Centre for the Future of Man, London, kindly allowed me access to several of Teilhard's unpublished essays. Prof. D. M. MacKinnon of Cambridge, and Profs. Ulrich Simon, H. P. Owen, and Father George Vass, S.J., of London read the manuscript in whole or part, each offering with his criticism great encouragement and hospitality.

Portions of Chapters II, IV, and VI have appeared in *Religion in Life, The Irish Theological Quarterly,* and *The Christian Century* respectively.

Chapter I

INTRODUCTION: IDEALS AND POSTULATES

God is pure act without alloy of potentiality.

. . . Some intelligent being exists by whom all natural things are directed to their end; and this being we call God.

—St. Thomas Aquinas

Since the appearance of Karl Marx's critique of capitalist society, Christian theology has been responding, in diatribe, apologetic, and dialogue, to the political and philosophical movement which he founded. In the contemporary dialogue, Marxist thinkers have been drawing the vitality and often the heterodoxy of their positions not from Engels, Lenin, or Stalin, but from Marx's philosophy of man. Since the relatively recent discoveries of early Marxian manuscripts, a lively "back-to-Marx" movement has developed, especially among those who wish to establish the humanistic credentials of communism and reinstate Marxism in the philosophical marketplace. As the philosophical authority for Marxist participation in dialogue and, more importantly, as one whose foundation in and rejection of Judeo-Christian ideas to some extent shaped the form of his economic system, Karl Marx must be the controlling figure of this study. In response to his continuing influence, it will take up only those theological issues which he explicitly or implicitly incorporates into his analysis of human evil and its transformation.

History has welded the names of Marx and Engels with the result that many writers treat them as one. For our purposes Engels's work is useful only where it clarifies Marx's thought. The degree to which Engels distorted Marxian insight and extended it into full-blown dogma will become apparent in nearly every chapter of the book. Engels' own modest evaluation underscores Marx's pre-eminence: "What Marx accomplished I would not have achieved. Marx stood higher, saw further, and took a wider and quicker view than all the rest of us. Marx was a

1

genius; we others were at best talented. It [the movement] therefore rightly bears his name.''

No study of the relationship between Marxism and Christianity can afford to deal with a notion of monolithic communism or a general view of Christianity. In Pierre Teilhard de Chardin is crystalized much of that hope in man—yet on a different basis—which excited the dreams and struggles of Marx and which has been received by unprecedented numbers of non-Christians with respect and great sympathy. Teilhard is thus chosen as one of the foci of interpretation not merely for his intrinsic interest, which is considerable, but also for his unique suitability as a respondent to the theologically-oriented system of Marx.

The first person to recognize the similarities between the Marxian and Teilhardian doctrines of man was Teilhard himself. Following him, those interested in dialogue, comparative religion, and anticommunist polemics have not hesitated to juxtapose the names of Marx and Teilhard. In fact, awareness of their relationship has persisted largely as a fashionable juxtaposition of names, to which one might begin to add provocative elements of resemblance. Both exceeded their specializations through broader and more evocative beliefs about the nature of man and the role he is destined to play at the center of economic or evolutionary processes of development. Their interest in human wholeness, moreover, led them to expose and remove the barriers between the moral sciences and the more precise disciplines of economics and paleontology. Under their influence so-called natural developments in nature and society were electrified by moral imperatives. It is through the speculative side of their respective specialities that Marx and Teilhard have won the greatest number of followers, and, indeed, much of their scientific work has been called into question by less daring but more disinterested researchers in their fields.

Marx and Teilhard habitually disparaged philosophy while often in the same breath making sweeping philosophical generalizations about man. They were not philosophers in the traditional sense, and philosophical analysis of their work does not yield an infallible key to the greatness of their thought and its popular appeal. Marxian communism was not designed as a philosophy of man but as a strategy of politics and social change. Similarly, Teilhard represents something greater than a philosophy of man and nature, something which does not stand or fall by the coherence of his apologetics; for Christianity offers itself to all people as a complete life of worship which often transcends the logic of its greatest interpreters.

Finally, the unity of theory and practice peculiar to each writer's hope for human transformation extended to or perhaps originated in the integrity of his personal life. Thus, disdain for compromise led each away from academic careers into exile, isolation, frustration, and an enervating series of conflicts with the authorities over the right to disseminate their visions of man. In 1883 Marx died stateless and intestate in London, in the only European country capable of absorbing his influence and neutralizing his force. Teilhard died in 1955 in New York City, twice-exiled, sentenced by his church to twenty-eight years in China and America, far removed from the heady stimulation of his beloved Paris.

One of the core principles shared by Marxism and Teilhard's evolutionism is that to be human means to change. Humankind is continually forming, kneading, and recycling the stuff of its civilizations in pathos-laden hopes of growth and improvement. Beyond the growth in scientific and technological information, the renovation of selected institutions and the periodic shuffling of national real estate, lies the hope of a more extensive and permanent kind of change; for as long as man has been self-reflective he has been trying to change his own nature, to become someone he is not. Such a desire, with its totality of scope and fervor of devotion, encompasses a *way* of living and dying which invites description and analysis in religious terms. Hence, in the minds of many, communism and evolutionism constitute a way toward human transformation in no less authentic a sense than the religion of Jesus was "The Way" to its earliest adherents.

The new ways did not develop in isolation from the tenets and traditions of The Way. In discovering the relationship between Christianity, communism, and evolution we shall test the anthropocentric systems of Marx and Teilhard against the fundamental Christian doctrines which, in a variety of ways, gave them life and form. The aim of this book is not to determine Marx's opinion of religion or Teilhard's of Marx, as necessary as this background is, but rather first, to identify the theological implications of each system *according to the claims it makes for itself and within the limits of its own terminology;* second, to compare the implications and claims of each in the light of the other; and, finally, to relate such conclusions as are possible to the needs of living human beings. The aim of any such method is the choice of two men whose comparative evaluation will suggest a truth greater or at least other than that yielded by isolated analysis. In this case it is hoped that a comparison of the achievements and the shortcomings of Marx and Teilhard will contribute also to a clearer theological understanding of man.

PRELIMINARY PREJUDICES

With the gravity proper to any New Beginning in philosophy or theology, Karl Marx and Pierre Teilhard de Chardin announced the open-minded empiricism which was to characterize their investigation into the whole phenomenon of economic and evolutionary man. The early pages of *The German Ideology* promised the dissolution of dogma and its replacement by the purely empirical study of the human condition. Similarly, Teilhard's preface advertised *The Phenomenon of Man* as a scientific treatise exploring only an experimental law of recurrence, beyond which the author himself hesitates to venture. Yet the first line of affinity between Marx and Teilhard exists in the dogmatic presuppositions which both writers brought to their analyses of man. One of the purposes of this chapter is to show that, despite protestations of scientific objectivity, Marx and Teilhard harbored a set of similar assumptions concerning the developmental and social nature of man, and that the presence of these assumptions generally corroborates this statement of Karl Popper: "At no stage of scientific development do we begin without something in the nature of a theory, such as a hypothesis, or a prejudice, or a problem, . . . which in some way guides our observations."[1] Without an understanding of each man's "prejudice" we can neither do justice to the fullness of his thought nor, for that matter, hope to present an intelligible appraisal of the Marxian and Teilhardian doctrines of man.

Marxian Ideals

Karl Marx founded an empirical sociology based on the activity of real people; yet he measured that activity against an ideal Man who never existed. The ideal was shaped by the philosophy of left-Hegelianism and his experience in the early 1840s as editor of the *Rheinische Zeitung,* a position which afforded him his first taste of bourgeois repressiveness in the form of Prussian censorship. Before he had come into contact with the French proletariat, the ideal was fixed in the Paris Manuscripts *(Economic and Philosophical Manuscripts)* of 1844. Throughout the tedious years of economic research in the British Museum, and during his active involvement with the working men of Europe, Marx harbored a belief about man the historicity of which he never attempted to establish in a systematic way.

According to the Marxian view, man exists in a perpetual state of becoming. His earliest manuscripts agree in principle with the view which is axiomatic in the writings of Teilhard de Chardin. Nothing appears in the world of nature and history except by way of birth and development in a temporal succession, so that each element in the universe, including man, forms a link in a great chain of becoming. The full implications of man as a creature of evolution could not have been grasped by Marx at so close a range to the momentous announcements of the 1850s. Nevertheless, as early as 1844, Marx had a rudimentary knowledge of the evolution of man through the philosophy of Hegel and the scientific precursors of Darwin, and was able to write, "The whole of history is a preparation for 'man.' . . . History itself is a real part of *natural history*, of the development of nature into man."² This "conscious process of becoming" proceeds from man's satisfaction of animal needs and his alienation from the community to the appropriation of an authentic human nature in a communist society "which assimilates all the wealth of previous development." The *Origin of Species* was published in the same year as the *Critique of Political Economy*. But Marx, who by that time had committed himself to a life of economic research, displayed only casual interest in the implications of Darwin's theory for the communist movement. Any ideological use which might be made of the theory he left for Engels to decide.

Indeed, the young Marx was more concerned to elevate man from the animal kingdom than to implicate him in it. In order to do this he resorted to an idealized picture of man as a self-determined being whose activity amounts to a continual process of self-creation. This apotheosis of the self entailed a near essentialist belief in "freedom" which, the young editor wrote in 1842, "is so completely the essence of man, that its very opponents bring it into being when they struggle against its reality."³ At the heart of this belief lay the Hegelian notion of the evolution and struggle toward freedom of self-consciousness in all its spheres. "The German nations," wrote Hegel, "under the influence of Christianity, were the first to attain the consciousness that man, as man, is free: that it is the *freedom* of spirit which constitutes this essence." Hegel was not surprised that such a discovery was made under the influence of Christianity, since human freedom is derived from that absolute perfect Being who wills "nothing other than Himself—His own Will." And the nature of his will—his nature itself—is freedom.⁴

But to name Hegel or any other philosopher as the father of the Marxian ideal of humanity is to slight the fullness of the heritage which shaped Marx's thought. The ultimate source of Marx's ideal man is St. Thomas's unconditioned Being, whose unconditionedness is one of his perfections essential to his nature. It was from the Thomistic description of God, as mediated by Hegel, that Marx unconsciously derived the view of man as properly a subject and never an object. The importance of this observation is that it illumines Marx's appropriation, not of a philosopher here and there, but of a fundamental catholic teaching about God. In the manuscripts of 1844 then, years before the historico-materialist inversion of the Hegelian dialectic, Marx had already displaced Hegelian idealism by reassigning God-values to an ideal Man. Such was Marx's radical humanism: "To be radical is to grasp the root of the matter. For man the root is man himself. . . . The criticism of religion ends with the teaching that *man is the highest essence for man*."⁵ By this inversion Marx excised from his imaginary man all ontological influences of God, spirit, soul, or any core of spiritual identity and declared the "self-active" residue to be man as he ought to be.

The despiritualization of man resulted most notably in a redefinition of the human essence. It was no longer possible to penetrate the layers of human nature to find a person at the center. Substance was resolved into function, and, in keeping with the post-Renaissance view of nature, the essence of human nature was identified with its ongoing formation. In the traditional theology which had preceded this redefinition, reason, conscience, free will, and other elements were thought to comprise the nature but not the absolute humanity of man. This nature may be degraded to animality, integrated in the truly human, or exalted to the divine, depending upon the relationship of the person, the "inner man," or the "heart" with God and its fellow creatures. Only in this relationship—with him who separated *me* from my mother's womb, called *me* by his grace, who loved *me* and gave himself for *me*—does the person truly know itself and receive assurance of its incommunicable value.[6] In Marxian thought, however, there is no core unit of identity, neither an immanent nor a detachable essence of man, outside the ensemble of social needs and the sum of productive forces.

Any precise definition of man as a *human* being therefore must take into account many factors. Between man's consciousness, his identity in society, his language, his interaction with nature, and his modes of production, there exists an intimate relationship which defies chronological ordering. The invariable in this functional approach is the social nature of man. In order to make sense of the Paris Manuscripts, which were never meant for publication, we may distinguish between man's prehistorical struggle to humanize nature, described by Marx in abstract, philosophical language, and the economic expression of it in the productive cooperation which eventually evokes self-consciousness and language.

First, in the struggle to humanize nature, both Christianity and Marxism imbue corporate man with the power and responsibility of creation. Just as Adam includes the whole race of man, so the Marxian individual is "equally the whole in his 'species-life.' " The command given Adam to join God in the ongoing task of creation, however, is rightly executed only by those who recognize themselves as created beings, whose identities depend not upon nature or social relations but upon the creative word of God. The divine commission in Genesis presupposes a mutual understanding of the derivative nature of all human creativity, from the use of language in zoological identification and poetry to procreation and the inhabitation of the earth. In the Marxian theory of nature, as opposed to the account in Genesis, man begins on an equal footing with nature, neither blessed as its steward nor cursed as its victim, and embarks upon a Promethean development of his own being: "By thus acting on the external world and changing it, he at the same time changes his own nature. He develops his slumbering powers and compels them to act in obedience to his sway.''[7] Man enters a symbiotic relationship with nature for the purpose of production, and in so doing, not only creates but verifies his own physical identity. Marxian naturalism posits an interdependence between man and his environment which is reducible to nature's dependence upon itself. For, unlike the scholastic term *natura humana,* by which man is understood as a spiritual-bodily composite, ''nature'' here is opposed to spirit. With the term ''human nature'' Marx was describing nature in a human, and the human's consciousness of his existence in and as nature. The process of symbiosis occurs only as man strives with nature, puts his human stamp upon it, and finally makes of it his inorganic body. The ultimate result of this interchange between man and man and between man and nature is ''the veritable resurrection of nature, the realized naturalism of man and the realized humanism of nature.''[8]

From another perspective on the process of humanization we may observe in a less abstract form the social implications of early Marxian naturalism. Man becomes conscious of himself as a human being by comparing himself to others of his kind. More specifically, he first verifies his natural identity in his relationship with the opposite sex. Changes in the quality of this relationship indicate to him to what extent his natural needs have become human and inextricably bound to another person. Marx followed Feuerbach's understanding of man's self-recognition in the ''I-thou'' relationship with other people only to this point of self-verification. Here, even in the early Marx, the social relationship which ensues is a practical one, with little textual evidence to warrant the overemphasis placed on mutual love by a psychoanalyst and a theologian.[9] On the basis of *need* and not love, the Marxian man not only realizes his own existence, but begins satisfying those needs through production and exchange. Thus, the most important criterion for the true humanity of man remains self-consciousness, albeit a highly selective *function* of self-consciousness—production.

However basic the need which appears as the matrix of human consciousness, man soon supersedes crude need and makes all his activity an object of his will. This mental ability, along with man's recognition of himself as an embodiment and a symbol of his zoological group, constitutes man's *species-being.* Although Marx soon abandoned the term as idealistic in his critique of Feuerbach, he retained the freedom it implies throughout the work of his maturity. Aware of his own and his race's need, and able to plan for the future on the basis of the present and the past, man begins to produce his own and a share of his neighbors' means of subsistence. The instinctual creations of the anthill and the beehive give way to the prescience of social man. ''What distinguishes the worst architect from the best of bees is this, that the architect raises his structure in imagination before he erects it in reality.''[10] It is important to note that, with few exceptions, only in the early manuscripts did Marx emphasize man's ability to differentiate himself from his activity, to produce even when he is free from the necessity of basic need, and to create according to the laws of beauty. This is the idealized form of work or "self-activity" which is not merely a task but the human essence itself. For the mature Marx, who largely put aside the problem of aesthetics, the ideal held, and the grand theme of the freely wrought humanization of nature and society remained inextricably bound to the sociology and economics of work.

It was a short step for Marx from philosophy to economics, from the essentialism of the organic ideal, in which man humanizes nature by interacting with it, to the essentialism of the labor theory of value. Stated simply, this theory evaluates the worth of any article, including gold, according to the amount of abstract, that is, quantitatively measured labor invested in its production or refinement. In its expanded "relative form of value," the theory states that any single commodity may be expressed in terms of countless other commodities, the common denominator being undifferentiated labor. Since such an unending series of equations is unworkable, the relative form of value is expressed in the socially accepted form, money. Marx's application of the theory, as received from Adam Smith, Ricardo, and Hegel, rejected an economics based only on the laws of supply and demand, values, prices, and business cycles, that is, a view of economics as a natural process in which human beings play the role of mathematical quanta rather than conscious subjects. Instead, Marxism dictates an intimate working relationship between man and nature, in which the resultant objects or products are mystically imbued with human properties: "As values," Marx wrote, "all commodities are only definite masses of congealed labour time."[11] The theory has been widely repudiated as mysticism; but Marx's intent is clear. By means of the labor theory of value, he hoped to put flesh on the dialectical ideal of freedom in order to reassert the centrality of man in the hitherto inhuman subject of economics. Economics, like all nature, was now to have man as its mover, maker, and purposive goal.

Teilhardian Postulates

As a scientist interested only in reading what the phenomena declare about the development of man, Teilhard never permitted himself recourse to an ideal that lies outside the possibilities opened by the phenomena themselves. But he did admit to presuppositions or "postulates" that emerged from his interpretation of the phenomena and that now may be assumed without proof to be valid as a basis for argument and further philosophical and theological development. We may isolate two vast themes, or better, conditions, under which all his postulates are subsumed: Man is a participant in evolution and a creature related to God. At the beginning of his seminal essay "My Universe" (1924), Teilhard elaborated these themes in four postulates. Although differing in purpose and style, three of the four are compatible with the assumptions inherent in the young Marx's ideal of man.

The first postulate Teilhard entitled the "primacy of consciousness." By that, he advised his readers, he meant to say "the goodness of being."[12] Teilhard reserved the word "good" for that which is attested to be in the ascendency by its stage of evolutionary progress. Since he did not wish to affirm or believe in something that cannot, as it were, present its natural credentials, he first established the structural presence of consciousness as the "soul" or the "within" of the lowest of organisms. This form of consciousness, rudimentary as it is, makes the thing what it is, and in this sense already exercises a position of primacy and anticipates the dominant role consciousness plays in human beings. Both Marx and Teilhard stressed the liberating aspect of self-consciousness, which allows man to plan the development of his own being, and both placed the fullest development of being at the *telos* of their philosophies of man. Marx would have further agreed, in some sense, that "complete being is conscious being"[13] insofar as production and exchange and, later, revolution can only occur not as the results, but as the indivisible concomitants of heightened forms of consciousness. In his belief in the primacy of consciousness Teilhard, however, did not limit the consciousness of man to crucial functions in the shaping and reshaping of society, but set before the consciousness an open horizon of thought and experience leading to human unity and culminating in humankind's ecstatic assumption into the divine life.

The second postulate, "faith in life," introduced two beliefs by no means foreign to the substance of Marxian teaching: The universe "has a goal" and "cannot take the wrong road nor come to a halt in mid-journey."[14] The teleological principle built into the evolutionary process Teilhard later called the Law of Complexity-Consciousness, under which the increasing physico-chemical complexity of a material arrangement unfailingly entails a higher degree of psychism or "consciousness" in that arrangement. The totality of the process, from its biological to its historical phases, is motivated by numerous factors, including the natural coalescence of elements, the coalescence of stems, the spherical shape of the earth which causes the physical compression of peoples, and the psychical curvature of the mind. Such an outline of life's ascent toward consciousness and spirit via the ladder of created matter reproduces the scholastic teaching that "the tendency of matter is toward the highest and most perfect form to which it can attain.

. . . Since, therefore, the human soul is the summit of all generation, it is toward this that matter tends, as toward the highest form which it can achieve.''[15]

Marx, of course, would have rejected a teleological view of life and history which takes into account any form of spirit. In fact, he saw in Darwin's theory the doom of "teleology" in the natural sciences, by which he probably meant the religious view of creation and history as processes directed by divine interventions toward an already-revealed goal. What he did not understand at close range, however, was that the replacement of the mechanical view of nature by the evolutionary would bring with it a new kind of teleology. Whatever develops not only attempts to maintain itself in its own being but also attempts to persevere in becoming that which it is not.[16] Despite his own offhand remarks to the contrary, the above-quoted passages from the Paris Manuscripts indicate Marx's adherence to a teleological form of evolution. Nature produces as its finest product man, who in turn produces his own history with a view toward the transformation of his own nature. No divinity other than the human wills this development and no fate other than the economic insures its performance.

The third postulate (fourth in Teilhard's list), "the priority of the whole,"[17] may be understood on three levels: the cosmic, the personal, and the social. All three levels find similarities of concern in Marx, but in the Paris Manuscripts the assumption of the social whole as the proper definition of man takes pre-eminence. On the *cosmic* level Teilhard saw all life as a unitive whole, stretching as far as the eye can see and the instrument can measure, from the abyss of the infinitesimal arrangement of atomic particles to the vastness of sidereal systems. Although science has succeeded in breaking down the *Weltstoff* through sophisticated methods of analysis, reducing all to the "new god," energy, we do not *see* the whole until we recognize the artificiality of analysis and apprehend the synthetic, unifying power of nature.[18] With regard to man this means that the human body, formerly thought to be a fragment of the universe detached from other bodies, is in reality *enkekosmismene*—rooted in the cosmos. The title of his essay, "My Universe" is descriptive of the author's own being as well as the physical world around him. In the title he extended a well-worn theme, "I am a little world made cunningly," without, we should add, succumbing to the dualism implied in the remainder of Donne's first quatrain:

> I am a little world made cunningly
> Of Elements, and Angellike spright,
> But black sinne hath betraid to endless night
> My world both parts, and (oh) both parts must die.

Add to Teilhard's picture of the physical interdependence of man and cosmos the organic nature of time as revealed in evolution, and we realize how thoroughly implicated in nature is the Teilhardian man. Teilhard's man participates in the dialectical struggle for "hominized nature" in the Marxian sense, but man's organic relation to nature is not in Teilhard expressed solely through the instrumental, exclusive medium of productive work. Even "struggle with nature" betrays in Marx the static image of two warriors locked in an eternally fluctuating, but not necessarily developing, opposition. Nature for Teilhard reveals itself as the opponent, the condition of the struggle and the informing force of man's development even as he emerges from the natural to the historical. This holds true because nature is evolution, and historical man is evolution become conscious of itself.

Teilhard's belief in God's separateness from nature rescued him from naturalism and romantic organicism and allowed him to posit the *personal* unity of the individual in his relationship to nature. Because Teilhard in principle followed Scripture and Catholic tradition in teaching that human nature is created, falls, is redeemed, and is glorified in its entirety, he was able to describe man's organic relationship to the universe both in material terms (as in the previous paragraph) and in spiritual terms. In *Le milieu divin* he wrote that each soul exists for God and enjoys a mystical union with him. All that is sensible exists for the soul, which is inseparable from the universe into which it is born. He concluded from these two sentences that "in each soul, God loves and partly saves the whole world which that soul sums up in an incommunicable and particular way." His final point in this "syllogism" was to declare that by virtue of the soul's immediacy to God *and* the material universe, the psychic, spiritual, and material aspects of man and the universe form a whole, and that God saves by acting *physically* in the person of Christ on that whole which exists microcosmically in each individual.[19] Because in its intellectual operation the soul can approach God only through "the things that are made" (Rom. 1:20), Teilhard, following Thomistic thought, assumed that God saves in a physical way, first through man's organization of his own unity, and second through the physical integration of that unity into the cosmic body of Christ.

We may excuse his equivocation of the operations of soul[20] in order to make the point that man's organic relation to the whole of the universe, including his society, and his special relationship to God depend upon a Hebraic understanding of man as ensouled matter. For the above syllogism to make sense, "soul" must be understood as the tangible, expressive, and living reality of man. The Bible tends to speak of the unity of the personality in its three interrelated functions, the corporal, the psychical, and the spiritual. In the New Testament this unitive concept of man finds expression in Paul's synthetic approach to anthropology, whereby man constitutes not a combination of elements but a whole which may be seen from various perspectives.[21] Closer to the heart of Teilhard's education is the unity implied in St. Thomas' description of the person as a microcosm composed of reciprocally interacting elements. God creates the soul and the body at the same time, for the soul is the body's proper actuality. The soul is united to the body, not as a separate source of automation, as Plato taught, but as the informing power of the whole.[22] Teilhard carried this view in the lumber room of his mind whenever he attempted a unitive formula that would embrace secular labor and spiritual aspiration, the activities and the passivities of human life, or the rigid distinctions between nature and supernature.

The desired wholeness of the person never sanctioned individualism for Teilhard (or Marx) but acted as a prerequisite for the unity of the *social* organism. Both believed that the social whole has a potential for action and achievement that surpasses the sum of its parts, and that this whole represents the essence of man-coming-of-age. Teilhard's vision of social unity presupposed the Hebraic view of the commonality of all men which in Scripture is based on mankind's descent from one man. Teilhard's view of social unity also reflected the more exclusive community of the children of Israel who formed a unit by virtue of their corporate personality. And, like ancient Israel, the processes of life and anthropogenesis can experience success or failure only as a whole. As opposed to Marx, Teilhard's emphasis on social unity also retained the obverse of corporate personality, the equally biblical principle of the responsibility and identity of the part within the whole. The first complete formulation of this principle occurred in "My Universe" in which Teilhard made the unification of elements the necessary condition of their individual definition. He was later to lend the formula "union differentiates" to his scientific theory of complexity-consciousness as well as to his doctrine of personalization. In the latter he echoed and enriched the Marxian theme of verification when he cited man's sexual relation to woman as a paradigm of self-discovery via union with another.[23]

The fourth (third in Teilhard's list) postulate was "faith in the absolute." In the apologetic context of "My Universe" this absolute represented a higher consciousness which is attained forever, "an absolute perfection."[24] The relationship of this human transcendence to Omega point, which he identified as "God our Lord," will be interpreted in due course for the light it sheds on the nature of man. But first it is essential to show that the eternal nature of the absolute in which Teilhard believed is founded on faith in the eternal God. He in several places established the separateness or givenness of God as pre-existent and transcendent, as the origin and impulse of life and holiness, and as the personal One who stands outside the process of evolution while communicating his personality to it.[25] Such statements, which isolate the attributes of God, are rare in Teilhard due partially to his method of apologetics and, more importantly (as he saw it), to the theological irrelevance of speaking of God or man in isolation from one another.

Were Teilhard faced with Popper's question, "How did you first *find* your theory?" (e.g., of the coincidence of Christ and Omega), he would reply in epilogues, biographical essays, and letters to friends with words in this vein: "And so exactly, so perfectly does this [Pauline Christology] coincide with the Omega point that doubtless I should never have ventured to envisage the latter or formulate the hypothesis rationally if in my consciousness as a believer I had not found not only its speculative model but also its living reality."[26]

In answer to Popper's second question, " 'How did you *test* your theory?' which alone," adds Popper, "is scientifically relevant," Teilhard presented an apologetics which coordinates the religion of Christ with life's irreversible evolution toward personalization. By taking a long-range view of all the phenomena, he isolated certain laws of life's development which are verifiable at all levels, thus enabling us to think in terms of a totality or a metaphysics. Involved in his ultimate arrival at God as Omega are proofs reminiscent of the proof from degrees of being or the proof from final purpose, both of which emphasize the finite being's propensity for the absolute.[27] Through constant recourse to analogy, metaphor, and illustrative diagrams which were subtly transformed into constitutive statements of Christian truth, e.g., the cone of time, Teilhard combed the phenomena and his own experience for indications of a universal tendency toward God.

The most passionate of his proofs were the psychological or, as he called them, proofs "from necessity." They relied, at one extreme, upon personal testimonials to his confidence in the universe, his need for its success in order to avert despair, and the utter perspicuity of his faith in the absolute: "Because I can read it so plainly in my own heart, . . . it must logically be shared by all my fellows."[28] At the other extreme he advanced his psychological proofs by means of the venerable literary device of the author-narrator-seeker of wisdom who is only reluctantly convinced of the truth: "With this coincidence as evidence, I begin to think in the most critical and positivist parts of my being that the Christian phenomenon might well be what it claims to be."

This "phenomenological" approach to the *whole* of human experience, including a serious examination of the interior life, is subject to the limitations of any inductive theological method. However, in conversation with the early Marx's dogmatic humanism, Teilhard's methodological limitations opened the horizon to a "Someone" who transcends the individual's subjective proofs "from necessity" or the community's claim of social empiricism. It is this Someone—eliminated by Marxian presuppositions, yet theoretically possible according to the rules of empiricism—who in Teilhard's universe experiences or guarantees man's drive toward unification. To Marx's inversion of Hegelian theology into radical, idealist humanism we may juxtapose words which obviate the possibility of an overly neat synthesis of Marxian and Teilhardian thought: "Faith in Man can and indeed must cast us at the feet and into the arms of One who is greater than ourselves."[29]

THE SOURCE OF PERSONHOOD

Marx and Teilhard set about their scientific interpretations of man with minds considerably more cluttered with presuppositions than the supposed *tabula rasa* of the inductive investigator. Before they came to the testing of their theories of man they had already set him in a framework of teleological evolution as the spearhead and culmination of life. Whether in the planning of production or in the growth toward social unification, the free exercise and development of consciousness played a central part in the presuppositions of both thinkers. For varying reasons they rejected out of hand all manifestations of individualism— in the French Enlightenment, the laissez-faire of modern capitalism, Protestantism, and, in Teilhard's case, twentieth-century existentialism—and presupposed a cosmic, social, and individual unity of man. The composition of this unity, moreover, operates according to the same relational principle by which the individual defines and verifies his place within the human organism.

But where Marx exalted the principle of relation in society while reducing its individual constituents to functions-in-a-field, Teilhard's belief in God as a Trinity of Persons caused him to retain both the principle of relationship and the value of the persons related. The metaphysical basis of his later doctrine of personalization was set down in accordance with the orthodox contention that the being and interpenetration of the divine Persons of the Holy Trinity provide the archetype of the essence and relationship of human persons. Hence the whole world's unification tends toward the personal because the divine Persons "at the most profound and primordial level of being" exist "only through a process of self-unification."[30] There is, furthermore, in each individual an "essence" of personhood, which Teilhard called "the very centre of our consciousness, deeper than all its radii," which Omega preserves and reclaims.[31] In other words, although Teilhard had little interest in the scholastic definition of the person as "an individual substance of a rational nature," he did not undermine its metaphysical basis but upheld the personal reality of the One in whom man discovers his own identity and worth.

In the transition from idealist philosophy to empirical science Marx also developed a greater concern for the well-being of the individual. In his sanctification of human labor, for example, he appealed by analogy to Luther's emphasis on each believer's worthiness in Christ.[32] Marx's values were such that he wished to set moral limits on the economic power which may be directed against the individual in a bourgeois state. His radical humanism *("man is the highest essence for man")* reverberates throughout *Capital* in words that all but shout "Man is not what he should be!" and surfaces again in its revolutionary corollary: *"the categoric imperative to overthrow all relations* in which man is a debased, enslaved, abandoned, despicable essence."[33] The assumed social essence of man, however, as defined in the Paris Manuscripts, neither presupposed nor anticipated Marx's later interest in the needs and capabilities of the individual.

Even when he used the word "person," as he occasionally did, to designate the authentic man, Marx did so without an appreciation of that word's theological roots in the doctrine of God. Teilhard, while presupposing no independent theory of personalization, was—at all stages of his career and in every phase of his self-confessed "profound tendencies toward pantheism"—aware of the living presence of a personal God and the catholicity of a doctrine about him. Belief in a personal God, therefore, established the canon of the person and reduced the need for an improbably faultless theory of evolution or revolution to contrive of its own chain of reasoning a community of persons.

Chapter II

THE SHAPES OF EVIL

. . . The bond of a common nature makes all human beings one. Nevertheless, each individual in this community is driven by his passions to pursue his private purposes. Unfortunately, the objects of these purposes are as such that no one person (let alone, the world community) can ever be wholly satisfied. The reason for this is that nothing but absolute Being can satisfy human nature. The result is that the city of man remains in a chronic condition of civil war. Hence, there is always the oppression of those who fail by those who succeed.

—*St. Augustine*

Human evil is approached through a review of its phenomenological appearances and an analysis of its inner life and causes. One may describe the appearances of evil with great insight and vivid realism and proceed either to accept the appearance as the essential evil-in-itself or seek by other less empirical methods to explain the reality of its hidden nature. Theology, not unlike other disciplines, such as sociology, cinematography, and journalism, graphically describes the shades and forms of evil in nature, man, and society. Unlike most other disciplines, theology never scrutinizes the phenomena on their own terms, but always seeks the unity of data and meaning, appearance and essence, event and cause. Marx and Teilhard, each in his own way, disregarded this theological principle. Following them, we shall restrict ourselves in this chapter to their perception of the appearances of evil while reserving for Chapter 3 the weightier matters of its origin and nature.

Marx insisted on the empirical nature of his investigation, and Teilhard stressed "seeing" as the key to human success. In that which follows we wish to discover what exactly Marx and Teilhard saw when they looked at human life, not as it was or might be, but as it is. We want to know the extent to which the implications and logical conclusions they drew from economics and paleontology transcended their respective disciplines and shed light on human unhappiness.

While holding similar presuppositions about man, Marx and Teilhard set him in a very different world. The Marxian man appears as an exteriorized function in the capitalist economic and social system. He is set within the interplay of forces whose antagonism serves only to prolong his physical suffering and his separation from a truly human essence, whose actualization Marx reserved for the distant future. For Teilhard's man, who also lives in an ascendant condition of becoming, time more than anything else separates him from the realization of his potential. The Teilhardian man is whole and reflective and therefore encounters the growing pains of an unfinished cosmos as an interior experience of alienation: anxiety. It is the conflict not of oppressed and oppressor but of despair and hope. The real point of contact between Marx and Teilhard in the phenomenology of evil consists in their indirect use of Christian doctrines to describe the fallenness of economic or evolutionary systems of development. In this, Marx's use of theology is the more blatantly falsifying, while Teilhard's represents a failure to communicate to the process of evolution the spiritual tensions which he so intuitively perceived in the individual.

FROM LUTHER TO MARX: ECONOMIC CONCUPISCENCE

In the act of productive labor man communicates his humanity to the material objects he creates. Through the systematically rigid control of his labor and the private ownership of his products, man is separated and threatened by objects embodying his own human essence. To describe this condition Marx used the words *Entfremdung,* "alienation" or "estrangement," and *Entäusserung,* "external projection into objects."[1] Marx became familiar with the category of alienation in the work of Hegel and Feuerbach, and his use of the term is a reaction against the abstract function of alienation in both philosophers. In Hegel alienation played its part in the odyssey of the Absolute Idea from its externalization in the matter of unconscious nature, through self-consciousness in man, and finally, by way of history, to its Prussian destination in the Hegelian reconciliation. Feuerbach descended from the realm of pure consciousness by denying the reality of the Hegelian Absolute Spirit and reassigning its process of alienation to the subconscious of the religious man.

Marx rejected the substance of the Hegelian and the Feuerbachian interpretations of alienation for their respective emphases on the primacy of absolute consciousness or the subjective religious consciousness. Marx, in fact, objected to any interpretation of man's estrangement that accounts for its origin, mode of appearance, or its eventual elimination solely in terms of mind or human consciousness. The alienation of mind in Hegel meant that mind has projected itself into a material form alien to its true nature. But, according to Marx, since man is a natural being, his creation of material objects cannot be construed as a relinquishing or an alienating of his pure being. Alienation existed for Marx only in the context of the act and results of productive labor. Because man is a collective creature whose social interaction produces estrangement between classes, the consciousness of alienation is of no consequence until it becomes the property of an entire class. While the young Marx alluded to the individual's *feeling* of alienation, he also made it clear that, like the consciousness of an entire class, true alienation can result only from the contradiction of class interests.

By reminding ourselves of this restricted function of alienation in Marx we restore a modicum of meaning to what has become a trite and exhausted concept, and we are in a position to assess the relationship of Marxian alienation to the Christian doctrines of evil and sin. To the evil he saw in society around him Marx imputed the traditional negativity which the Fathers, St. Augustine, St. Thomas, and Scholasticism termed "privation." Alienation describes the absence of completion which prohibits a being from fulfilling its own nature. Marx and Teilhard agreed with St. Thomas that the movement of any being toward its own fulfillment, or, in evolutionary terms, toward its ascendant transformation, is an unqualified good. Privation differs from simple negation in that the former requires a positive subject. We may draw the parallel between Marxism and Christianity by naming the ultimate subject in which privation exists, as it were, and contrast the methods of that subject's rectification. The Marxian subject is the human essence, which, as the "ensemble of the social relations," defines a social structure built around a particular method of production—in this case, capitalism. The defective existence of the organism Marx attributed to the economically-induced isolation of its individual members. The separation which Marx condemned is that of an objective situation in which man is deprived of objects (and the wealth which purchases objects), and in which one class is separated from the privileges of life's fullness. On the basis of the early manuscripts we may speak of man's desire to reunify his daily existence with the human essence (keeping in mind its social definition) through the reappropriation of the objects into which he has squandered his life-forces.

The importance of "essence" in this context recalls Tillich's judgment of Freud and Nietzsche, who both failed to differentiate man's essential and existential being and who describe man solely on the plane of existential concupiscence.[2] Marxism and Christianity, to the contrary, distinguish between the existence of man and the essence from which it is separated, but Marx proposed the negation of the physical conditions of production as the single condition for the reunification of existence and essence. In Christian doctrine the ultimately good subject which supports the negative reality of evil is the person, whose humanity consists formally in the exercise of reason, language, and creativity, but essentially in the responsibility-relationship of the "inner man" to his Creator-Redeemer. Alienation, in its current usage as one's separation from that to which he belongs, consists in the shattering of the Image of God, the loss of original righteousness, and the absence of God's integrating presence within man and his various communities. It is theologically expressed in idolatry, hypocrisy, and formalism. Alienation is prolonged whenever man rejects the divinely appointed Mediator whose task it is to reconcile man to God, and, in so doing, to reintegrate the unique attributes of man into a truly human essence.

Alienation in the world reflects estrangement from God; unbelief is the greatest sin, for it effects the primal and most profound alienation. It is not sufficient to see alienation as a result of the absence of belief. As a state of separation from God alienation expresses not only the negativity of a lost unity but also the concupiscence of a debased relationship. Every act or condition therefore which results from a lack of faith, that is, disunity with God, is automatically incorporated in the perverted relationship which St. Paul terms "sin." As Tillich puts it, "Man's predicament is estrangement, but his estrangement is sin."[3]

All traditional theology recognizes the validity of this unitive relationship, although the German reformers, in defense of the *sola gratia* principle, chose to identify concupiscence with man's original and continuing separation from God. *The Apology of the Augsburg Confession*, for example, selects those quotations from Augustine, Bonaventure, Thomas, and Hugo of St. Victor which mention the positive force of concupiscence, and rejects any view of concupiscence by which it is understood as a mere punishment or result of "deficiency" (Art. III). Luther characterized original sin as that which effects total separation from God. "Over and beyond this," however, "it is the proneness toward evil; the loathing of the good; the disdain for light and wisdom but fondness for error and darkness."[4] Concupiscence is lust, not necessarily sexual, that desires to draw the whole of reality into itself. Tillich gives the examples of Nero, Don Juan, and Faust, whose insatiable desires were set not so much on power, sex, or knowledge in themselves, but on the *totality* of the conquest.[5]

By doing away with the venerable distinction between *imago* and *similitudo* in his theology of God's image, Luther hoped to demonstrate the corruption of all the faculties of body and soul, especially the will and the intellect, in order to reaffirm man's powerlessness to contribute to his own justification. To this end he dismissed not the unique rationality of man but the idea, as St. Thomas expressed it, that this faculty naturally inclines man toward the truth about God and peaceable life in society. Concupiscence, according to Luther, is so much the condition of man that his seemingly rational organization of his life in government and society amounts to a necessary restraint of his corrupt human nature. Luther's designation of sin as the nature and essence of man was only unraveled and thoroughly explained a generation after his death in the refutation of Flacianism.

The positive, rebellious nature of concupiscence gives rise to Luther's well-known hypostatization of the powers which militate against unification with God. Among those powers which he, with St. Paul, imbued with the authority to ruin man's capacity to be the subject of his own actions are flesh, world, law, sin, Satan, and Anti-Christ. The virulence and realism with which Luther re-presented the above Pauline categories, his identification of total concupiscence and original sin, and finally his doctrine of the bondage of the will, advanced in terms which lent themselves to a dualist misinterpretation, contributed to the epithet contained in the Tridentine condemnation of his doctrines: *Manichaeus redivivus.*

Insofar as Marx related his concept of alienation to the theological understanding of privation, he remained at least formally within the Catholic tradition. The genius of the Marxian analysis of society, however, and the substance of his disagreement with Teilhard's strictly privative view of sin and evil, lies in his assimilation of Lutheran extremities and his sociological and economic re-presentation of them. As a secularized Jew and an unbelieving baptized Lutheran, Marx was introduced to the fundamentals of his denomination in secondary school where he was expected periodically to give evidence of his faith and knowledge in the form of theological essays.[6] Although his studies in social and economic history brought him into contact with the various phases of the German reformation, his knowledge and use of Lutheran doctrine are characterized by superficiality and cynicism. This did not prevent him, however, from incorporating into his work the Lutheran emphases on concupiscence, the positive forces which dominate and pervert man's relationship to society, and the total depravity of rational, civilized man.

Marx peered into the "innermost essence" of nineteenth-century capitalism and exposed the concupiscence of an entire economic system which lives and multiplies not for the sake of production or use-value, but solely and insatiably for the sake of profit and its need "to capture the whole world." In his analysis of capitalism Marx also proved that profit is made only at the expense of labor, so that concupiscence finds its necessary expression in the exploitation of one class by another. Following Luther, Marx refused to separate alienation, the privative state of the human social complex, from concupiscence. Dehumanization is always a perversion. His insight into man's inhumanity to man—indeed, his hatred of it—will act as a secular corrective to Teilhard's naive oversight of exploitation and his strictly privative view of evil. Marx's hatred of exploitation reflected in an industrial context the rage of the prophets and was not out of step with the prohibitions of usury and exploitation in St. Thomas, the schoolmen, and Luther. In this respect, R. H. Tawney called Marx "the last of the schoolmen."[7]

But Marx's construction of the exploitive situation is, again, more reminiscent of the extremism with which Luther attacked the perverse, active, and all-pervasive reality of sin. Marx's division of all humanity into two hostile camps, the oppressors and the oppressed, and his moral absolution of protagonist and antagonist alike set the conditions of exploitation into Manichean bas relief. Where certain scholars are inclined to interpret Marx as a secularized descendant of the medieval Cathari,[8] I believe his lineage ought to be traced to his Lutheran background, such as it was, and to hyperbolisms such as this one: "So man's will is like a beast standing between two riders. If God rides, it wills and goes where God wills. . . . If Satan rides, it wills and goes where Satan wills."[9] The powers and principalities in the Marxian universe are economic, and in their own way more mysterious than those that plagued St. Paul and Luther, for in Marx they are as yet unconquered.

Marx wrote of a society in which the objective powers of dominion and greed, in the form of objects, owners, and an entire economic system itself, hold sway over learning and all areas of civilized life. Indeed, he echoed a particularly Lutheran theme when he based the negative side of his case for revolution on the bankruptcy of human reason. Existing in a totally fallen and alienated environment, how does the Marxian man recognize his plight as an aberration from the true standards of humanity? Marxism's answer coincides with modern Lutheran alternatives to the seventeenth-century dogmaticians' reliance on "relics" of the *imago Dei* to explain the unique rationality of man despite the totality of the Fall. Man retains contact with his essential humanity, and, in Lutheran doctrine, an awareness of his fallenness by means of the grandeur and sublime hope contained in *needs* which are not satisfied by food and shelter.[10]

In his willingness to sort out the active forces and causes which result in the phenomenon of alienated man, Marx appears to employ the category of sin. This chapter, however, is about the appearance of evil because Marx (and to some degree Teilhard) detached the phenomenon from its cause and essential nature. In his rejection of the primal self-estrangement of consciousness as advanced by Hegel and Feuerbach, and in his sublimation of so-called Lutheran determinism, Marx failed to reproduce the latter's concern with man's responsibility before God. He therefore drove a wedge between the empirically observed phenomenon of alienation and the human decisions which cause and perpetuate it. An understanding of the social, economic, and materialist context of Marx's use of alienation, therefore, is necessary if we are to read the attractive analogies that follow as Marx's purely formal adherence to some of Christian theology's categories of sin and evil.

The Power of Objects

The primary result of man's objectification of his labor is his idolatrous bondage to commodities. The Marxian man lives in a society that thrives on the multiplication of commodities and the continuously created need for new commodities. The worker himself is infected by the desire for objects and exchanges his delight in his own creative virtuosity for a preoccupation with the commodities he creates. Through no fault of his own he is blinded to the deformed human content of these objects and grows to value them as things which are intrinsically desirable. In *Capital,* Marx called this universal preoccupation with the object or the commodity by the term "fetishism." He confirmed the idolatrous nature of fetishism with an analogy drawn from Feuerbach's critique of religion: "As in religion man is governed by the products of his own brain, so in capitalist production he is governed by the product of his own hand."[11] The analogy is neat but does not explain precisely how commodities, even those whose use-value is nil, are able to assume a "mystical character" in their dominance of man. The labor theory of value goes some way toward explaining the mystical power of commodities, but Marx did not portray the worker as enjoying insight into the human content of his own productions. Nor did Marx investigate the worker's subconscious longing for reunion with self. The labor theory of value, moreover, entails an abstraction of the species-life, Man, from the everyday experience of industrialized men—an abstraction which Feuerbach made and for which he was repeatedly criticized by Marx. The human content of commodities also does not in itself explain why prices fluctuate or why certain factory-produced commodities exert greater influence over man than other similarly produced products. Clearly the labor theory of value cannot answer this or many other related questions without recourse to the profit motive, the law of supply and demand, and, most important for this study, an inquiry into some of the noneconomic aspects of the laborer's plight.

The worker encounters his own objectified labor not only in concrete commodities but in the money with which he purchases the work of his own hands. Few institutions or individuals are treated to a greater portion of Marxian vitriol than the common expedient, money. Money, in Marx's analysis, is intrinsically evil and exercises its power in ways independent of human decisions. Its fetishistic power over man is absolute: "Money is the jealous God of Israel, by the side of which no other god may exist, . . . and this alien being rules him, and he prays to it."[12] Money in the form of wages plays its part in the degradation of man. As a result of the capitalist's manipulation of the working day in order to create surplus value (profit), the worker finds himself working for compensation which allows him to eke out only a bare existence.[13] He does not live for work; he works in order to live. The products he makes are not the expressions of his personality or the cooperative enterprise of society. The alienated man produces for himself only wages.

The self-activity which is objectified into wage-labor makes of man's work a commodity to be bought and sold. Here the power of objects reaches its dehumanizing conclusion: since all the activity which goes into work amounts to a definition of the human essence, the man who sells his labor time sells himself and becomes "the consumption of the commodity purchased."[14]

Labor as Estrangement from Nature

One of the goals of Marx's philosophical and economic criticism was the portrayal of real people. The objectification of labor gives way to a second aspect of alienation, that of man's estrangement from the processes of industrial labor, in which we begin to see more clearly the suffering of individual men. Labor, Marx once observed, is "the everlasting condition imposed by Nature upon human existence."[15] Man humanizes himself and nature, however, only when his labor is characterized by the exercise of imagination, a fulfilled sense of purpose, and joyful attraction to the work for its own sake. When these conditions are not met, man's specifically human powers and his conscious mastery of nature are reabsorbed into the animal world of instinct. Just as religion externalizes the creatures of human fantasy, so Marx wrote, industrial labor transforms the active essence of man into an alien task, from which only the rare moments of leisure or the indulgence of animal functions—"eating, drinking, procreating"—offer refuge and coherence. Philosophically, therefore, since a definition of humanity consists in a healthy interaction with nature, the manipulation of the labor process spells an alienation from nature and the degradation of human life.

Marx's description of this form of alienation reproduces in a secular form the Genesis account of the first man's dislocated place in nature after his expulsion from the Garden. The biblical story portrays a shift from one dynamic situation to another by means of the deceptively static image of the first couple's expulsion from a *place*. Adam's initial position, nevertheless, involves creativity and activity in the naming and managing of his fellow creatures. After the Fall his creativity continues only by means of extreme pain and the Sisyphean dynamism of his struggle for survival in the face of nature's hostility. Finally, after a life of unremitting toil, the only unity with nature Adam can hope to achieve is a mingling of dust in death. The Genesis account does not coincide with Marx's version in several critical aspects. The biblical man enjoys a harmonious relationship with nature, but, by reason of his unique answerability to God, he is never described, even at his origin, as undifferentiated nature. Man's pre-eminence is such that when he rebels, God does not hesitate to levy a curse upon nature as a means of punishing him. To Adam God says, "Cursed is the ground because of you." Nature is not in Genesis the neutral territory or the field ripe for humanization as it is in Marx. Rather God rules it as his unreflective creature and disfigures it with thorns and thistles for the sake of his relationship with his highest earthly creature. Just as man's primal unity is not with nature but God, so his destiny holds more than the Marxian rationalization and perfection of the essentially natural relations which obtained in his innocence.

Industrial labor, however, ruins human nature by effecting a general loss of spontaneity and an impairment of full mental and physical development. The chief sin of industrialization is the division of labor. Despite vast improvements in wages and conditions of production over the past century, Marx's denunciation of the division of labor carries an insight and a contemporaneity that cross political boundaries. The unspeakable monotony of piecework and assembly lines exists in all industrialized societies. The division of labor's one-sided emphasis on a single minute skill continues to make specialization a very dangerous procedure for the worker. For as soon as his mechanical function is changed or eliminated he descends as a "crippled monstrosity" into the army of unskilled labor, thereby reducing the value of his labor, and increasing the capitalist's rate of surplus value.[16] The division of labor furthermore coerces the worker to adapt his activity and finally, Marx added, his entire personality to the monotonous operation of a machine. Since it never stops working and thereby extends the working day "beyond all bounds set by human nature," the machine is transformed into the productive subject and man into its dehumanized appendage.[17] The mechanized division of labor also removes the human element from production in the separation of physical and intellectual activity, so that the laborer is removed from the sphere of interaction between planning and physical activity and comes to regard intellectual work as the privileged function of the ruling power.[18]

It is important to note that Marx never advocated the abolition of machinery in favor of a return to the halcyon days of individual craftsmanship or agricultural feudalism. He realized, perhaps better than anyone else in his day, that man's destiny is bound to the machine, which, if rightly used, contains the possibilities of the alleviation of human misery. His outrage became the greater when the machine instead extended the working day, intensified labor through piecework, did away with the need of muscular coordination, and removed all interest from work. An impromptu speech at the anniversary celebration of a socialist newspaper in 1856 reflects Marx's ambivalent attitude toward mechanization, and, in its tone, captures the rarely-glimpsed moral bewilderment in one who hoped to lay bare the secrets of capitalist society.

In our days everything seems pregnant with its contrary. Machinery, gifted with the wonderful power of shortening and fructifying human labor, we behold starving and overworking it. The new-fangled sources of wealth, by some strange weird spell, are turned into sources of want. The victories of art seem bought by the loss of character. At the same pace that mankind masters nature, man seems to become enslaved to other men or to his own infamy. . . . All our invention and progress seem to result in endowing material forces with intellectual life, and in stultifying human life into material force.[19]

The Loss of Community

In the third and decisive aspect of alienation, that of man's relation to the community, Marx followed the Christian diagnosis of fallen man who, having exchanged the truth of God for a lie about himself, manifests his spritual bankruptcy in an unending series of conflicts with his fellow man. In Christianity and Marxism, chronologically following man's rupture with nature, man finds himself at war with his fellows. In the Genesis account alienation from spontaneous creativity is succeeded by drudgery, fratricide, and the fragmentation of humanity into different races and languages. The fragmentation of humanity forms a theological motif which has persisted throughout the history of Christian theology. But fragmentation as an alienation from nature is itself the result of estrangement from God. For Marx, however, the rift in nature, which is expressed in industrial labor as "the negative form of self-activity," not only accompanies social estrangement but causes it as well. Never did Marx reverse the process and posit a personal or social form of alienation as the cause of man's disjunction from nature.

As an effect of something else, therefore, Marx portrayed social division and isolation in imagery comparable to that of St. Paul's depiction of his inner struggle with sin or Luther's striking description of human self-interest: "Due to original sin, our nature is so curved in upon itself [*incurvatus in se*] at its deepest levels that it not only bends the best gifts of God toward itself in order to enjoy them, . . . nay, rather, 'uses' God in order to obtain them, but does not even know that, in this wicked, twisted, crooked way, it seeks everything, including God, only for itself."[20] In Marx, as we shall see in the following paragraphs, all elements of this quotation are present: atomization, selfishness, ignorance of the depth of one's own perversion, and the concupiscent desire for the All. In his mature work Marx applied the self's interior struggles with sin, God, and other forces to the battlefield of an industrialized society, so that the conflict is primarily recognized and consciously enacted as class war or competition within the classes. Man's highly personal and sinful withdrawal into the false security of the self, which Luther called *incurvatus in se,* Marx applied to the economic policies of various individuals and companies as well as to entire social classes.

The proletarian's divorce from his active creative essence expresses itself in the destruction of his family life and in his isolation from any sense of human values, education, and the human community itself. His world becomes a vicious parody of bourgeois society where each individual inflates himself to the size of an atom; that is, in Marx's definition, "to an unrelated, self-sufficient, wantless, *absolutely full,* blessed being," and where the ideal of the cooperative fulfillment of needs is debased by economic competition.[21] The members of bourgeois society thrive on possessions gained through the creation and fulfillment of false needs. In a system of private property, Marx wrote, "every man speculates upon creating a *new* need in another in order to force him to a new sacrifice, to place him in a new dependence and to entice him into a new kind of pleasure and thereby into economic ruin."[22] In his emphasis on the "new" Marx anticipated the planned obsolescence of modern manufacture and the cult of novelty in contemporary advertising. With this picture of economic guerrilla warfare in mind, it is no wonder that Marx once cryptically spoke of the bourgeoisie as being "more subjected to the violence of things," or that Engels delighted in fitting Darwin's theory of the survival of the fittest, in Aesopian fashion, to bourgeois society.

This condition of *bellum omnium contra omnes* is regulated by the state, and its competitive nature held up before the proletariat as a guaranteed freedom. This separation of words and ideas from material conditions in order to maintain the status quo Marx called "ideology." The classical definition, before later Communists neutralized the word, states that the ruling class, that is, the class which has the means of production at its disposal, controls at the same time the means of mental production. "The ruling ideas are nothing more than the ideal expression of the dominant material relationships." The ruling class, embodied as the state, solidifies its intellectual hegemony by assimilating the best minds of the ruled class. While seemingly exempting himself from the following procedure, Marx declared that any class represents its interest as the common interest of all the members of society and invests it, as the "general good," with the form of universality. Ideology represents its client's policy as the only rational, religious, or natural course of action to be followed if the rights of the more unfortunate are to be protected. The detachment of ideas as natural or universal truths from the material conditions which produced them leads to the creation of religion and the falsification of history.[23] Philosophically, this form of alienation also dissociates ideas, for example, the idea of man, from their class setting, and advances impotent rationalizations as analyses of society. Philosophy alone, said Marx, himself a paragon of rationality, not only fails its task of understanding man but, by overlooking man's social needs and his economic exploitation, also hinders his transformation.

The self-isolating competition within bourgeois and proletarian society is stimulated by the pronouncements of the state. The state itself, however, is a phony entity which elevates itself above society through naked power and ideology. Its rulers then proceed to equate the political structure of the state with human social life, or, as does Hegel in *The Philosophy of Right,* with the supreme ethical realization of the Spirit. Man in this state leads a double life: the self-determination which belongs to his true essence is legally removed, and in its place he receives citizenship in the state—with all the rights and privileges thereof. One of these rights, said Marx in a commentary on the French and American constitutions, is that of equality. One of the privileges granted by the state, however, vitiates the ideological word "equality." The privilege of private property creates and idealizes the egotistical individual who is beguiled by the image of his own independence, which in reality is a form of slavery to the privileges awarded him by the state.[24] It is this individualist ideal, typified by Max Stirner's motto, "Ich hab' mein Sach auf Nichts gestellt," which the bourgeoisie uses to maintain atomization, in the form of competition for jobs and commodities, within a hopelessly divided working class.

Another aspect of the proletarian's social alienation might be labeled the reification of relationships.[25] In the sphere of morality, reification transforms the other person into a "case"; in business and advertising it takes the form of the obliteration of the distinction between true and false needs and the translation of people into "the market." Politically, the state as Marx knew it reified relationships by recognizing the egotistical individual as the true embodiment of man and by bestowing upon him the title and the legally inelastic rights of "citizen." In a system of capitalism people are relegated to personifications of the commodities they wish to exchange and the economic relations existing between them. As members of the working organism, people exist as special modes of capital whose power seems to them inexplicably derived from nature. This reification, which Marcuse has explicated most thoroughly in the context of contemporary society, gradually permeates all social relationships. It sets forth social relations as a totality of objective, economic relations, thereby concealing their origins, their means of perpetuation and the possibilities of their transformation. Above all, the worker loses sight of the human content of these relationships and is unable to escape from an entire economic and social system which confronts him as a rational, naturally-endowed power.

COMPASSION AND PROTEST

The passion of Marx's literary protest against conditions in English factories invites comparison with the protest literature of his day. Blake and Elizabeth Barrett Browning portrayed the pathos of victimized children; Carlyle preached a self-redemptive doctrine of work; Dickens's *Hard Times* created a daguerreotype of the tedious desperation of "Coketown" with its inhabitants "who all went in and out . . . with the same sound upon the pavements"; and Marx encouraged the negation of suffering through revolution. The gradual improvement of the worker's lot through parliamentary reformism proved to be the ultimate solution in which few of the literary protesters had placed serious hopes. In *Capital* the ill effects of objectification, the division of labor and social estrangement—from tenement "cave dwellings" to the pathos of child labor—were documented with a quality of meticulous detail and compassion that added flesh and feeling to the abstract categories of the *Economic and Philosophical Manuscripts*. The noncommunist world has attempted to dismiss Marxian economics, but it cannot ignore the moral thesis woven into the questionable predictions of a nineteenth-century economist: man must combat unnecessary human suffering as an intrinsic evil. This is to say that Marx grasped human suffering, especially in its social manifestations, as both his moral and economic point of departure, as well as the guiding concern of his own personal commitment to communism.[26]

To summarize the vitiated and debased existence of humankind, so thoroughly documented in *Capital,* Marx employed, as Teilhard would after him, the figure of immaturity. Although he manifests unique properties and abilities, man in Marx and Teilhard is truly human only by virtue of the potentiality lodged within the squalor and confusion of his actual existence. They were both therefore fond of the term "prehistory" as a caption for man's present stage of development. Where Teilhard understood this prehistory as a natural and therefore acceptable stage of humankind's growth, Marx attributed to it the inhumanity of reification and the shame of animal life. It is prehistory in this sense which Marx never accepted nor tolerated but always willed to destroy. Far from a benign stage of development, man's prehistory is characterized by conflicting forces whose antagonism is ripening in hatred and violence toward a social explosion and the emergence of something—or someone—new.

EVOLUTIONARY PRIVATION

In the preface to *The Phenomenon of Man* Teilhard de Chardin announced that he had chosen man as the center of his phenomenology and around him would establish a coherent scenario for all life. By assuming the primacy of the psychic in the world, he continued, his work would be built around the pre-eminent significance of man in nature. Although Teilhard, like Marx, wished to set man at the center of the universal condition of life—the evolutionary rather than the economic process—Teilhard was both blessed and limited by an inability to reproduce the contemporary human phenomenon as it actually *is*. As a fossil paleontologist his keen sense of observation approached the legendary among his co-workers. But his preoccupation was with the future. *"The past has revealed to me how the future is built,"* he wrote to his cousin in 1935, "and preoccupation with the future tends to sweep everything else aside."[27] The postulates which he advanced concerning man's fulness of consciousness, planetary unity, and his ultimate success all had as their orientation a point somewhere in the distant future.

Man as he is, therefore, was not usually the standard by which Teilhard measured the effects of good or evil. Even in the midst of the most complex and horrendous social developments, Teilhard adhered to a norm which we might label the *not-yet* of evolution. Evil consists in those manifestations of human (and nonhuman) life which have not yet attained to the culmination of evolution. The dynamic quality of this privation goes some way toward vitiating the word "evil" itself, for in a system of evolution whose direction, at least, is irreversible and whose success is highly probable, certain forms of human evil appear as natural and necessary stages in the ascent toward perfection. Teilhard, like Marx, understood the privative nature of the human situation: man is not yet what he could be, what he ought to be, nor what he shall be. He suffers temporal and existential separation from the completion of his being. Teilhard, however, did not join Marx in a healthy respect and hatred for the independent power of evil. His view of evolutionary privation never issued into an in-depth analysis of a particular evil as it exists on its own terms.

Coupled with this futuristic perspective (and its implied doctrine of progress) was Teilhard's reticence to adopt the perspective of anything so diminutive as a class. He instead championed the cause of humankind as Teilhard envisioned it will some day be born, thereby exposing himself to the same criticism which Marx leveled at Feuerbach: "When . . . he sees instead of healthy men a crowd of scrofulous, overworked and consumptive starvelings, he is compelled to take refuge in the 'higher perception' and in the ideal 'compensation' in the species."[28]

Teilhard adopted the perspective of one who is somehow outside and above the entire span of evolution. He quite understandably, therefore, tended to picture wars, social upheavals, and institutions in broad, generalized strokes. When the events surrounding World War II are billed as "superficial chaos" and the Cold War as a biological imbalance, we have some indication of the methodological distance from which the movements of humanity, including evil, are being diagnosed. This particular facet of Teilhard's method, then, including his native optimism ("Everything that happens is adorable"), plainly endangers an accurate qualitative assessment of events to the extent that his overall conclusions may be considered suspect.

Forms of Unconsciousness

Of the Teilhardian postulates reviewed in Chapter I above we may note in their turn the deficiency that he observed in the first three categories of existence: consciousness, irreversibility, and unity. The fundamental importance of human consciousness or "seeing," by which Teilhard meant the individual's self-understanding and ultimately the entire race's co-reflection, was set down in the preface to *The Phenomenon of Man*. As one might expect, it was characteristic of Teilhard to see "unconsciousness," where higher consciousness is possible, "as a sort of ontological inferiority or evil since the world can only fulfill itself insofar as it expresses itself in a systematic and reflective perception."[29] The passive form of this unconsciousness is typified by the eastern religions, whose unprogressive spirit Teilhard found oppressive and wasteful. His dismissal of the most reflective religions of India and the Orient demonstrates his view of the evil that lies in static reflection. In a letter to his cousin he spoke of his experience in China: "Nowhere, among the men I met or heard about, have I discerned the smallest seed whose growth will benefit the future of mankind. Throughout my whole journey I have found nothing but absence of thought, senile thought, or infantile thought."[30]

Keeping in mind Teilhard's view of the expanding, revolutionary role of consciousness, it comes as no surprise that he was receptive to the intellectual possibilities of a communist revolution in China. Although he felt the Bolsheviks deserved their defeat in China in 1927, he nevertheless admitted to some "*good* elements in the communist awakening." Twenty-two years later in the wake of a successful Chinese revolution he was to reiterate these sentiments.[31]

The active form of unconsciousness, as opposed to passive withdrawal, appeared in Teilhard as the mistaken notions of those who do not *see* the movement toward mass co-reflection, and who instead employ their rationality in the service of individualism and private gain.

Although Teilhard believed that "all history bears witness to the fact that nothing has ever been able to prevent an idea from growing and spreading and finally becoming universal," he made slight provision for the growth and universalization of wicked ideas.[32] This is not to suggest that he was insensible to the reality of ideology in its classical Marxian sense; rather, he did not expand upon his rudimentary intuition of ideology so as to come to grips with the neutrality of ideas and their mercenary deployment as weapons. Teilhard criticized the misuse of thought, not so much for its power to enslave, as for its potential to inhibit man's slow inevitable progress toward co-reflection.

The most blatant misuse of ideology, however, occurs in the misrepresentation of the venerable slogans of egalitarian democracy. The Enlightenment advertised its Rights of Man as an advance in the cause of humankind, but in reality these rights bred an individualist system of units at the expense of the "incommunicable singularity of being" which man achieves only in a loving social relationship. These units moreover are wrongly assumed to possess not only legal equality but also biological and cultural parity, with the result that the special biological and cultural groupings necessary to lead humankind to totalization are levelled and relativized.[33] In the third and most compelling of his restatements of the Rights of Man, Teilhard set down an inalienable right applicable not only to French democracy but to communist dictatorships as well: ". . . for no reasons must the forces of collectivity compel the individual to deform or falsify himself (by accepting as true what he sees to be false, . . . which is to lie to himself)."[34]

Stagnation

Knowledge exists for its own sake, wrote Teilhard in *The Phenomenon of Man*, but even more certainly it exists for power. Power in turn is exercised for increased action, which, in the form of work, becomes the agent of noogenesis. Teilhard's second postulate (pp. 9–10 above) provides for the proper direction of man's working energies toward the fulfillment of a goal. The deficiency in this respect which he observed, but did not thoroughly analyze, is the evil of stagnation. As early as Neolithic times man was beginning the process of "mass formation," or planetization, which has climaxed in modern man's infolding upon himself. Societies and civilizations have reached such a degree of physical proximity, psychic communion through mass communication systems, and economic interdependence—a universalization Marx called the world market—that they can no longer develop save by interpenetration of one another. In the century after the industrial revolution's greatest abuses, machinery, by liberating man from the struggle for the basics of human existence, has brought with it the hitherto unknown phenomenon of leisure time. Machinery, in other words, "fulfills the dream of all living creatures by satisfying our instinctive craving for the *maximum of consciousness* with a minimum of effort!"[35] Teilhard viewed the enforced leisure of modern man as a vast and yet unsounded pool of resources. While these potentialities remain untapped, man continues to suffer, as a direct result of technological progress, the twin manifestations of stagnation in the noosphere: unemployment and boredom.

There was in Teilhard as well as Marx an implied ambivalence over against technological progress. Automation, for example, taken for granted to be the *sine qua non* of man's eventual humanization, for the present plays a large part in human suffering and stagnation. Marx went to great lengths to show that capitalism necessarily produces cycles of unemployment by its manipulation of the industrial reserve army, its competition for labor in boom times, and its intensification of production through mechanization. These are accompanied by a rise in wages and the cost of production, thus bringing increased production and prosperity to an end and inaugurating a new season of unemployment. Contrary to this, Teilhard interpreted unemployment as one more manifestation of the Law of Complexity-Consciousness. Writing at the nadir of the Great Depression, Teilhard offered this assessment of unemployment: "Under contingent and local appearances, it expresses the inevitable result of the loss of equilibrium brought about in animal life by the appearance of thought."[36] Because he took the long-range evolutionary view of this transition from mechanized activity to freedom for thought, he made the unrealistic suggestion that the unemployed need not be returned to mechanized labor. Surplus labor instead was to follow the trend of developing consciousness as it was being revealed in technological unemployment and apply itself to scientific research.[37] There is, of course, more than a touch of incongruity in this due to Teilhard's conceptualizing of this harsh reality as a mode of consciousness, and his naive, utopian solution. The victims of the Great Depression (as well as today's unemployed) would have taken little solace in Teilhard's analysis of their "liberation" into the psychic sphere of development.

The universal boredom which Teilhard associated with man's unused psychic capacities is more often than not relieved in the exercise of war. Teilhard believed that war wastes the overflow of psychic energy, drains man's capacity for peaceful research, and transforms it into the development of increasingly destructive weapons. Yet the subject of war also provides a good illustration of Teilhardian optimism. Although he experienced as a stretcher bearer the fatigue and horror of Verdun and the Chemin des Dames, Teilhard displayed an unmistakable romanticizing of the Great War. The war that finally crushed the optimism of nineteenth-century theology seems to have had a liberating effect on

Teilhard and renewed his zest for progress. He subscribed to the myth of *Dulce et decorum est pro patria mori* with an adolescent fervor that belied his thirty-four years and the intellectual rigor of his Jesuit training. His enthusiasm was not dampened by his first encounters with battle and life in the trenches. In "Cosmic Life" he wrote, "When I am fired by enthusiasm for war between two cultures, I believe in a superman, and I am grateful to God for making it possible for me to expose myself to a ghastly death in order to win the day for an ideal of civilization."[38]

The early "war papers" present few intimations of the synthesis of mass co-reflection in the noosphere, but in them Teilhard had already formulated in embryo his thesis that man advances only via a series of unifications. It was in this spirit of solidarity for the sake of the human advance, or we might say solidarity at any price, that Teilhard hailed the cause of war, and in so doing equated any kind of solidarity or unified sense of purpose with the good of a "higher spirituality." Teilhard was not writing, of course, to glorify war, but to encourage his readers to seek a peaceful impulse which is equally suited to rally the forces of unification. Like Marx, who, as we noted in Chapter I, located man's drive toward socialization in the most fundamental physical wants, Teilhard realized that human solidarity is most often occasioned by threat and war. The attempts of both writers to establish a positive, noncompetitive locus around which to build human unity will occupy us in the latter half of this study.

Although he was removed from the scene of action in World War II, or perhaps *because* of his distance from the events, Teilhard sustained his optimism with regard to the processes of unification already at work in the world. After the war he assured the delegates to the World Congress of Faiths that the war's superficial turbulence marked only the growing pains of a human race which had suddenly come alive to the possibility of higher being. In Paris in 1946 Teilhard engaged in a public debate with Gabriel Marcel, who questioned Teilhard's doctrine of man's ascendent consciousness: "I ask myself why such a consciousness should necessarily produce a spiritual value. By 'spiritual' I understand a reference to certain values which are very precise. Let me take the example of the doctors at Dachau. On this level, can one be optimistic? What is the integrating consciousness of these scientists worth? I see nothing hominizing there." To this Teilhard replied that "man, to be man, must have, as a man, tried everything to the very end"—"an assumption," adds Teilhard's biographer, "that seems morally questionable in the highest degree, and one that Teilhard himself would have been the last to follow through to its logical conclusion." Teilhard argued that to possess an integrating vision of the world is to partake in a spiritual activity, an argument Marcel characterized as Promethean and unchristian.[39]

Teilhard's overall assessment of two world wars stressed the growth of human unification which has proceeded from war and which in turn will prevent future wars. The examples given are the wireless and aviation from World War I, and from World War II the control of atomic energy whose destructive potential would render armed conflict impossible. In general, Teilhard did not allow enough space to the moral and spiritual implications of these and other scientific discoveries. For one who, like Marx, stressed the inter-relationship of a variety of disciplines, Teilhard had a strangely amoral tendency to divorce technological investigations from the society in which they are conducted. This attitude, which is so unlike the fundamentally moral posture of the Marxian science of economics, may be traced to his belief not only in the evolutionary primacy but also the moral goodness of intensifying unification and consciousness. We might add, finally, that aside from references to man's cognitive misunderstanding of the uses of force and his zoological immaturity, Teilhard did not explore the specifically human origin and character of the great technological advances. Some of man's most cherished accomplishments would have been inconceivable, or at least interminably delayed, had it not been for the impetus of war or other, less strident forms of nationalism. The V-2 rocket, and all that inspired it, is the father of man's scientific exploration of the solar system.

Distortions of the Whole

The evolutionary process of unification has reached its physical apex in the human nervous system, and with the appearance of reflection now jumps to a nonphysical plane in the many forms of psychic communication among people. The physical and, in the early essays, the metaphysical matrix and reverse of unification is multiplicity. In the social context multiplicity appears as individualism, which is not, Teilhard emphasized, to be equated with the personalism which results from union with another.

In his distrust of individualism Teilhard alluded to many Marxian themes and revealed an acquaintance, at least, with the problems which Marx analyzed generations earlier (e.g., the insufficiency of philanthropy to cure poverty). Whereas Marxian realism aimed its missiles at the liberal optimism of an industrial society in sore need of moral awakening, Teilhardian optimism shone as a lonely light in the gray years of existentialism, post-war pessimism, and in the generation of the absurd. Despite the difference of milieux, Teilhard well understood, as we have noted, the sense of isolation that prevails in a society established on the guarantee of individual rights. His list of the rights of personhood, which he substituted for the Rights of Man, retained the much-needed emphasis on constitutional sanctions, while awakening the social responsibility of each person. Marx, we shall see, eliminated all constitutional rights before he had perfected the social mechanism capable of replacing them.

On the subject of specialization, which in Marx is the industrial correlative to social fragmentation, Teilhard maintained largely a biological perspective. Although Teilhard knew that the universality of mechanization has denatured the world, he nevertheless insisted that man has escaped its ravages. This is true, because man, alone of all the animals, has not allowed the overspecialization of an organ to make him a prisoner to his own process of development. "Specialisation paralyzes; ultra specialisation kills."[40] Since human development has centered in mental growth, man has steadfastly refused to use his limbs and teeth as tools and has consequently devised—without becoming somatically involved—first crude implements and now sophisticated systems of automation that extend his efficiency while preserving his intellectual freedom. As a generalization about the species, homo sapiens, all of this is true. But as Teilhard himself admitted, with regard to the individual such biological optimism is only reasonable "virtually and in aspiration." Marx harbored a similar optimism with respect to the potential of mechanization, but he also implicated man in the specialization characterized by the animal's bondage to his own restricted instincts. Although both men stressed the uniqueness of man, only one aptly applied a fundamental biological truth to an open and observable situation in society. It was the economist and not the naturalist who understood the intellectual, cultural, and vocational dead end which, despite increasing wages, still awaits every man whose specialization has made of him, as Marx put it, an appendage and prisoner of the machine.

The most blatant form of individualism occurred in Teilhard's lifetime in the racial specialization of German National Socialism. Neither Marx nor Teilhard were adverse to characterizing and slurring racial peculiarities, and Marx is often accused of anti-semitism. But the doctrine of the Master Race, Teilhard wrote, has an especial perversity and appeal because it *appears* to accept and extend nature's pattern of "the success and domination of a privileged group." But the biological feasibility of racial isolation and the Nazi movement's inner solidarity constituted a "subtle deformation of a great truth" whose perversity lay in its myopic restriction of the human synthesis to a single race.[41]

Of more importance to Teilhard and to postwar generations was another, less subtle deformation of the biological doctrine of convergence. This is the phenomenon of communist collectivization, over against which Teilhard maintained an attitude of guarded ambivalence. As the obverse of individualism, communist totalitarianism constitutes the other half of the biological imbalance from which the whole world is now suffering. The collective represents the necessary stage in the trend of evolution toward convergence and will not therefore end in man's dehumanization. Rather, it presages a "biological super-arrangement" whose structure will necessarily place people in such an intimate physical and psychic proximity that they will mesh, center-to-center, not in an act of annihilation but in one of personalization. He retained this optimism not without levying a criticism at communism or "terrenism" which is reminiscent of Marx's indictment of the division of labor within a capitalist factory. "The Million standardized in the factory; the Million motorized—and all this only ending up with Communism and National Socialism and the most ghastly fetters. So we get the crystal instead of the cell; the ant-hill instead of brotherhood."[42]

Although Teilhard believed that a society based on love rather than compulsion will evolve from the totalitarianism which he described, he did not offer by way of explanation anything more than biological principles transferred to psychic and social planes. For example, his theory of the round earth's compression of people as a leading factor in socialization appears to be more a poetic conceit than a serious scientific explanation. Just as the individual's reflection leads naturally to self-centeredness rather than co-reflection, the curve of the earth might just as well lead to pulverization and a new multiplicity. Indeed the earth's compressive force is leading to just that—in the forms of overpopulation and dehumanization through overcrowded living and working conditions. Moreover, people flee to the cities and arrange themselves in great molecules of physical complexity called high-rise apartment complexes, in order to escape the unguarded mutuality of old-style relationships and to establish highly selective new ones.

Or let us consider a biological law laid down by Teilhard. By insisting on the *moral* value of increasing natural and social complexity, he overlooked a historical trend which has been identified by many, most notably Reinhold Niebuhr: the more organized and highly structured the group or state, the greater is its hypocrisy and abuse of power. But Teilhard's long-range optimism with regard to totalitarian arrangements, that is, that they are only transitory biological heresies, does not do justice to this dark side of complexification (although it does go some way toward explaining his popularity among Marxist intellectuals). His optimistic stance carries with it the danger of a quietistic indulgence of repressive regimes, a quietism which assumes the apparently natural inexorability of human liberation through the lengthy processes of humanity's coming of age.

THE FEELING OF ALIENATION: ANXIETY

Teilhard de Chardin's literary effort was not so much an analysis of the dehumanizing conditions that produce alienation as it was a personal response to man's *feeling* of that alienation. In his response to anxiety, he lifted it from the restrictions of its social expression in class rivalry and placed it into a more universal context. Man, whose nature it is to be alone in the world, has begun to perceive the enormity of his loneliness. The individual understands himself as family, tribe, or nation, but humanity has not yet found other humanities around it "to lean down and tell it where it is going." The awful beauty of this cosmic isolation inspires man's fear but also his worship of a universe that is too beautiful to be comprehended. Man's obsession for analysis, however, drives him to break down synthesis after synthesis and so to depersonalize all that he most admires. As his preoccupation with scientific analysis overcomes his natural inclination toward adoration, man becomes less at home in the machine he calls his world. In his discovery of the "crushing number of living things and of stars," moreover, man has merely uncovered further evidences of his own physical insignificance. Although anxiety is bound up with the advent of reflection and is as old as man himself, modern man's greater knowledge of his position in an evolving universe and his endurance of socialization and mechanization have rendered his experience of becoming, or his genesis, painful and disquieting.

The cause of that disquiet lies in the increasing delitescence of the absolute. In the foregoing sections we examined the evil which hinders the realization of three Teilhardian postulates: forms of unknowing suppress consciousness; man's working energy stagnates; human wholeness suffers distortion through individualism and totalitarian collectivism. These three deficiencies may be equated with evil only when they are related to Teilhard's fourth postulate, faith in the absolute. The modern anxiety, which Teilhard himself experienced repeatedly in the forms of ennui and severe depression, lies in man's recognition of the discrepancy between the finite nature of all human projects and the infinite, which as a great yawning chasm appears to devour and absorb man's noblest works.[43] His quest for an absolute was in reality the desire for a "suitable outcome" or a "way out" for the individual personality and the achievements of civilization.[44]

Hence, the essence of anxiety does not consist in mechanization, analysis, or loneliness in themselves. It is rather, Teilhard concluded, "in the inner fact that men have despaired of God's personality!"[45] This profound insight does much to explain the nature of twentieth-century anxiety; but Teilhard did not submit the diagnosis as the cure. He refused to treat the revelation of God's *issue* for man and the certainty of Christ's universal sovereignty as formulas for the automatic removal of the contradiction in human life. Nor did Teilhard ever describe or counsel spirituality as though he or his reader were living in a world hermetically sealed from doubt and fear. To do so in the twentieth century, of all centuries, would have been most dishonest. The Christian's experience of anxiety is as real as the divine milieu; there was no attempt in Teilhard to avoid this paradox.

In this same vein, he did not give absolute scientific assurance of the successful outcome of evolution. Although his faith in God's promises inclined him toward scientific optimism, he believed that the "supra-phenomenal" nature of faith necessarily leaves all the anxieties in place, even in the hearts of believers. Although a priest, he was nevertheless in close enough contact with the world to understand that "the realities of faith are not felt with the same solidity as the reality of experience. . . . And so inevitably, providentially, there must be terror and bewilderment when one has to pass from one to the other."[46] From one perspective Teilhard's retention of the paradox marks his failure to fulfill his most heroic ambition, the creation of a synthesis of theology and natural science. But from another perspective, it reveals an honest reading of his own experience and the preservation of the uniquely human contradiction between the limitless freedom inherent in Christian belief and the physical and intellectual finitude of each believer.

We are now in a position to evaluate some of the differences between Marx and Teilhard de Chardin. Where Marx began with the social phenomena of suffering and injustice, Teilhard addressed himself to man's search for meaning amidst the many scientific discoveries of the twentieth century. The young Marx isolated the contradiction in human life and in the *Economic and Philosophical Manuscripts* touched on the *feeling* of alienation in those who are deprived of commodities, manipulated in their work, and isolated from society. But these categories of suffering were used solely as instruments to describe a socio-economic situation. Marx occupied himself with a "way out" for humankind only in his portrayal of an entire class's need to escape the vicious cycle of capital→profit→increased capital. He saw his role as that of a social scientist, determined to solve the whole human predicament by restricting himself to a single dimension—the observable economic and sociological one—of human experience.

Teilhard, to the contrary, depicted the human predicament, that is, the loss of meaning which he interpreted as a spiritual crisis, only after he had refracted it through his own personality. This procedure in many places opens onto an insightful description of modern man, particularly the spiritual man, who carries with him the most sublime hopes for the universe as well as "a burden of inconsistencies and unfulfilled aims." Teilhard's personal analysis in fact yields the cause of anxiety; the abandonment of God's personality eventually leads the modern world away from love and grace to chance and the comfortless dogmas of materialism. If Teilhard's refraction of modern anxiety contained an accurate portrayal of the inner conflict between unbelief and hope, it nevertheless failed to identify the anxious world's alternative to belief in a personal God. When he attributed modern nonbelief in Christ to man's heightened awareness and worship of the universe, he was projecting his own particular temptation, his "profound tendencies toward pantheism," onto a modern man of straw. In this he missed man's preoccupation not with the splendor of nature but with the pleasures of self-infatuation. Since Teilhard himself never experienced a sense of indifference toward the ultimate issues in science and theology, he never quite comprehended the massive indifference of a secularized, industrial society toward such questions. The majority of this society probably does not perceive the world as too beautiful to share man's adoration with any other Being. The image of Teilhard's own personality has undoubtedly stamped itself on this aspect of his profile of man. In fact his method of culling from his own experience the spiritual climate of an entire generation, in an effort to portray the whole phenomenon of man, was bound to fail more often than succeed, for its reach inevitably exceeded its grasp.

There is then this basic difference between Teilhard and Marx: while Marx's sociological empiricism tended to limit his reach (if not his pretentions), Teilhard boldly attempted to explicate the relation between the whole of human development and humankind's emotional and spiritual understanding of it.

THE USES OF PASSIVITY AND DEATH

We now pass from Teilhard's response to anxiety into another human problem which, in the individual, Marx left untouched. This is man's experience of passivity and the various forms of diminishment which culminate in death. We have alluded to the rigidity of the categories into which Marx installed the ideal man and the empirical man. The former is essentially active, the latter passive. This categorical understanding of man, however, does not adequately represent the tension between the forces of activity and passivity which exist in all people irrespective of their political or economic stations. In Le milieu divin Teilhard divided the passivities into two groups. The passivities of growth present the individual with the situation or the conditions under which he is to develop his mental and physical life. The passivities of diminishment, or the "real passivities," constitute the external obstructions to human growth and the internal forces of erosion in every human being. Among the internal forces of diminishment Teilhard included failure, disease, physical suffering, old age, death, and sin (pp. 54–62).

In sharp contrast to Marx, Teilhard knew a dialectical transformation of man which is operative on the personal level. For the moment we shall suspend judgment on this dialectic's viability in social transformation and concentrate on its meaning for the individual's effort to utilize and transform his suffering. The premise of any consideration of suffering is that God does not will that evil should overwhelm his children. The corollary to this, therefore, encourages Christians, who believe in the goodness of God, to struggle against evil and attempt to reduce it to a minimum. This struggle on the part of one who suffers diminishment represents not only his desire to conform to God's will but also a yearning to live in obedience. In other words, he engages in activity for the sake of submission or passivity. But our finite and sinful actions are bound to fail, and with that failure come the death of the ego and the collapse of all individual and collective achievement. At this spiritual bottom a new reality opens before man. "I can only unite myself to the will of God (as endured passively) *when all my strength is spent*, at the point where my activity, fully extended and straining toward betterment, . . . finds itself continually counterweighted by forces tending to halt me or overwhelm me. Unless I do everything I can to advance or resist, I shall not find myself at the *required point*—I shall not submit to God as much as I might have done or as much as He wishes."[47]

In this passage Teilhard revealed the dialectical tension between activity and passivity, resistance and submission, which exists in every Christian. At the very point of defeat, when the power of suffering has reduced a person to a state of impotence and passive acquiescence, the individual discovers God in the *willed* act of submission. In this submission a reversal, or what Teilhard termed an "excentration," takes place by which man dies to himself and begins to live only to God. What Teilhard did not make clear, however, is that where suffering is embodied in sin and its direct consequences, this excentration corresponds to the more traditional word: repentance.

In the nontheological and neutral language of passivity and diminishment, Teilhard reproduced the personal dialectic revealed to St. Paul: "My grace is sufficient for you, for my power is made perfect in weakness." God requires in each person a point of moral, mental, or physical diminishment, which in the moral sphere traditional theologians called *passiva contritio,* in order that the divine love may be grace and our knowledge, faith. Only the rending of human pride and achievement prepares the way for the new creation of the whole. This is the Christian's dialectic captured by Donne in one of the *Holy Sonnets:*

Batter my heart, three person'd God; for you
As yet but knocke, breathe, shine, and seeke to mend;
That I may rise, and stand, o'erthrow mee, and bend
Your force, to break, blowe, burn and make me new.

Luther had expressed the same truth earlier at the inception of the Reformation: "When God begins to justify a person, He first condemns Him; when He wants to build up, He first tears down; whom He wants to heal, He first batters to pieces; whom he wants to bring to life, He first kills."[48] It is this dialectical sequence—human action (in conformity to the will of God), inevitable diminishment, death of the self, willed submission, God's gracious action, and new, more sublime life—which permeates God's relationship to humankind and each believer's private existence amid the currents of interior diminishment. It occurs as a cyclical motif throughout the history of God's chosen people; it emerges in the life of the Messiah and, as we shall discover, in the socialized secularization of that life in the proletariat's violent distortion of its messianic identity.

Teilhard reproduced a general outline of this scriptural dialectic and applied it to the suffering of the individual. He reduced the inner force of this dialectic, however, in several ways. He did not give sufficient attention to the judgment of God, which is a precondition of all human suffering taken in its broad sense, and therefore did not allude to the discrepancy between judgment and the grace which offers an utterly unique avenue of escape. Whenever he attempted to relate the dialectic of personal diminishment and rebirth in Christ to the collective realm, his presentation affords little comfort and opportunity for spiritual growth. Pain, for example, is an intensely personal experience which cannot be satisfactorily explained by the fact that "the world, seen by experience at our level, is an immense groping, an immense search, an immense attack; its progress can take place only at the expense of many failures, of many wounds." Those who suffer are "casualties fallen on the field of honour" who are "paying for the forward march and triumph of all."[49]

Suffering drives people to the cross of Christ, the symbolic power of which, however, Teilhard depersonalized by associating it with an evolutionary "law common to *all* life."[50] Thus, at the end of his famous little essay, "The Significance and Positive Value of Suffering" (in *Human Energy*), Teilhard did not turn his readers toward the *event* which has once and for all removed the pain par excellence of suffering and death, but toward a *process* led by the divine vanguard who "bears the weight and draws ever higher towards God the universal march of progress." Significantly, then, the final sentence does not recall the redemption, but, in the phrase "let us act like him," enjoins imitation.

Marx and Teilhard experienced their share of personal suffering. Teilhard, on the one hand, developed his view of human suffering on the basis of his own inner conflict, and was thus more concerned with the sublimation of mental anguish into spiritual power. His understanding of evil as evolutionary privation led him to overlook the intrinsic horror of physical suffering and to condemn only those mass regressions and failures of nerve which stall the human ascent. Marx, on the other hand, produced a protest out of the matrix of the physical sufferings of others and did not allow his personal problems, such as poverty and illness, to influence consciously his analysis of evil.

Three of Marx's children died early in childhood, and a fourth as a young adult. Seven of Teilhard's ten brothers and sisters died prematurely. Only Teilhard attempted a literary response to this ultimate diminishment, and only Teilhard, for that matter, reflected on man's universal anguish and frustration in the face of death. "Seen in the future," he wrote, "death is the epitome, and the common basis of everything that terrifies us and makes our minds reel."[51] It casts a pall over the most vibrant and optimistic of human actions and colors every earthly hope with a shade of absurdity.

"We owe God a death," Shakespeare says flatly; but what is the nature of man's dying? Speaking as a physical scientist, Teilhard described an animal's death as the reabsorption of radial energy into the tangential. Man disintegrates like an animal, but in him death represents a critical change of state in which radial energy is liberated from its dependence upon the tangential and from entropy. All people, by virtue of spirit's mastery of material arrangements and evolution's drive toward personalization, are liberated from reliance upon physical necessities and achieve at death the purely spiritual life of personality. In his earlier essays Teilhard described this liberation in terms of the "immortality of the soul," although his early views on the material origin of the spiritual element in man separate that venerable phrase from its traditional usage. But whether he spoke of the immortality of the soul or the conservation of persons, as he tended to do in his later work, at back of his innovative image of the two energies and his shifting theological vocabulary lay an extension of the same dialectic which operates in the sublimation of all human diminishments. The ultimate point of excentration occurs at death: "God must, in some way or other, make room for himself, hollowing us out and emptying us if he is finally to penetrate into us. And in order to assimilate us in him, he must break the molecules of our being so as to recast and remold us."[52] Thus in death, as in all the passivities of diminishment, the excentration, the reversion to God, takes place only in the person's willed act of surrender.

In the Christian's surrender of his being into communion with God death is revealed as the final passivity which is undergone *and* as a decisive historical action. One of the important differences between Marxism and the Christian tradition is Christianity's emphasis on the historicity of death. Since the individual's death as an event in itself is not subject to a Marxian analysis, we can only assume that, to one whose entire philosophy is a historical interpretation of man, death lies outside the purview of history. Only men have and make true history; for Marx a man's dying, however, is unhistorical, for it represents only the animal's return to undifferentiated nature. In contrast to this, Christianity treats death as an event, the last important event of a person's life. Far from being a simple abdication to matter, the nature of any one act of dying may be shaped, according to the circumstances of death, by the individual's attitude toward it. A man may often choose a reasoned or desperate, heroic or cowardly, resigned or despairing response to death and allow that response to stand as a final witness of his personality and philosophy of life.

Most important, however, is the witness made before God. This witness, Teilhard wrote, takes the form of a willed communion with God which serves as the consummation of one's historical existence and as the introduction to a new dimension of life. The culmination of the individual's life is "death in union": ". . . Grant that I may willingly consent to this last phase of communion in the course of which I shall possess you by diminishing in you. . . . Vouchsafe, therefore, something more precious still than the grace for which all the faithful pray. It is not enough that I should die while communicating. Teach me to *treat my death as an act of communion.*"[53] Because man's act of surrender contributes to this final communion, the Christian prepares for the event of his death—not with maudlin sentimentality but with athletic rigor and discipline. This sense of preparation, in the form of an intensifying awareness of the "Christic," pervaded the last years of Teilhard de Chardin. In letter after letter he expressed his hope "to end well" and to "keep in form" so as "to persevere to the end in doing all I can to bring about the coming of His Kingdom as I see it in my dreams."[54]

Teilhard prepared for death with an understanding of its dialectical functions as a destroyer of visible forms and a liberator of spiritual ones. Since Teilhard's Christ encompasses the whole world, the death of Christ carries within it the potential excentration and surrender of all people and effects the transition to the spiritual life. Christ's sacrificial action in the face of death serves not only as a moral *exemplum* (as Teilhard says that it does), but it radically changes the nature of death "by suppressing its evil effects" and "reversing its sting." True to his vocation of observing the whole phenomenon of man, Teilhard resisted an easy spiritualization of man's life and victory in the midst of death. The realities of life are always experienced with a greater intensity than the realities of faith. The death and resurrection of Christ do not remove the contradiction between our efforts to grow and the many forms of resistance these efforts encounter. The created framework of the cosmos itself does not allow Christ to remove the diminishments but only to integrate them, though not without changing them, in a new spiritualization of our lives.

On a social level, beyond the destiny of each individual, Teilhard and Marx were susceptible to a different kind of immortality and braced themselves against a different form of anguish. The individual in Teilhard and Marx labors for a cause whose goal of social renovation lies in the distant future. For the Marxian man, as Ernst Bloch has shown, the certainty of a class's revolutionary consciousness looms on the horizon as the only "novum against death." Marx himself, however, did not offer this crumb of solace to the individual, but instead dispatched the problem in one laconic sentence: "*Death* seems to be a harsh victory of the species over the individual and to contradict their unity; but the particular individual is only a *determinate species-being* and as such he is mortal."[55] Although his own life demonstrated his unswerving dedication to a cause whose fulfillment lay beyond his lifetime, Marx did not pontificate upon the individual's immortality in his species or social class. The realist in him would have seen through this theological disguise. The Communist, therefore, who labors purely for the true and lasting consummation of Marx's hope—a universal classless society—must be driven, despite Marx's repudiation of self-sacrifice, by an uncommon altruism.

This immortality in one's cause has its place in Teilhard's view of death: "What fascinates me in life is being able to collaborate in a task, a reality, more durable than myself. . . . If death attacks me, it leaves untouched these causes and ideas and realities, more solid and precious than myself."[56] The reality of massive co-reflection, toward which the individual's effort, suffering, and death have made some contribution, will not be realized in his lifetime. Josef Pieper briefly criticizes Teilhard's casual attitude toward death and speculates on the fate of the "hopers" who die before the ascent of life has been completed.[57] The brevity of Pieper's criticism does not do justice to the spirituality of Teilhard's meditation on death in *Le milieu divin;* but we are again reminded that the vertical relationship that each Christian enjoys with Christ disrupts the symmetry of natural progress. It is *now* possible for the individual Christian to attain on earth and at death communion with God. This is not to say that Teilhard missed this point, but only that, like the problem of individual suffering, it was not adequately integrated, nor could it have been, into a collective scheme.

Although Teilhard in a number of places insisted on the possibility of evolution's failure, as one who believed in the existence of God and the conservation of personalities at death, he never credibly advanced the possibility of a total death of the universe. His belief in the necessity of a new genesis of other noospheres throughout the universe, should this planet's die, compares with Engels' wistful hope in the eternal regeneration of mind.[58] As Engels' speculations prove, one need not be a Christian to be caught in the contradiction between a thirst for the absolute and the scientific pessimism which feeds upon and indeed revels in the second law of thermodynamics. While the need for an absolute that transcends total death is theologically well-founded, Teilhard's exposition of it relied too heavily on a questionable psychological hypothesis: should it be proved to man that in so many million years the earth will cease to support his effort and that the human race will die, man would immediately "cease to act" and shut down his civilization.[59] This is a suspect piece of psychology for three reasons. It attributes to the ordinary person (farmer, machinist, academic) a cosmic vision which he does not in reality possess. It leaves out of account the universal voice of man's infatuation with momentary achievement and pleasure: *carpe diem;* and on the practical level it does not account for the activity of millions of Communists who, living in the shadow of Carnot's law rather than the sunshine of Engels' fancy for the absolute, strive nonetheless for a perfect society in a finite world.

THE FAILURE OF THE SYSTEMS

Indirectly and directly Christianity provided a theological framework for two very different phenomenologies of evil, one set within an economic order, the other an evolutionary process. With its doctrines of election, creation, original sin, and personal salvation, the Christian faith erected a backdrop against which Marx and Teilhard evaluated the individual's or the person's role in impersonal systems of development.

The brilliance of Marx's conception of alienation lay not in its application of Hegelian ideas to human consciousness (Feuerbach had already done that), but in its collectivizing use of Christian doctrine. Despite the early Marx's sensitivity to man's feeling of alienation, his creative achievement came in his later projection of the human condition into the class structure. He further appropriated the Pauline and Lutheran description of fallen man's separation from God and bondage to fleshly and cosmic powers and applied it to the situation within capitalist society. By depicting the economics of sin in capitalism's voracious concupiscence he effectively demonstrated the universal nature of evil which, as an act, prescribes the character of the exploiting class, and, as a condition, afflicts the exploited with physical and mental suffering.

The design of Marx's scheme, ignoring as it did the personal dialectics of the Christian life, resulted in the simplification of human nature. For the ideal of self-determination, which he never empirically established as a norm, does not in itself represent "truly human" nature any more than his evocation of total proletarian passivity constitutes the accurate results of sociological investigation. Here, above all, Teilhard provided a remedy to Marx's simplification of human existence. By establishing the problem of meaning as his apologetical point of departure, and by heeding a simple truth—that classes do not fear death, but people do—he restored the person, with all the human tensions between finite and infinite intact, to the center of the religious and evolutionary drama.

With great boldness Teilhard transposed the privative deficiency of man's failure before God to the evil aspects of the not-yet of evolution. Hence in Teilhard's collectivizing of the phenomenon of evil, the refusal to love appears as man's retardation of evolution and his dangerous potency to will a general strike in the noosphere. Teilhard, moreover, complemented the universality of social and economic injustice in Marx's analysis by reflecting upon the individual's anguish in his encounter with personal diminishment and the inevitability of death. In fact, his profile of man is most salutary in its acceptance of the realities of activity and passivity in every life and their spiritual synthesis in the life of the Christian.

As a system-builder, however, Teilhard's shortcoming emerged in his failure to communicate his devotional awareness of the dialectics of diminishment and growth in Christ to his optimistic system of evolution. Whereas Marx inflated the powers of his universe by the breath of his hatred for them, Teilhard, by his method of farsighted tolerance and his spiritual and psychological view of alienation, *deflated* the powers to the extent that their authority to diminish on an evolutionary scale becomes negligible. Teilhard's failure to integrate thoroughly the personal diminishments and their sublimation into a system of evolutionary progress calls into question the feasibility of fitting that which is essentially a personal relationship based on faith, obedience, and love to an impersonal movement of the collected forces of civilization. Even the collective entities, Israel and the church, participate in the dialectic of obedience and faith, judgment and grace, by assuming the personal images of son or bride in their relationship with God. The basic weakness, therefore, which emerges from the Teilhardian and Marxian *systems* is their depersonalization of man's fallen condition. The full extent of this depersonalization will be revealed only in their analyses of the origin and nature of evil, to which we turn in Chapter III.

Chapter III

THE ORIGIN AND NATURE OF EVIL

What appears as the congenital sinfulness of one generation is conditioned by the sinfulness of the previous one, and in turn conditions that of later; and only in the whole . . . progressive development of man, do we find the whole aspect of things denoted by the term, "original sin."

—*Friedrich Schleiermacher*

It does not seem likely that man will succeed in transforming evil until he understands it. Marx and Teilhard were aware of this and therefore did not content themselves with a description and denunciation of evil but sought its origin and ground of historical development. In order to transform humanity as a whole and to inaugurate a society of an entirely different order, they needed to explain how evil affects not just the person but the whole process of becoming in which humanity is enveloped. Although Marx and Teilhard humanized the economic and evolutionary processes—by making humankind their mover and goal—we shall observe in this chapter the intensifying disjunction of person and process which constitutes the major deficiency of their systems. Caught in this contradiction, Marx and Teilhard chose the coherence of the whole at the expense of the unique properties of the person. The desire for systematic coherence led them to abandon the quest for a historical man and a personal decision which, taken long ago, created a milieu of sin, suffering, and death. Instead they preferred to begin with the milieu, that is, the condition of human development, and proceeded to demonstrate the necessity of its sinful character. All that remained, then, was the identification of the person with this all-pervasive economic or evolutionary mode of becoming, and the groundwork for the erosion of man's personal and spiritual responsibility was complete.

REJECTED IDEOLOGICAL EXPLANATIONS

In the *Economic and Philosophical Manuscripts* Marx promised that he would never resort to a "legendary primordial condition" or in any way attempt to go behind history in order to shed light on the current state of human nature. Hence he steadfastly refused to create a speculative picture of the human situation prior to the class struggles accessible to historians and observable in his day. He was not adverse to describing the early and what he believed to have been more peaceful periods of man's existence, but he was unwilling to *explain* or *justify* man's present condition on the basis of a nonhistorical, prelapsarian era, or to deal with the transition from myth to history. In this refusal he has been joined by many representatives of modern theology, including Teilhard de Chardin, who insist upon the total historical accessibility of man, and who will only reluctantly ascribe to human existence conditions of a transhistorical origin.

All bourgeois justification of the bourgeois position in society has as its foundation the doctrine of creation. Like Teilhard, Marx did not minimize the importance of creation. The Marxian and Teilhardian man, in fact, acts as the agent of a continuing creation. What they both opposed is the static view of creation which sanctifies the status quo and eliminates all possibility of change. Aside from his nonbelief in a transcendent Being, Marx opposed the idea of creation on the principle that it makes of man a dependent creature. To one such as Marx who idealized self-determination, the doctrine of creation was not only psychologically harmful but politically dangerous owing to the rationale it provides for the givenness of human misery. Instead he advanced the spontaneous generation of life as an alternative to the notion of an infinite regression of causes to the first cause, the creative God. For man to search for an alien being and to name him "Creator" amounts to a disavowal of the supreme reality of the dialectical struggle between human creativity and nature by which man creates himself.

In his many references to the suppression of the proletariat, Marx isolated two general ideological fronts, theoretically founded on the immutability of the creation, which capitalism mounts against the lower class in order to justify an imbalanced status quo. The first form of ideology is based on the unquestioned goodness of nature. It extrapolates from the competition within the animal world and the necessary existence of victors and victims in order to explain the exploitation and abasement of the poor. But nature, said Marx, does not decree that one man must exploit another, nor does nature produce on the one side owners of money or commodities, and on the other people possessing nothing but their own labor power.[1] Bourgeois ideology moreover claims to find a natural basis for free trade, free labor (as opposed to trade unions), and the huge economic disparity between the classes. In practice capitalism reduces the living standards of the worker to the subsistence level and then characterizes that level as standard or natural. In no context did Marx ever equate the strivings of men with natural competition. Whether nature is characterized as peaceful or competitive, its law is never man's good, infallible guide in submission or revolution. Only man's materially conditioned, historical consciousness can serve that purpose. In the light of bourgeois ideological uses of Darwinism and the importance which Marx ascribed to man's unique historical consciousness, it is, incidentally, puzzling that both Engels and Marx felt obliged to attempt a correlation of communist doctrines with the theory of evolution.

The second form of ideological explanation is more theological in substance. When the proletarian tries to see outside the vicious circle of capital→surplus value→capital in order to understand the origin of the process, he is confronted with a theological moralism. Rather than admit that the proletariat's state is traceable only to the capitalist mode of production, the oppressors, Marx claimed, posit the primal existence of two kinds of people: the frugal and the wasteful. The frugal man accumulated; the wastrel did not. "This primitive accumulation plays in political economy about the same part as original sin in theology."[2] More accurately, the wealth resulting from the so-called primitive accumulation was too often associated with the Protestant doctrine of the Calling, as it was used to justify both the poverty of one class and its immediate cause, the voracious economic activity of another.

As we have seen, Marx himself was not adverse to dividing the human race into two types, the exploiters and the exploited. But on the crucial question of the origins of this division, he derided as an ideological approach any analysis of human nature. And of course he was right in lampooning the perverted ethic which equated financial success with righteousness. He performed a valuable service by demythologizing history to expose the violent, murderous sources of wealth. With St. Augustine, he would have agreed, "What else are the great kingdoms but great robberies?"[3] By such a moral revelation, however, Marx failed to lay bare the origins of alienation and exploitation. He did not dare to ask *why* man conquers, murders, and exploits. In Marx the question is so often abandoned to ridicule—as in his parody on the "True Socialists" and their notion of the "corrupt essence of the rentiers"—because he consistently refused to consider any facet of man that cannot be set into an economic context.[4] The persistence of the question in a humanized study of economics, however, forced Marx to make certain tentative statements concerning the origin of alienation. In his ambiguous treatment of the problem, examined in the next two sections, we can begin to note some of the inadequacies of this theory of alienation which will carry over into his prediction of revolution and a new society.

REMNANTS OF A PERSONAL THEORY
OF ORIGINAL SIN

Despite Marx's lack of interest in theological explanation and his immunity from its knottier problems, scattered throughout his system of economic determinism and existing as implications and logical corollaries of it are remnants of a personal theory of original sin. In the Paris Manuscripts Marx refused to begin his explanations "from a legendary primordial condition." Fourteen years later, however, in the recently discovered preparatory draft for *Capital* (the *Grundrisse)* Marx made his only thorough pilgrimage back to the idyllic days of tribal life. In this work he set the stage for the fall of man by introducing a quasi-historical creature whose nature does *not* consist solely in his productive activity, but rather in his relationship with his fellows and his communal, cooperative *ownership* of the land. He did not follow Engels' *Origin of the Family* and exaggerate the benign character of tribal communism, but he did examine man's early relations to the land, from the time he held it with his fellows as a divine grant, to man's early consciousness of private ownership, the land as "mine." In that epoch, Marx wrote, men were joined by blood, community, language, and custom and, as a community, they acted as proprietors of the land. Only as an embodiment of the community could man think of himself as an owner of the land. For our purposes the most remarkable discovery in these studies is this: in his view of communal ownership of the land, Marx envisioned a tribal entity, a corporate *man* who was once upon a time "something more than the abstraction of the 'working individual.' " This man possessed "an objective mode of existence in his ownership of the earth which is antecedent to his activity and does not appear as its mere consequence."[5] Thus the Marxian Fall consists not in the ownership of property per se, but in the individualism which first differentiated the self from the land and therefore from the community.

By what agency did man lose this communally sanctioned ownership? How was this ownership perverted into hateful property relationships which alienate man from the products of his self-activity and divide the human race into warring classes? According to Marx the fall from primordial unity with the self, the community, and the land occurred as a primitive kind of division of labor. There are natural and yet alienating forms of this division owing to differences in sex, age, and position in the family. As alienation, it developed into the unequal distribution of labor and its products, in short, property, through the acquired power of disposing of the working activity of others. This power may develop within the established communal setting or may be claimed as the right of the victorious after a period of intertribal warfare.

The only concrete cause Marx advanced for the rupture of tribal unity and the subsequent rise of owners and workers is the inevitability of wars and the occupation of land belonging to others. With the onslaught of war, the communal nature of man became a negative thing, a mere defense against other tribes. Hoarding of family land in a defensive manner led to greater private property until the strongest became protectors and ultimately owners of what had formerly been the *ager publicus*.[6] Although Marx's description of man's self-differentiation from the land and community implies a lengthy process, Marx capsulized the long train of events in a historical instant and thereby created a rival symbol of the Fall, replete with para-miltonic anguish at the loss of innocence: "This is the time when the very things which till then had been communicated, but never exchanged; given, but never sold, acquired, but never bought—virtue, love, conviction, knowledge, conscience, etc.—when everything, in short, passed into commerce. It is the time of general corruption, of universal venality."[7]

Implicit in this sin against the community is man's seemingly innate greed for power, land, and, at a latter stage of his development, for money. With regard to Marx we can say only "seemingly innate," for he never followed Engels' unequivocal statement of man's innate perversity, but understood the inception of private property as the victory of the principle of Having over that of Being. There is a noneconomic aspect of this greed which Marx suggested in his emphasis on the acquisition of power in social and intertribal relationships. He returned to the theme of power in *Capital* where he introduced a long quotation from Luther by saying, "Taking the usurer, that old-fashioned but ever renewed specimen of the capitalist, for his text, Luther shows very aptly that the love of power is an element in the desire to get rich."[8] The moral side of the story is concerned with the greed which motivates even the most primitive exploitation. Although Marx, as will be evident in the following section on economic determinism, denied the possibility of a personal or a universal sin which contradicts the properties of human nature, as a moral economist he was forced to face the questions: Why are tribal, as well as class wars, inevitable? Why do the most natural divisions of labor, such as sexual or family roles, develop into exploitive relationships based on power? Why are these relationships—and all others—solidified on the basis of the possession of private property?

It would be a misrepresentation of Marx to pretend that he ever systematically addressed himself to these questions. We find in him a thorough grasp of the effects of sin: the universality of corruption in the form of world industrial complexes, which obliterate natural and ethnic distinctions and change all kinds of international and interpersonal relationships into money relationships. This set of circumstances—and not St. Paul's reminder of the universality of death in Romans 5—measures the Fall's universal consequence. Moreover, Marx harbored two explanations of the mechanism by which the condition of universal bondage is transmitted. The moral theory indicted the avarice and desire for power common to human nature wherever it is found. The economic theory, to be dealt with in the next section, proposed the amoral mechanism of the situation, which operates according to its own predictable logic independent of moral decisions. Save for the ill-defined period of blessedness in the paradise of precapitalist society, to which Marx himself gave a legendary cast, the first man encountered by both the moral and the economic explanations already possesses a background of sin and evil. It was not possible for Marx to locate historically the *first* act against the community, for any such act would have been committed by one already separated from the community.

In an effort to divert the problem, if not to solve it, Marx introjected the traditional sequence of the innocence, temptation, and fall of Adam into the heart of the individual capitalist. In a remarkable passage which characterizes sin as a historical continuity and as a kind of Kierkegaardian "leap" in the individual's present, Marx portrayed the existential manifestation of original sin.

At the historical dawn of capitalist production—and every capitalist upstart has personally to go through this historical stage—avarice and desire to get rich are the ruling passions. The capitalist's necessary prodigality has always lurking behind it the most sordid avarice and the most anxious calculation, yet his expenditure grows with his accumulation, without the one necessarily restricting the other. But along with this growth, there is at the same time developed in his breast a Faustian conflict between the passion for accumulation and the desire for enjoyment.[9]

For the Christian theologian the identification of Adam and "me" represents a healthy emphasis on the vertical relationship with God, unconditioned by historical circumstances, by which every man is accounted responsible for his own actions. Such an approach adheres to Kant's opposition to every attribution of effects in moral character to causative occurrences in time. "In the search for the rational origin of evil actions," Kant stated, "every such action must be regarded as though the individual had fallen into it directly from a state of innocence."[10] The absolute identification of "me" or the human race with Adam, however, fails to answer, or even to contest, the question of how sin began in the world or why each individual necessarily encounters in himself not only the recapitulation of Adam's experience but also a background of sin which in every way precedes his personal sequence of innocence, temptation, and fall. For Marx the evasion was more serious. For the existential recapitulation of economic history would remove the Marxian man from the only arena in which responsibility, sin, and redemption are possible—the reality of history.

THE SIN OF THE ECONOMIC PROCESS

In his definitive explanation of human evil, Marx attributed the exploitation, alienation, and suffering of man to a universally verifiable situation, or, in its historical perspective, to an economic process. This situation itself is derived from the Marxian man's identity as a mode of the community's life of production and exchange. Hence, when we say that economic determinism draws its validity from human nature, we are envisioning man as Marx understood him, and not as a person responsible and precious in the eyes of God. Because Marx, as I shall show, so closely associated the nature of man with an inexorably corrupt mode of economic life, it is clear that his man can bear no responsibility for the corruption of his own life and no creative power to change it. While this appears to overlook Marx's own condemnation of all ideologies which attempt to package evil as a necessary component of human nature or the biological order, it is just this equation of man's evil with the given mode of human development—the economic—which diminishes the credibility of Marx's (and to some extent Teilhard's) doctrine of man.

Despite the imagery of concupiscence and the categories which Marx borrowed from Lutheran theology, his explanation of man's fallen condition bypassed traditional theology's refusal—since Augustine and before Schleiermacher—to equate finite existence with evil. We are therefore justified in separating Marx's talk of sin, with its implied moral responsibility, from his deterministic understanding of sin's true origin and nature. At the core of the Marxian man's unhappy existence is the economic limitation of his own finite nature. The misery of sin arose from the matrix of man's social nature and his physical needs; it developed in his attempt to satisfy his needs through exchange and was exacerbated by the most primitive forms of the division of labor. The sin is now identifiable by that which man suffers as the result of his natural and historical development. The Marxian sequence, then, moves from what man is, to what he does, and finally to what is done to him.

In Engels' brief eulogy at his friend's grave he summarized Marx's discovery of "the law of development of human history" with these compact observations:

Mankind must first of all eat, drink, have shelter and clothing, before it can pursue politics, science, art, religion, etc. . . . . Therefore the production of the immediate material means of subsisting and consequently the degree of economic development attained by a given people or during a given epoch form the foundation upon which the state institutions, the legal conceptions, the ideas on art, and even on religion, of the people concerned have been evolved, and in the light of which they must therefore be explained instead of *vice versa*, as had hitherto been the case.[11]

Engels was reiterating the Marxian dictum set down thirty-seven years earlier: "Life is not determined by consciousness but consciousness by life." The economically based conception of history rejects mind as the criterion of human nature and the source of civilized life and substitutes for it the needs of the body. Man, the social animal, naturally draws upon the community for the fulfillment of his basic wants. The need for mutual sustenance through production and exchange therefore forms the most important component of the social nature of man. After the *Economic and Philosophical Manuscripts* we hear no more of man's relationship to woman, of the other person as need. As early as *The German Ideology* (1845–46) Marx and Engels claimed to distinguish man from the animals by the former's production of his means of subsistence. The reciprocal satisfaction of need becomes human by reason of man's dawning consciousness of the process of production and exchange.[12] Thus the nature of man as he *is*—a creature wholly dependent upon his community and environment—determines what he must do and leads directly to the more immediate cause of his suffering.

Out of man's need and natural inclination toward commerce arises the division of labor. From the beginning, the division of labor manifests itself as an agent of alienation. While Marx knew that there can be a perfectly natural division of labor, as in the family, he hastened to add that this initial relationship always becomes exploitative. The mystery of its corruptive power may be sounded to the depths of man's structural need to live in the community and to sustain himself through production and exchange—but no deeper. In *Capital* Marx explained man's preoccupation with objects in this way: "This fetishism of commodities has its origin . . . in the peculiar social character of the labor that produces them" (p. 31). Or with Adam Smith, he knew that it is not the innate differences in men which give rise to the division of labor, but the division of labor which produces different kinds of men.[13]

The *origin* of the sinful or alienating aspect of the division of labor is lost because man's status as a responsible person has been taken from him. A distillation of the process of economic determinism tells us only that man exploits and is exploited because his essentially commercial nature demands such action. According to Marx, the essence of man *is* a complex of material, that is, trade relationships. Yet Marx condemned the capitalist for transforming all relations into material processes of exchange, a strange accusation, as Berdyaev remarked, to be made by a historical materialist. In the Marxian world of economics, in which the possibility of a human nature, character, or personal decision antecedent to the mode of production is a priori excluded, one has no choice but to identify the nature of man with an impersonal system of production which has manifested its own corruption from the beginning. And this is exactly what Marx did: "The sum of productive forces, forms of capital and social forms of intercourse which every individual and generation finds in existence as something given, is the real basis of what the philosophers have conceived of as 'substance' and 'essence of man.' "[14]

The totality of man's enslavement to a condition of existence is such that in the last analysis he does not recognize its alien character and therefore cannot effectively plan his resistance. By entering into the consciousness of all men, "industry as self," by virtue of its inner identification with the natural processes of social life, becomes greater than the sum of all exploited and exploiting individuals. It is the condition of capitalist industrialization alone, Marx wrote to Annenkov, which determines exploitation.[15] In a more polemical context in *Capital* the imagery of capital suggests an insatiable organism whose forces "consume" the worker "as the ferment necessary to their own life processes" and whose dictates all within its social system must follow (p. 150). Hence the capitalist must exploit his laborers in order to make a profit, and the worker must alienate himself from his fellows in competition for jobs. As in the Old Testament, the sin which this system generates and perpetuates becomes the condition of bondage, the penalty, of all. Action is fate. Economically, then, as well as theologically, alienation begins with man's conscious idolatry before the powers and principalities which oppress him, and ends in his internalization of them and nondeliberative resignation to a life of bondage.

The Manichean opposition of the oppressed and the oppressors with its emphasis on the *sin* of exploitation amounts to nothing more than a system whose tendency to malfunction lies buried in the recesses of man's social metabolism. So obscure is the original man and his original sin that even in Marx's penetrating mind the system, with its scientifically observed laws, has supplanted the proper study of mankind. Instead of man, the maker of systems, we are confronted with the system, for which men are mere illustrations: "But here individuals are dealt with only in so far as they are the personifications of economic categories, embodiments of particular class relations and class interests. My standpoint . . . can less than any other make the individual responsible for relations whose creature he socially remains."[16] Marx, the economist, was justified in making such an abstraction. But in a moral economics which hoped to raise human nature to its highest dignity, the effacement of personal responsibility was a retrograde step leading to a new dehumanization.

Marx showed that all people are caught on an economic wheel of fire, and therefore all are absolved of personal responsibility for its horror. He did, however, take up the cause of one portion of humanity and dramatically portrayed its passivity and sacrifice. The proletariat can claim no identity which is unconditioned by material forces. Through no conscious decision has it fallen, and through no inner perversion does it give itself to the idols of its own hand. Its greed, competition, atomization, and hatred have in no way been self-induced, but are the inevitable results of evil in another being more powerful than itself. The proletariat's essence is suffering *(passio)*; and, as a totally nonethical bloc, it is inured to the hard Christian truth that "the state of the Christian soul is conditioned by a sense of transgression committed and not of injury received."[17]

Although freedom is the greatest component of the Marxian ideal, the proletariat's freedom exists only in a state of suspension and is scorned for the time being as an ideological word and a tool of oppression. When the complex of economic conditions and the entire superstructure built upon them are changed and can no longer determine man, then the proletariat will have emerged from its human prehistory into the Marxian kingdom of freedom. In the meantime the worker finds no renewal in Christianity's eschatological tension between the past and the future. The freedom that the Christian now enjoys through faith in a future which has already been historically and sacramentally realized in the victory of Christ is completely foreign to the Marxian man. In the endless historical present, therefore, the capitalist representative of economic force and its faceless victim are locked in a position of stasis by the laws of economic determinism. The immutability of roles, which dominates capitalism and the proletariat, seems to mock all criticism and moral exhortation to alter societal relationships and creates, finally, a protagonist and an antagonist necessarily immune to the moral demands Marx laid upon them.

THE MATERIALIST STRAIGHTJACKET

Marx never used the term "historical materialism." When it is associated with his name it is usually in terms of the metaphysical theories of matter propounded by Engels and later Communists. Marx himself was repelled by crudely reductionist theories of matter, such as the mechanical patterns of Hobbesean materialism, which he pronounced *"hostile to humanity."* But Marx's economic determinism did not abolish the metaphysical *conclusions* of the earlier and more mechanist forms of materialism but built upon them by applying them to the historical condition of man in society. Marx's idea of matter, even understood from the nonmetaphysical perspective of human needs and a host of economic circumstances, not only precluded the possibility of a divine spirit, but also claimed that physical forces determine and take primacy over the human mind and spirit.

Too much, I believe, has been made of a text in *The Holy Family* (p.172) in which Marx appears to say the opposite and to anticipate Teilhard de Chardin's spiritual "within" of even the most rudimentary forms of matter. Marx wrote, "The first and most important of the inherent qualities of *matter* is *motion,* not only *mechanical* and *mathematical* movement but still more *impulse, vital life-spirit, tension* or, to use Jacob Bohme's expression, the *throes* [Qual] of matter. The primary forms of matter are the living, individualizing *forces of being* inherent in it and producing the distinctions between the species." R. C. Zaehner places great importance in this passage for its emphasis on "qualities we usually associate with living things."[18] This is less than a revelation, however, when we remember that Marx transcended earlier forms of materialism by enlarging, as it were, the minute moving particles which constitute reality until they attain the size, flesh, and flexibility of interacting classes and institutions. Indeed, Marx's materialism, as opposed to Engels' (and Teilhard's) investigations of the *Weltstoff,* was always related to the *Umwelt* and the practical needs of living people. But for the destruction of meter, he might well have added Engels' name to the first line of this early epigram:

> Kant und Fichte gern zum Aether schweifen
> Suchten dort ein fernes Land,
> Doch ich such' nur tuchtig zu begreifen,
> Wass ich—auf der Strasse fand![19]

In *The Holy Family* passage, moreover, Marx does not even seem to be presenting his own view but, judging from the context, appears to be offering an exposition and an implied criticism of the theological residue in the materialism of Francis Bacon. In *Novum Organum* Bacon wrote of matter, "Let the required nature, therefore, be the action and motion of the spirit enclosed in tangible bodies; for every tangible body with which we are acquainted, contains an invisible and intangible spirit. . . . "[20] Although the wretched organization of *The Holy Family* makes it difficult to distinguish with certainty between Marx's own views and those of other materialists, this passage seems merely to be part of an exposition of the history of British materialism. It is a questionable procedure, therefore, to ground an interpretation of Marxian materialism on one passage, especially this one from *The Holy Family.*

Assuming, therefore, that Marx was not a mystical materialist but simply one who believed that mind evolved from matter and continues in subservience to it, we must note Marx's failure to explain the genesis of ideas. Marx taught in *The Holy Family* (p.176) that man draws all his knowledge from that which is accessible to the senses. In a world where matter is *all,* in the sense of its primacy over consciousness, we might question how the preponderance of the all is recognized and evaluated and how it produces sublime and often erroneous ideas. We might in fact begin by probing for the origins of the Marxian ideal of human freedom and cooperation, worked out as it was in a society blanketed by alienation and in a world whose history has never yielded the ideal man of

Marx's imagination. Marx even claimed to detect growth toward this ideal in the consciousness of the proletariat, but could not explain the origin of this consciousness. He cited material need as the source of the proletariat's growth in consciousness toward a hitherto unrealized ideal. But this negated his own critique of religion in which he characterized man's *need* for a higher being as a socially-induced illusion. Nor will the Marxian theory account for the motives of those ideologues of other classes—Marx himself!—who descend into the proletariat to join in its struggle. Finally, the Marxist law itself, devised by a lover of Aeschylus and Shakespeare, fails to explain the genesis and enduring appeal of great literature and works of art.[21] Indeed, logic and a multitude of historical exceptions argue against the law of economic determinism. Rather than give careful attention to the intellectual, religious, and political roots of institutions and to the variables and invariables of human nature, Marx provided a single stencil to be used again and again to rewrite the history of any epoch. Certainly, as M. M. Bober wrote, "Man must eat before he can turn to philosophy, . . . but to erect a necessary condition into a comprehensive and sufficient cause is hardly a proper way of building the corner stone of social philosophy."[22] Voicing a similar criticism, Teilhard remarked, "To think, we must eat. But what a variety of thoughts we get out of one slice of bread!"[23]

From the beginning, according to Marx, economic conditions shaped the nature of man and his tribal society. While not overemphasizing the strictly economic factor, anthropological studies of contemporary primitives had revealed a similar stereotype of man as a being whose feelings and thoughts are impressed on him by external forces. Anthropologists, however, no longer unanimously hold the opinion that individual initiative and creativity have no part in primitive society. It was thought that tradition and custom were unswervingly obeyed through mental inertia or group instinct. This concept of the rigidity of tribal law and custom, however, distorted the reality of native life. Although the primitive has great respect for tradition and is indeed influenced by his basal needs, there is another force at work. In words equally at home in a critique of Marxian determinism, Ernst Cassirer concluded, "A life of mere pressure, a human life in which all individual activities were completely suppressed and eliminated, seems to be rather a sociological or metaphysical construction than a historical reality."[24]

If physical needs and the conditions of production were the dominating factors in man's development, we should have a race characterized by unvarying mediocrity, a race of J. Alfred Prufrocks:

> I should have been a pair of ragged claws
> Scuttling across the floors of silent seas.

The Marxian formula not only fails to convey the continual interaction between thought and all forms of physical production, but it also disregards the higher, specifically human needs which indeed lead to production—but often to the production of works and ideas which transcend elemental wants and the conditions of environment.

Engels was the first to hedge on the severity of the Marxian formulation by citing the dominant but not exclusive role of economic factors in determining consciousness and history. He allowed that elements of the superstructure, e.g., politics, religion, law, philosophy, exert their respective influence and may even give form to historical struggles. In a famous letter to J. Bloch written in 1890 Engels confessed, "Marx and I are ourselves partly to blame for the fact that the younger people sometimes lay more stress on the economic side than is due it. We had to emphasize the main principle *vis-à-vis* our adversaries who denied it." Engels, however, in the same letter contradicted his own spirit of concession: "We make our history ourselves, but in the first place, under very definite assumptions and conditions. Among these the economic ones are *ultimately decisive.*"[25] Economic determinism, therefore, with its erosion of human responsibility and its constriction of human creativity, remains the inviolable foundation stone of Marxism.

REJECTED THEOLOGICAL EXPLANATIONS

Teilhard shared with Marx a refusal to view the past, especially any area inaccessible to scientific or historical study, as a source of explanation of current developments. On three fronts Teilhard held, "Nothing is so delicate and fugitive by its very nature as a beginning."[26] To demand a demonstration of the origins of even the most well-known and universal phenomena is to call into question the entire historical enterprise. Access to the first Greeks or Romans, the proto-alphabet, or to the original automobile is necessary neither to an understanding of their contemporary counterparts nor to a recognition of their developmental character. Likewise in biology, the precariousness and brief duration of the peduncle or the bud of any living branch necessarily blots out all vestiges of its biological origins, so that all that can be said with certainty is that nothing appears except by way of birth. It is not science's business to go behind the great chain of becoming. Thirdly, and most importantly, Teilhard for theological reasons rejected all explanations of man's present condition that rely on the tradition-bound dogmas of creation and the Fall. All such explanations that represent the creation and Fall of man as solitary events in the past, are, in Teilhard's word, "ungraspable." Since the beginning of the process of becoming lies outside the province of science, the origin of the universe remains a genuinely theological problem. But theology's only answer, said

Teilhard, overlooking the traditional doctrine of *creatio continua,* has been the divine fiat of Genesis 1.

The instantaneous fiat of God was rejected by Teilhard for scientific and theological reasons. Scientifically speaking, God's instantaneously willed creation of the universe implies fixism, and therefore endangers the truth of evolution. For this reason Teilhard rejected an absolutist interpretation of creation *ex nihilo* by dwelling on the recessive elements of myth in the Genesis account, for example, the dualism implied in God's mastery of chaos, and by allegorizing the formation of Adam from the red earth to mean the "prolonged effort of 'Earth' as a whole."[27] The divine intervention according to Teilhard amounts to *"God making things make themselves,"* a formula which in *The Phenomenon of Man* was translated into his acceptance—with Marx and Engels—of spontaneous generation as the evolutionary explanation of the origin of life.[28] As a scientist Teilhard could not posit a temporal beginning of things, for whatever is scientifically registrable is known only as the successor or product of something previous to it. Nor could he theorize about a preevolutionary creation which lies outside the chain of becoming, although in a few footnotes he allowed for "the notion of an ontological beginning of the universe."[29] He did toy with the idea of "involution," that is, an instantaneous creation of Adam and a precosmic fall, both of which preceded the world's historical condition of evolution. This "Alexandrian" phase of creation and the fall proved unsatisfactory to Teilhard, not because it makes God the direct cause of evil, but on account of its gratuitous, inorganic, and nonhistorical character that renders it unintelligible to the modern world.[30]

As we shall discover in the next sections, Teilhard could solve the dilemma only by making evolution the sole condition of creation, and by radically altering God's role as the timeless originator of all that exists. Teilhard was right, of course, to say that creation does not consist in one precosmic event, but he was wrong to adopt the language of agnosticism by attributing the origin of the earth to an accidental detachment of stable atoms from the sun. Similarly, Teilhard's acceptance of spontaneous generation, set in the whole context of his theological and metaphysical writings, merely illustrates a way in which God creates by "making things make themselves." But standing alone in *The Phenomenon of Man* it has inspired a somewhat misleading correlation with Engels' comparable views in *Dialectics of Nature.* In fact, since Teilhard and Engels refused to designate a temporal beginning of moving matter, and since they adopted a similar position on the passage of inorganic matter to life, French Communist Roger Garaudy has gone so far as to claim that Engels and Teilhard agreed on the inception of life.[31]

There must be a moral in this misinterpretation: If any theologically-oriented synthesis of science and Christianity wishes to avoid the contempt of the scientific (or unscientific) materialist, it must maintain the clarity of God's presence in the world. With considerable insight Engels said that "God is nowhere treated worse than by the natural scientists who believe in him." Engels likened their rationalizations of God's activity to the surrender of one army division after another "until at last the whole infinite realm of nature is conquered by science and there is no place left in it for the creator. . . . What a distance from the old God—the Creator of heaven and earth, the maintainer of all things—without whom not a hair can fall from the head!"[32] Thus there is a great danger in Teilhard's undertaking, for regardless of how one conceives of God's creative method, the words "accidental" or "spontaneous," as they are often used to denote fortuitous occurrences, not only give the impression of excluding the grace and prescience of a creator God, but also minimize the unique moment when God acted upon absolute nothingness in order to create the world which he continually preserves, renews, and directs. While there is no doubt of Teilhard's adherence to some form of a doctrine of creation, that is, creation by an "extra-cosmic" and not Bergsonian force, the phrasing of his scientific-apologetic works—coupled with his tendency to relegate the transcendent acts of God to footnotes as though they represented adiaphora of marginal interest—does not adequately integrate the majesty of divine creation in the stream of evolution.

In addition to scientific principles, Teilhard advanced a theological argument against the doctrine of creation *ex nihilo*. Where traditional theology has always emphasized the freedom and the grace out of which God created all things, Teilhard alluded rather to a sense of arbitrariness which denies Christ's organic relation to the whole process of becoming, and which therefore threatens the value of the created order. He characterized the notion of participated being, by which Christian metaphysics thought to solve the problem of the world's relation to God, as presenting "an entirely gratuitous creation, a gesture of pure benevolence with no other object for the absolute Being than to *share* his plenitude with a *corona* of participants of whom he has strictly no need. . . ."[33]

There is a way in which God is bound to creation, not, as Teilhard would have it, for the sake of human dignity, but rather as an expression of God's love for humanity. The love of God, as manifested in the creation, forms the basis of his covenant with Israel and all peoples. Genesis 1:1 depicts the beginning of a juridical relationship destined to be repeated in the Garden, with Noah, and again and again in the long history of Israel. The nothingness out of which God creates his earth and its chosen people, as well as God's self-imposed bond with them, is exemplified in Hosea's promise to Israel:

> And I will have pity on Not pitied,
> and I will say to Not my people,
> "You are my people";
> and he shall say, "Thou art my God" (2:23).

When we confess that in the beginning God created the heaven and the earth we do not call into question the totality of God's involvement with man. Rather we verify the covenant of love which God originated and restores—with interest, as St. Thomas Aquinas says—as often as man breaks it.

Before we get into Teilhard's understanding of original sin and the part which God's creative activity plays in it, it is necessary to understand why Teilhard rejected the traditional view of the Fall. Here again his rejection came on the grounds of science and theology. The scientific objection was summarized by Teilhard's admission in a 1924 essay: "Since, in the series *known to our experience,* everything happens as though there were no Adam and no Eden, then it must be that the Fall, as an event, is something which cannot be verified or checked."[34] This position entails the rejection of monogenism, the belief in an original, solitary man, as a viable scientific hypothesis. Primitive man, as Teilhard wrote in *The Phenomenon of Man, "in the eyes of science . . .* can only be *a crowd"* whose *"infancy* is made up of thousands and thousands of years" and whose nature is best ascertained by the tools he leaves behind.[35] Thus revelation may demand an individual agent of death in order to enhance a second individual's subjugation of it, but science does not distinguish between individuals and populations. Teilhard rejected the theological interpretation of monogenism, moreover, on account of its false construction of two fully formed homo sapiens "capable of bearing responsibility for original sin." It is against the laws of nature, wrote Teilhard in words reminiscent of St. Irenaeus, that man should be born an adult.[36] He concluded his discussion of mono/polygenism by proposing the theory of monophyletism wherein Adam symbolizes a solitary stem of primates which appeared in one geographical area in one geological time period.[37] As a scientific hypothesis monophyletism does not solve the problem of primitive man's moral immaturity, but rather turned Teilhard's eyes to the future by confirming and promising the uninterrupted nature of the human ascent.

For Teilhard the origin of all impediments to that ascent, the *original* sin, is buried within the nature and experience of man:

> Wise was the fangless serpent, drowsy.
> All this, indeed, I do not remember.
> I remember the remembering, when first awakening
> I heard the golden gates behind me
> Fall to, shut fast. On the flinty road,
> Black-frosty, blown on with an eastern wind,
> I found my feet. Forth on journey
> Gathering thin garment over aching bones,
> I went. I wander still. But the world is round.[38]

Theologically, these lines by C. S. Lewis reflect Teilhard's (and Marx's) understanding of modern man, who makes his way in the world groping and advancing in his optimism, and to whom the past as a source of explanation or solace is a suppressed memory. The memory of a first couple's infectious disobedience threatened Teilhard's cosmic Christology and was for that reason, among others, rejected. Taking as his starting point the cosmic nature of Christ, the fulfillment of evolution's progress, it was axiomatic to Teilhard that what Christ has not assumed he does not redeem. If the original sin of man amounts to "an accident which took place toward the end of the Tertiary era in some small corner of the earth," Christ's redemptive power is constrained and his identity as him "by whom all things consist" is localized. All that remains therefore in any such localization of sin and redemption is the purely juridical assertion of Christ's expiation of the sins of the world.

Theologically, in Teilhard's eyes, the traditional view of the Fall trivialized sin and therefore unwittingly depreciated Christ's victory over it. In this judgment Teilhard failed to see the mysteriously real value of the symbols, covenants, or, in his words, the juridical arrangements by which God communicates himself to man. When a man gives his word of promise, it may or may not be fulfilled. Even if it is fulfilled, there always exists in man a discrepancy (the origin of ideology) between word and act. God's word, however, regardless of its metaphysical, historical, or literary genre, always coincides with its actualization. "And God said, 'Let there be light,' and there was light." The deliverance of Israel represents the historical aspect of God's covenantal agreement, just as in its final expression, the Logos is made flesh, and Christ is revealed, in von Balthasar's fine phrase, as the Language of God. The most juridical of the divine arrangements, therefore, such as Christ's ransom for humankind, or man's corporate responsibility in Adam, do not suffer from a lack of realism and are not improved upon by attempts to find their physical or natural equivalents. Even the divine language, by virtue of its involvement in linguistics and thought forms, is a symbolic exercise. It can only be replaced, however, by another less effective set of symbols. This is borne out by the elaborate metaphysical *imagery* with which Teilhard is forced to describe Christ's real presence in the evolutionary ascent.

THE METAPHYSICAL BASIS OF EVIL

Very early in his career Teilhard identified the progressive unification within any group of organisms with an increase in being itself, and therefore characterized all manifestations and levels of disunity as deficiencies in being. The ultimate deficiency, pure multiplicity, he equated with the "empty concept" or "pseudo-idea" of nothingness.

Although Teilhard retained the orthodox *nihil,* his notion of pure multiplicity, like every theological or philosophical attempt to define nonbeing, suffered from a definable existence of its own. Teilhard's wrestling with nothingness recalls St. Augustine's effort to explain "to those of duller mind" the changeability of formless nothingness. Where Augustine tentatively settled for "a nothing something" or an "is, is not," Teilhard established two poles of being: "the Multiple, made nothing by its very essence," and the unified and concentrated absolute Being of God.[39]

The problem then consists in unifying the Multiple—this nothingness which has an essence—in order to produce growth toward unification. But what is to be united and what subsequently is to be produced? The answer which the naturalist/theologian provided is a surprising one. The evil multitude Teilhard early equated with matter, from whose unification or complexification will proceed soul, spirit, and finally, in the mature expression of Teilhard's hope, personal life. Teilhard's initial deprecation of matter in favor of a spiritual monism appears to contradict his own apotheosis of matter in *Hymn of the Universe.* It is not only uncharacteristic of a scientist, but it also goes against the theological mainstream which places ultimate responsibility for evil in the heart of man. Nevertheless, in the embryonic stages of Teilhard's transformist system of theology, whose ultimate goal is the spiritualization of man, the development of reflective consciousness and spirit from materiality appeared as the only means of explaining the residue of evil in the world.

Indeed Teilhard retained an ambiguous theological attitude toward matter. On the one hand it is the holy agent of man's spiritualization; on the other hand, it represents the entropizing pull toward disintegration from which the Christian must escape. In his famous "Hymn to Matter" Teilhard emphasized its former function, lauding not its inherently redemptive nature, but the dialectical effectiveness with which matter drives man beyond itself and into the arms of God:

Blessed be you, harsh matter, barren soil, stubborn rock; you who yield only to violence, you who force us to work if we would eat. . . . Without you, without your onslaughts, without your uprootings of us, we should remain all our lives inert, stagnant, puerile, ignorant both of ourselves and of God. You who batter us and then dress our wounds, you who resist us and yield to us, you who wreck and build, you who shackle and liberate, the sap of our souls, the hand of God, the flesh of Christ: it is you, matter, that I bless.[40]

At the time of its composition, then, Teilhard's "Hymn to Matter," repugnant to many spiritual sensitivies and inspirational to the practitioners of natural ascesis, had its setting in a universe whose only basis is spirit. To the young Teilhard the material world is dormant or ossified consciousness. The disappearance of evil in the universe will correspond with unity's victory over the multitude, with the spiritualization of the physical universe, so that in the end, "Spirit will have absorbed matter."

A step beyond the stage of matter's alienation from spirit is the softening of the antinomies in what Teilhard called "spirit-matter." "In a concrete sense there is not matter and spirit. All that exists is matter becoming spirit."[41] With this sentence Teilhard echoed a Hegelian theme and placed our heritage of Cartesian dualism into a dynamic context by picturing evolution as a single continuum, rooted in material multiplicity and destined for absolute spirituality.

The idea of spirit-matter or matter becoming spirit, however, was absent from the last twenty years of Teilhard's work. He replaced the sharp antithesis between matter and spirit and the spiritual monism of his earlier years with the idea of personalization, which becomes possible now by virtue of the intimate relationship which exists between the spiritual and the material in the most rudimentary forms of matter. The matter which God complexifies in his continual creative activity now bears spiritual freedom as its determining component. It is this psychism of matter—attributable also to Engels, but not to Marx—which, when complexification has reached the necessary "temperature," creates something new in the world of nature or society.

While indicating Teilhard's agreement with Engels on the tension between the material and the spiritual in each particle of moving matter (energy), we need to emphasize Teilhard's distance from Marx's concept of man. Teilhard believed that, although human freedom can be broken down into its deterministic compartments, the world as a whole is based on freedom. With this in mind he asserted that an organism, a tiger, a man, ultimately a society, acts in continuity with and at the direction of its essence. The tiger's carnivorous instinct develops because the tiger's fearful symmetry encompasses the "soul of carnivore." This also has its social applications. Economic changes in a system no longer based on the soil and real property, industrial mechanization, and social changes rooted in the French Revolution only *appear,* according to Teilhard, to have a material and economic impetus. In reality they are psychically motivated and represent a change of soul or thought. Teilhard, in other words, unlike Marx, isolated a pure need for unity in human nature which is not identifiable with external economic pressures. Whereas in Marx existence chronologically and constitutively precedes essence, and life determines consciousness, Teilhard taught that on successive levels of being consciousness first determines and finally absorbs material life.

Teilhard's position raises scientific as well as theological questions. At what point does consciousness become determinative in matter, and how does it operate in mutation to influence genetical diversity.[42] Since consciousness dictates the nature of even nonreflective creatures, such as the tiger, we must admit that psychism and the freedom and spirit which Teilhard associated with it in some way prepares for man's special reflective form of psychic activity. We are confronted with an aspect of life which threatens, despite Teilhard's antimonistic intentions, to assume the guise of the *all*. Since this is the case, Karl Rahner's criticism of materialism—to the effect that any totality cannot define and identify itself—applies also to a system of evolution which is immersed from its origin in some form of the psychic.[43] The presence of the psychic in prehuman evolution makes it more difficult to explain the novelty of human consciousness, for, as one critic objects, as an evolutionary *effect,* psychism cannot itself be the product of an already existing, inferior mode of thought.[44]

Man's arrival at reflective consciousness is the result of increased complexity in his social arrangement. When this complexity is brought to the boiling point, as Teilhard pictured it, the creature undergoes a change of state and becomes a man:

When the anthropoid, so to speak, had been brought "mentally" to the boiling point some further calories were added. Or, when the anthropoid had almost reached the summit of the cone, a final effort took place along the axis. No more was needed for the whole inner equilibrium to be upset. What was previously only a centred surface became a centre. By a tiny "tangential" increase, the "radial" was turned back on itself and so to speak took an infinite leap forward. Outwardly, almost nothing in the organs had changed. But in depth a great revolution had taken place: consciousness was now leaping and boiling in a space of supersensory relationships and representations.[45]

But tepid water, to prolong one of the ten or twelve images in this brief passage, will not boil. If Teilhard is to be taken seriously in his contention that consciousness is not merely the result of psychic and physical properties brought into harmony, he needs to introduce Omega's activity in heating the critical point of transition and drawing the increasingly psychic process toward itself. Here Teilhard broached a possible reinterpretation of the traditionally recognized activity of the Holy Spirit. Teilhard's work, however, contains no doctrine of the Holy Spirit but rather transfers the Spirit's being and role to the cosmic Christ. Without a place for the Holy Spirit, his theological introduction of a Spirit-like function for Omega led to the obscuring of the difference between the Spirit of God and the spiritual determinator resident in the infinite varieties of matter. One spirit arises through the complexification of material particles and ultimately is transformed into a finite form of transcendence, which allows man to center the entire space-time continuum in the private cosmos of his own mind. On the other hand, the

Spirit of God, in Karl Rahner's words, has nothing to do with a "dialectical unity of spirit and matter," for he is "not a part of the world but its comprehensive ground."[46] Although Teilhard did not explicate the difference in the spirituality of matter, man, and Omega, that is, how Omega communicates his love by "warming" the critical nodes in hominization, Teilhard's metaphysics of matter and spirit contributed in a pioneering way to theology's conversation with Marxian materialism.

THE SIN OF THE EVOLUTIONARY PROCESS

The discovery of consciousness, freedom, and spirit at the heart of the material world might have prepared for the integration of personal responsibility and evolution. But such an integration does not occur in the work of Teilhard de Chardin. For an explanation of sin and evil Teilhard, like Marx, fell back upon the necessary workings of a process. Beneath the surface of their analyses of society the Teilhardian and Marxian explanations are at one in their willingness to equate sin with the unalterable conditions of existence. Economic exchange and evolutionary progress, with their accessory evils, arise from man's essential need for unified existence.

The necessity of sin and evil stems from the creation of the world. Given the theory of Complexity-Consciousness and its metaphysical antecedent, the existence of a disorganized, primordial multitude, God's creation must take the form of unification, which Teilhard compared to the trinitarian relations within the Godhead. God's process of self-unification is thus communicated to creation, which "now appears as a kind of symmetrical duplication of trinitization."[47] The analogy of course breaks down as soon as we realize that the world's unification represents a growth in complexity and therefore, according to Teilhard, an increase in being, to which the full and immutable God need demonstrate no corresponding growth. "Trinitization," if taken as more than analogy, also plunges the Creator into the finite world of time, again submitting him to duration, growth, and perfectability. Teilhard did not teach that God must create, but that only one method of creation, evolution, is open to him.[48] Accordingly, creation continues by the trial and error method of gradual unification and the "groping interplay of great numbers" whose goal is the physical and spiritual completion of the universe. Under the conditions of evolutive creation, evil is not an accident (in the Aristotelian sense) of the universe. "It is an enemy, a work which God raises up inevitably through his solitary decision to create." God's creative action automatically involves him in a struggle against evil, for evil is an "unavoidable by-product," "a shadow which cannot be separated from creation."[49]

When the process of evolutive creation arrives at human reflective consciousness, man's transcendent freedom allows him to create his own nature by directing the course of his own evolution. The same biological, chemical, and social complexification which boils over into the creation of man causes man to center the world in his own ego. The same freedom which enables him to dream dreams and see visions directs him to isolate himself from the community, to say "I" and "mine," and finally to refuse to join in the evolutionary ascent. Reflection brings with it personalization, a new awareness of time, the development of art, culture, religion, and many other uniquely human factors. It also introduces the seed of a new kind of disunity which continues to plague man. "The seat of the evil we are suffering from is to be found in the very foundations of thought on earth."[50]

On the one hand Teilhard exclaims that a rise in psychic temperature automatically produces a better social arrangement. Spiritual perfection (conscious "centreity") and material synthesis (complexity) are two aspects of a single phenomenon. On the other hand, this material and chemical arrangement produces at the same time a mysterious "granulation" which closely resembles that which Luther (and Marx) knew as *incurvatus in se*. "With the dawning of Reflection, each conscious unit isolates itself and, one would say, tends increasingly to live only for itself, as though . . . the phyletic sense were submerged until it finally vanishes."[51]

Teilhard at times attributed man's distorted egocentricity to the nature of complexification itself, as though the Law of Complexity-Consciousness must have as its corollary the production of people curved in upon themselves. Most often, however, Teilhard identified inordinate self-interest with disorganized multiplicity itself which has not yet undergone socialization. Dominating Teilhard's approach to the problem of evil is the idea that sin exists before man as well as in the human state of disorganization. He admitted that human socialization has not shown itself to be especially productive of virtue, but he explained the brutality and intractability of the masses as "effects, not of complexity, but of unorganized large numbers."[52] The important point is that whether sin originates via complexification or in the state of multiplicity that precedes it, it remains for both Marx and Teilhard the necessary result of the universal condition of human development.

As a solution to the problem of sin and evil Teilhard proposed a universal law of wastage. Multiplicity in the process of social arrangement is subject to the influence of chance. As the multiple finds unity, therefore, it must willy-nilly give rise to evil through incompleteness, pain, and failure. "It is necessary that temptations come," Teilhard never tired of repeating.

The Fall and original sin in such a solution may be interpreted existentially in the person's struggle with his own passivities or statistically in the aesthetic overview of evolution. We have examined Teilhard's devotionally sound meditation on the individual's experience of the Pauline dialectic, "My strength is made perfect in weakness." Fall and redemption, excentration and communion are recapitulated in each person, for, with Yeats, Teilhard knew that " . . . nothing can be sole or whole/That has not been rent." When Teilhard attempted to apply this dialectical, positive valuation of sin to the large numbers involved in evolution, his theology faltered. In his conflation of divine creation and redemption with human achievement and sin, the person's spiritual dialectic was flattened and its movement from unity to disunity toward greater unity destroyed. In Teilhard's system of evolutionary theology the Fall represents humankind's innate need to rise toward a goal which lies ahead. It "leaves no mark at all, since its visible penalty is contained in Evolution, with *expiation* coinciding with work."[53]

With no meaningful Fall, the problem of sin's transmission vanishes. Although there is no historical first sin, there is, according to Teilhard, an ontological original sin, which is transmitted in the mechanism of evolution. Evolution, in fact, *is* original sin. By the necessary failures and missed connections which attend any condition of becoming, evolution creates a general situation of defeat, to paraphrase Rahner, which embraces all men prior to their own personal free decision. Deemphasized in Teilhard is the place of personal decision in original sin, and absent altogether is an explanation of its historical beginnings. As with Marx, so in Teilhard, a historical understanding of the origin of sin is lost within the nature of the mode of development, so that ultimately the system is identified with original sin and made to bear responsibility for it. Hence Teilhard wrote, "Original sin expresses, translates, personifies, in an instantaneous and localized act, the perennial and universal law of imperfection which operates in mankind *in virtue* of its being 'in fieri' " (in the process of becoming).[54] It is the price of progress. This is made embarrassingly clear in "Christology and Evolution": "We may say that all that would be needed to modernize Christology would be to clarify the notion of *sin,* as used in theological and liturgical formulas, by that of progress. . . . That is not asking much, surely?" It is not surprising therefore to hear Teilhard voicing opposition to expiatory theories of the Atonement which attempt to eliminate that which is an integral part of human nature.[55]

Teilhard not only implicated evolution in evil, but he identified that evil with original sin. He thereby reduced sin to a natural law of development and elevated physical evil in the prehuman, subhuman, and infrahuman spheres to a theological position of unwarranted centrality.[56] In effect, Teilhard naturalized personal sin and, through an abuse of terminology, personalized natural evil. Teilhard's idealist view of evil understood it as a unity whose various modalities, such as incompleteness, plurality, sin, and death, pervade the whole range of evolution. It is this totality of evil which in Teilhard's vocabulary constitutes original sin. Having established sin as the condition of life's development, Teilhard had no qualms in confessing death's entry into the world via sin. In fact, in the passing away of stars, and in the dead ends of countless species and phyla, death, and therefore sin, existed long before man. An original sin, therefore, cannot be intended to explain the origin of human suffering and mortality. It is this exegetically perverse conclusion drawn from Romans 5:12 ("death by sin") that Teilhard proposed as "the general solution of the problem of evil."[57] It is perverse because in the same breath St. Paul also says that sin entered by one man. Regardless of the interpretation placed on the "one man," whether it be construed as an individual or the human race's solidarity in Adam, Teilhard's equation of evolution and original sin cannot be brought into harmony with the Pauline typology. The evolutionary explanation does not solve the problem of evil but merely transfers responsibility from man to God, whose creative medium is restricted to an evolutionary sequence which necessarily engenders evil.

It is generally recognized that sin can be defined only in terms of personal accountability. What is sometimes disputed, however, is that physical evil in nature and man can be reckoned as evil only from the point of view of human needs. Galactic catastrophes, the dead ends of species, and even the repulsive life cycle of the liver fluke cannot be indicted as evil until they have touched human beings. Evil exists only in relation to man because man alone has been invested with absolute value. The creation announces man's right to judge, manage, and take responsibility for the world of nature. Since the value of nature is linked to man's position before God, God does not hesitate to deface nature in order to punish the only creature made in the divine image. The whole creation groans and travails in pain not because of an inherently degenerative force in matter, but because man's abuse of nature—the obverse of the Marxian and Teilhardian humanization of nature—has brought it low. He has neglected, worshiped, polluted nature, and used it as an uncomprehending tool in his work of self-destruction. Nature is not only judged, but also redeemed, in tandem with man. The Incarnation confirms the absolute value of man, for the Logos has become the subject of a human nature. The Incarnation also shows, as St. Athanasius reminds us, that of all the creatures in the chain of being man is the only creature in need of redemption. Sin, the judgment of evil, and the true perception of pain, therefore, begin with man and remain with him.

I have shown that Teilhard's "solution" to the problem of evil is based on the denial of this truth and that it, as such, represents the depersonalization of sin and the removal of man from his rightful position as the arbiter of natural and physical evil. Here again, however, the paradoxical nature of Teilhard's system comes to our attention. For there are several places in which he installed the *person* as the originator of sin and the only criterion for judging physical evil. We have seen how he established (in some passages) a mysterious nexus between inchoate reflection and egocentricity. In *Le milieu divin* (p. 61) the purely physical evil of death is exacerbated by "the wrong use of our freedom"; likewise, in "Sketch of a Personalistic Universe," Teilhard wrote, "It can truly be said that real pain entered the world with man, when for the first time a reflective consciousness became capable of observing its own diminution. The only true *evil* is suffered by personality."[58] In selected passages, then, pain and death are evil, according to Teilhard, only insofar as man is aware of his diminishment in them. This recorded ambiguity reveals the breach between person and process in Teilhard's theology. For standing against the personalist side of his doctrine of man we have discovered an impersonal aestheticism which, in its embrace of the whole phenomenon of evolution, not only obscures the perverted character of sin, but attempts to justify the existence and even the beauty of evil, sin, and hell as essential elements in evolution's success.

THE IMAGE OF GOD

Marx and Teilhard de Chardin each isolated a basal prerequisite by which man is judged a human being. Briefly summarized, the Marxian man lays claim to humanity when his bodily needs stimulate his participation in and planning of production and exchange. Enough has been said in outrage at this strangulation of human diversity by partisan and nonpartisan alike: Marxologists, philosophers, anthropologists, historians, psychologists, and theologians have all had their indignant say. Since I have already expressed my agreement with Marx's motive in demythologizing history and my disagreement with the dogmatism with which he pursued his One Idea, I would like to consider a theological alternative to Marx and to the broader criterion of humanity set down by Teilhard de Chardin. Teilhard subsumed the many functions of consciousness, such as culture, art, tool-making, and Marxian economic interchange, under the panoply of reflective consciousness. Man may be considered human once he is able to make his own awareness an object of thought. One criterion, Marx's, appears as a limited function of consciousness, and another, Teilhard's, covers every conceivable form of reflective activity. Yet, from a theological perspective both criteria are too narrow, for they represent only the increase of functional proficiencies, whether economic or cognitive, but reveal no accompanying *attitude* in man toward his new-found proficiency and toward others who share it with him. Man may demonstrate the externals of his humanity by making symbols or flint axes, fire or totems; he may bury his dead, harness the animals, and paint the walls of his cave, but, theologically speaking, until he has evaluated his new skills in the light of his relation to God and the needs of his fellow men, he has not come up to the original standard of humanity intended to live in the image of God.

Living in the image of God does not represent another function for man, *homo religiosus,* to be included under a larger category of reflective consciousness. Nor do we promote the image of God as the true criterion of humanity simply because science is showing us every day that it can duplicate in the laboratory or discover in the animal world the functional equivalents of skills previously limited by definition to humans. The image transcends the subhuman and human proficiencies which contribute to hominization, for its reflective activity is derived from God and is sustained in awareness of him. Thought from God becomes human only when it is returned directly to him in worship or indirectly to him in love for the community. Even the three divisions of consciousness made popular by St. Augustine cannot in themselves form the true nature of man. If memory, will, and mind, Luther warned, constitute the image of God, then Satan also possesses God's image. St. Thomas recognized this when, in deference to the Fathers, he reluctantly prolonged the distinction between *imago* and *similitudo.* For he knew that rational reflection is not a neutral proficiency but a gift from God designed for the knowledge and appreciation of God.

The mind's adventure with God introduces a form of transcendence which takes man to the upper limits of his humanity. It has been said many times by non-Christians that reflection gives man a kind of transcendence. To Marx this meant that man escapes the beehive and plans for future production. To Teilhard this transcendence allows man to plan—on a broader scale—the future course of evolution. But these forms of transcendence have to do with the temporal order, and by no means exhaust the possibilities open to his reflective consciousness. This theology has associated with the mind's ability to reflect upon the revelation of an infinite Spirit and in so doing to transcend the finite order. Anything less than this latter form of transcendence falls short of the "truly human," of which Marx and Teilhard were so fond, and, while not obliterating man's humanity, threatens it with brutishness and a return to natural principles. The only point we wish to clarify, then, is that until man adopts an attitude toward his consciousness or sets it in a specific context (by recognizing its divinely transcendent origin and purpose), his social or mental complexification remains a part of the mechanics of the situation or the natural order.

The attitude that identifies man living in the image of God is answerability or its equivalent, responsibility in love. The ego that man discovers in reflection is not merely the outcome of need or material arrangements, but is the residential being which enables man to evaluate successive needs and experiences while maintaining its own, to some extent, timeless identity. Man becomes an "I" when he is addressed by God as a "Thou." Human identity results from the natural processes into which God, in a special act of creation, breathed a personal and historical word. Having received the power of words via the creative word, man is meant to answer. Since his answerability is directed to the infinite God, man's use of words takes on an open transcendence which distinguishes itself from the sophisticated signals of the higher mammals and from human symbols, whose shades of meaning and validity are limited to the finite order. Man responds in obedience and love because he has received a communication from outside himself. The image of God consists not only in man's ability to make words, but, more fully, in his relationship to the Word made flesh who is the foremost exhibition not only of God's reason but of his love. "So," concludes St. Thomas, "the divine image should be looked for in man in terms of *the word conceived out of awareness of God, and of the love flowing from that.*"[59] The rationality, therefore, which characterizes the divine and human word procession is incomplete without the accompanying gracious love which wills the creation, the communication of words, and the transcendent relationship which puts man in touch with the infinite. Man in the image of God is destined, then, not only to answer, but to respond in the love by which he was created.

We do not seek the true nature of man, that is, the definition of the image of God, by speculating on the constitution of the first man or first tribe of men. The New Testament has shown a better way by revealing the perfection of the image to whom man turns for the confirmation of his calling and justification by God. The primal Word was present at the beginning, presided over the communication of words to men, and witnessed the rupture of the divine-human relationship, which Genesis portrays in Satan's duplicity with words and the confusion at Babel. Only Christ reveals the true meaning of the image of God by virtue of his relationship to the Father. By demonstrating perfect unity with God, Jesus at once reveals man's distance from the Father and his need to regain the image in its perfection. As the perfect image of the Father and as a historical figure, Jesus mediates the restoration of the relationship between God and man and exalts the image beyond the simplicity of its origins to that into which we are changed, from glory to glory, by the Spirit of the Lord.

The relational character of the image of God makes it clear that sin is primarily a revolt against Christ and a revulsion against the realism with which he demonstrated the true nature of the Image, that is, as a dying to the world and a renewal of life in God. Man does not now merely contradict the splendor of his original situation, nor, by a kind of evolutionary immaturity, does he merely sin against his unrealized potential. His sin is against the perfector of the image and is a rejection of the way in which that perfection has come about. To explain sin as the necessary concomitant of any kind of process immediately nullifies that uniqueness of man which lies in his responsibility to confirm or deny that which through God's gracious initiative has been accomplished in him. It is this linkage between the infinite God and the person's finite will which led Luther and Kierkegaard to assert that the reality of sin can be confessed in faith only by one in a position of spiritual responsibility toward God. And it is this view that informs Brunner's sound belief in sin as that which divides man from the animals, for only one made in the image of God has the spiritual resources to sin.[60]

In their treatment of sin Marx and Teilhard utilized a definition of man which all but omits the dimensions of will and responsibility. Marx used the New Testament categories of sin but only to dramatize the frozen antitheses within the economic order. He borrowed the *form* of dualism as presented by St. Paul and Luther without realizing that in the Christian life these theological categories become a dualism of decision. Once addressed by God as a rational, free creature and once offered a way of redemption, man may choose light or darkness. Instead of describing alienation as the willful turning from that to which one belongs, Marx concentrated on the inherent sinfulness in the mode of production, property, money, and the class structure of society. He failed to see that these institutions are neutral and subject to the will of those who would corrupt them and use them for personal gain. St. Augustine spoke straight to the Marxian man when he explained, in his own way, the personal origin of alienation and of man's bondage to money and things:

Thus some men make evil use of these things, and others make good use. And the man who makes evil use clings to them with love and is entangled by them (that is, he becomes subject to those things which ought to be subject to him, and creates for himself goods whose right and proper use require that he himself be good); [the good man, however,] must be ready to possess and control them. . . . Since this is so, you do not think, do you, that silver or gold should be blamed because of greedy men, or food and wine because of gluttons and drunkards, or womanly beauty because of adulterers and fornicators?[61]

Like Teilhard's statistical approach to the problem of evil, Marx's notion of sin is a collective affair which makes small provision for interpersonal evil or for the turning inward which both constitutes and motivates human sin. As I have emphasized, this motive and this guilt can have no ground of existence in the Marxian man, whose social nature eludes the Christian's accountability in the depths of an ego which cannot be diffused into a pattern of socio-economic relations.

In contrast to Marx, Teilhard held a personal theory of sin which applies to individual Christians. His effort to systematize it and to fit it into the context of evolution, however, drove him to a statistical law of wastage. We have insisted that sin is a personal event between creature and creator and that it presupposes a certain degree of spiritual maturity in the will which dares to rebel against God. That is to say, organizations, governments, and other collective movements do not, strictly speaking, commit sin. The people who transmit sinful orders and those who mindlessly carry them out impart to situations the character of sinfulness. It is not the situation of economic injustice or evolutionary failure which initially engenders sin. Sin occurs when humankind attempts to justify greed, hatred, rivalry, and willingness to be used as inevitable manifestations of the sinful situation. Like Marx, Teilhard in one aspect of his theology hoped to surmount the impersonality of the system by placing great importance on the person. Just as Marxian economics centered on the human value of labor, evolution was said to be progressing toward a phase of heightened personality. The importance of the person, however, gave way in both thinkers to an explanation of sin which relied on independent and inhuman laws applicable only to aggregates. This is not to say that statistics cannot convey the predictable facts of exploitation, failure, and sin. Coroners' statistics predict with great accuracy the number of people who will take the personal and free decision to commit suicide. But a statistical approach to sin engenders only a spirit of fatalism by compiling, ex post facto, impersonal laws to explain and govern the person's transcendent relationship with God.

Now it might be objected that the "groping" and "trial and error" that mark life's advance show the need for sins of experimentation if we are to get anywhere in the universe. The only sin which could not play a part in the progress of the world, in this interpretation of Teilhard, would be the absolute sin, the rejection of Christ.[62] Although one is tempted to read Teilhard in this light, his doctrine of sin does not revolve around the rejection of Christ. Aesthetically as well as practically such a rejection in fact seems to be a necessary structure of the spiritual universe.[63] In his evolutionary *system* of theology the unforgivable sin has little to do with the person's rejection of Christ. The decision which Christ requires in respect to his identity and demands surfaces in Teilhard's system as man's duty to believe in the future. Humankind is divided into two camps—not exploiters and exploited—but believers in progress and pessimists who retard the human ascent. We are again reminded that the individual's sin, if repented, may indeed lead to an enriched reception of God's grace in forgiveness. For the individual, however, this sequence is not developmental but dialectical. In no Christian sense does the person *develop* in his sin along the lines Teilhard suggested in his evolutionary model. What Teilhard did not admit is that in a system which explains sin as evolutionary wastage countless persons made in God's image are tossed onto the slag heap of progress. God, who would have all people to be saved, cannot be conceived as willing, cooperating, or participating in this kind of progress. Rather man and his sin must retain a transhistorical dimension whereby man fully participates in progress while maintaining a relationship with God which depends not on the movement of history toward the Parousia but the transcendent presence of God in history.

By implicating the dominant modes of human development in sin, Marx and Teilhard located sin at the heart of man's finite condition. Although they both *believed* that man possesses a nature superior to that which is now manifested in him, their failure to discover its historical basis caused them to suppress their beliefs. Teilhard could only place that unity which every Christian has with God at the end of the evolutionary rainbow. And Marx could discover that freedom which is the essence of man only in the needs of an alienated class or in a society of the future. In either case, Marxian freedom remains a negative concept. Failing therefore in their historical quest to differentiate man from his mode of development—which they agreed inevitably engenders sin—there was no option open to them but the identification of person and process. Thus the essence of the Marxian man is "the sum of productive forces, forms of capital and social forms of intercourse which every individual and generation finds in existence as something given. . . . "[64]

In the same vein Teilhard wrote, "Man discovers that *he is nothing else than evolution become conscious of itself*" or, what amounts to the same thing, "hominized Nature."[65] The gravity of these passages lies in what P. B. Medawar terms "nothing-buttery," for, while they allow that man acts *as* a mode of the process, their restrictive definition of man seems to rob him of the initiative to act as a person *in* it or *against* it. Whenever the equivalent of "nothing but" introduces a definition of God's most complex creature, let the reader beware. In this case we are confronted with a reversal of the Christian teaching on original sin. Not man's finitude but his haughty refusal to recognize it forms the core of human sin. But in systems which identify sin with the condition of existence, pride and rebellion are of no consequence. Nor are we likely to hear the eternal question, "Adam, where art thou?", for Marx and Teilhard have in their systems laid the foundations for a doctrine of sin-without-guilt.

Chapter IV

AGAINST CHRISTIANITY

Thus they apply Christianity tranquilizing . . . whereas instead it is in the deepest sense arousing, disquieting!

—*Søren Kierkegaard*

Marx and Teilhard de Chardin demanded and in one sense attempted to accomplish in their own systems nothing less than a revolution in the church's doctrine of sin and redemption. Their criticisms contained a sweeping indictment of Christianity, which, from its vantage of power above the people, had failed to increase man's stature and to summon him to his true destiny. In its studied disregard of the true earthly needs and aspirations of man, Christianity had not only abandoned the cause of humanity but had also contradicted its own essential principles. Since Marxism considers the principles themselves to be false, its critique of religion has about it the illusion of finality; Christianity is not to be reconstituted but abolished. So devastating was Marx's attack on Christianity that apologists since the latter part of the nineteenth century have found themselves under constant obligation to answer it. Teilhard was no exception. Although he rarely mentioned the Marxist critique of religion, he was in constant dialogue with it and showed considerable sympathy toward it. Unlike Marx, Teilhard pressed his critique in faith and therefore faulted Christianity not for what it is but for how it is presented. Nevertheless, in his criticism of Christianity, it may be said that Teilhard joined Marx in the task of sweeping away the old forms of the Christian religion in preparation for a radically new order.

THE WILL TO ATHEISM

A prelogical will to atheism occupies a position of importance in Marx's philosophy and method comparable to that of Teilhard de Chardin's postulated belief in God. No amount of romantic or scholastic-like qualifications of Marx's rejection of God can alter the absolute atheism upon which his critique of bourgeois society and his

77

hope for the transformation of man were based. The mistaken notion that Marx's atheism, since it allows for the category and even the possibility of a rejected God, is something less than total, is shared by thinkers as diverse as Leslie Dewart, Karl Rahner, Erich Fromm, Roger Garaudy, and Pierre Teilhard de Chardin.[1] Yet not only did Marx reject the notion of God as an existent being as well as the necessarily imperfect literary representations of that existence, but he also excluded the possibility of any divine reality or presence independent of man's purely human self-transcendence. Although this atheism is regularly attributed to Marx as a logical result of a previous position, e.g., humanism, materialism, scientism, we are truer to the facts to record the prior existence of the vacuum, which was only later in young adulthood filled with positive beliefs.

The vacuum in Marx took the shape of a profound lack of interest in religion. It is generally acknowledged that Marx never passed through a period of religious idealism, never underwent a religious experience, and was never seriously affected by baptism into the Lutheran faith, to which his father, out of expediency and a genuine admiration of Frederick the Great, had subjected the entire family.[2] He thus escaped the direct influence of the Judaism of his ancestors as well as the overtly Christian pietism which had afflicted the young students of theology Bruno Bauer and Ludwig Feuerbach and his closest friend, Frederick Engels. Whereas Engels, at age nineteen, admitted to praying "every day, indeed almost all day" in an effort to regain the orthodox faith of his childhood, Marx at a comparable age was exalting a Promethean hatred of all gods and the divinization of man. Before he had accused Christianity of serving the ideological interests of the oppressors of the proletariat, Marx had already without a struggle dismissed religion as a non-entity.

Early in his career he showed impatience toward the Bauer brothers, Max Stirner, Feuerbach, and anyone else who analyzed religion as though it existed as a reality separate from the impoverished life of the proletariat. He retained this outspoken detachment from religion throughout the years of his political activity, as he, for personal, philosophical, and tactical reasons, constantly opposed those who wished to make anti-theism one of the foundation stones of communism. Such a procedure he felt evaded the task of prior importance, that of criticizing the political conditions that give rise to religion. As the editor of the *Rheinische Zeitung* he chided his contributors for their stylish, effete atheism: "And finally I told them that if they wanted to deal with philosophy they should flirt less with the idea of atheism (which is reminiscent of those children who loudly inform anyone who cares to listen that they are not afraid of the bogyman), and do more to acquaint the people with its meaning."[3]

Marx soon transcended his own atheism by transforming it into a positive, political humanism. Socialism, he proclaimed in 1844, recognizes no essential reality save the interaction of man and nature as it occurs in a concretely historical situation. As we have seen in Chapter I, this socialism is built upon the transference of the divine attributes of freedom and creativity to an ideal of man, with the result that Marx defined his humanism as "positive human *self-consciousness,* no longer . . . attained through the negation of religion."[4]

In one sense, then, the critique of religion was of peripheral importance in Marx's understanding of man. In another sense, however, Marx could write, "For Germany the criticism of religion is in the main complete, and *criticism of religion* is the premise of all criticism."[5] A number of literary events had, to Marx's mind, concluded the critique of religion. D. F. Strauss's *The Life of Jesus* had stressed the myth-making qualities of the early church, and yet had retained the core principles of Christianity as examples of fine philosophy. Bruno Bauer in his *Critique of the Evangelical History of the Synoptics* dismissed Strauss's idea of the primitive community and recognized only four falsifiers of history, Mark and his three imitators. This criticism led him to a position of intellectually militant atheism—and to trouble with the police. In the hands of the Left-Hegelians the master's philosophy of Spirit had been despiritualized and the full implications of its atheism made public. The Hegelian God, said Ludwig Feuerbach in *The Essence of Christianity,* who experiences alienation in the consciousness of himself as finite man, is actually a mere reversal of the experience of the religious man who projects his own consciousness into the role of almighty God. The criticism of religion became for Marx the premise of all criticism not merely by virtue of its challenge to Hegelian intellectual authority or its confirmation of Marx's personal disbelief, but also because the Feuerbachian method lent itself to criticism of any humanly-created institution which has come to dominate man. The critical analysis of religion presages the end of sacred idealism's reign in economics, politics, and ethics, and foreshadows a reunification of the human essence through full participation in the political as well as in the socio-economic functions of the state. The methodology of the religious critique, in short, tolls the knell for the ideology of capitalism, the fetishism of money and commodities, and finally, the authority of all absolutes.

ALIENATION AND *THE ESSENCE OF CHRISTIANITY*

The Essence of Christianity is Ludwig Feuerbach's attempt to explain the survival and the appeal of Christianity long after its central tenets have been intellectually demolished. He discovered the authenticity of Christianity's doctrines not in the nature of God or history but in the human psyche. He accomplished this by arbitrarily equating religion, including Christianity, with man's feeling of overwhelmed finitude. Man unknowingly projects (*entäussern*) his feeling of finitude onto the infinite possibilities of consciousness, which he discovers in his general nature or species-life, and gathers all these possibilities into an imaginary actuality outside himself. This process according to Feuerbach is the primal self-alienation which establishes the existence of a spurious God: "Religion is the disuniting of man from himself; he sets God before him as the antithesis of himself."[6]

Once we have observed the Feuerbachian inversion, most of what follows in *The Essence of Christianity* reads as predictably as an amateur detective story. In addition to the alienation of man from his species-being, which involves the depreciation of man in proportion to the exaltation of a transcendent God, Feuerbach delineated other modes of alienation. Chief among these is man's alienation from nature. In the doctrine of *creatio ex nihilo* the human subject invests his God with arbitrary powers that cancel the laws of nature. Nature has been downgraded, said Feuerbach, because of Christianity's absolutization of personality in the myth of a personal God. Feuerbach claimed that, since there is no way to argue philosophically from the impersonal world of nature to a personal God, Christianity has been forced to invent the doctrine of *creatio ex nihilo*. Further indications of alienation from nature are to be found in Christianity's aversion to normal sexual functions in its doctrine of the virgin conception and the practice of monastic celibacy. The gifts of nature, as well as nature's inexorable processes, are spiritualized—and thereby alienated—in the misuse of water, bread, and wine, and in the supreme manifestation of unconscious egoism, the doctrine of the resurrection of the dead and eternal life. It does not matter that here and there Feuerbach distorted the Christian tradition to make it fit the central thesis of his psychology of religion, for, as Karl Barth defiantly asserted, "Anyone who is not able to laugh in his face at this point will never get at him with whining or with angry criticisms of his views of religion."[7]

Feuerbach approached the historical phenomenon of Christianity armed with an ancient naturalistic theory (*Primus in orbe timor fecit deos*) and a Prusso-Promethean heritage, and transformed the Hegelian religion of the absolute into a manifestation of human psychological needs. A peculiarly German ingredient in Feuerbach's theory of religion was his wholly subjectivist understanding of Luther. Where Marx tended to sublimate the objective side of Luther, for example, his emphasis on the powers, anti-Christ, and Satan, Feuerbach concentrated on his subjective side, paying special attention to the believer's ability to know God only as God is revealed *pro me* in Christ. Although Feuerbach possessed great insight into Christian doctrine, the differences between him and Christianity are as irreconcilable as psychological explanations of the notion "God" and the divine self-revelation. At stake is the existence of God. As a principle of interpretation he made a state of neurosis normative for his judgment of Christianity and all Christians.

This he accomplished by blurring the distinctions within the Christian tradition between godly and ungodly alienation. In one sense *alienatio* is never deemed an impoverishment of human capabilities or a negative estrangement from self.[8] It is rather the self-forgetfulness which prepares man to transcend the discursive realm, in which knower and known are distinguished, and to enter into an ecstatic participation in the divine. In the self-transcendence of this form of alienation man discovers the heightening of his own identity. Teilhard de Chardin has his place in this tradition, as I shall show in Chapters V and VI, with his doctrine of self-transcendence through action and his prediction of ultimate self-discovery through ecstatic union in God. Now, the ungodly sense of alienation both Scripture and theology themselves recognize, name, and prohibit. St. Paul condemned those "who have changed the truth of God into a lie and worshipped and served the creature more than the Creator." In commenting on Romans 1:25, Luther, whose so-called subjectivity Feuerbach exploited repeatedly, made a prophetic distinction between the true God and man's projection of his own best qualities, wishes, and good intentions.[9] Nevertheless, Feuerbach usurped this great aberration, first thoroughly identified and proscribed by the Judeo-Christian tradition itself, and designated it as the soul of Christian thinking and behavior.

Feuerbach's inversion of the Hegelian dialectic was to remain the key for Marx's critique of society. For a brief period of his career, however, Marx embraced not only Feuerbach's methodological approach but also the whole content of his psychology of religion. He especially enjoyed Feuerbach's interpretation of Luther. In *Luther als Schiedsrichter zwischen Strauss und Feuerbach* (Luther as Arbitrator between Strauss and Feuerbach), Marx lightly decides to allow the great authority Luther to judge between Strauss's and Feuerbach's views of miracles. He then proceeds to choose quotations from Luther which appear to substantiate Feuerbach's anthropological approach to Christianity. For example, Luther: "For what we can not do, He can do; what we do not have, that He has." To this Marx adds that only Feuerbach, the antichrist, can reveal to Christians the true and undisguised form of their own religion: "And there is no other way for you to truth and freedom than through the stream of fire [Feuer-bach]. Feuerbach is the purgatory of the present age!"[10]

Engels once recalled that with the appearance of *The Essence of Christianity* the idealism of the Hegelian system seemed to explode:

"Enthusiasm was general; we all at once became Feuerbachians." Marx too felt the "liberating effect" of the book, and, as we shall see, the best known of his utterances on religion merely reproduce Feuerbachian ideas.

THE KERNEL OF TRUTH IN THE CHRISTIAN PROTEST

Marx's acceptance of Feuerbach led him directly into a paradoxical position. He denounced Christianity as an agent of alienation and at the same time accepted its ethical aspirations as true indicators of human nature as it is meant to be. The human essence, as transmitted from Feuerbach to the young Marx, is exemplified by the Christian's longing for community (albeit with a spurious "Thou"), his desire to fuse work and worship, and his belief in loving cooperation. In other words, Christianity bears in an inverted or alienated form a universal truth about the nature of man. Marx, echoing Feuerbach, opposed the imposition of a mediator, be it Christ or a priest, into any loving relationship between man and man. By its doctrine of the Mediator, however, Christianity expresses a desire for unity and a *protest* against the present condition of fragmentation, which in themselves convey an essential truth of man. Hence it is most natural that, in his essay "On the Jewish Question," Marx should characterize the truly democratic state, in contrast to the so-called Christian state, as "the realization of the human basis of religion in a secular manner."[11]

It is the Feuerbachian Marx with whom theologians are most comfortable, for despite his personal, humanist, and revolutionary atheism, Marx seems willing to seek out the inalienable core of Christianity. This core has to do with man's ability to transcend in thought the squalor of existence by measuring it against an absolute essence. In Christian theology the reality of God makes this transcendence and evaluation possible. Following St. Augustine, theology has identified the essence and preconditon of truth with God. "Where I have found the truth, there I have found my God, the truth itself." Tillich traces this process of identifying *veritas* with God in his elaboration of the two traditional types of meeting with God.[12] In Teilhard de Chardin's psychological proofs "from necessity," based on the individual's need for an absolute, and in his description of a cosmos evolving with and toward Christ, there is effected a fusion of the ontological and the cosmological validations of God as truth. Because God exists, man is able to question the disorganization of his present life and to project himself in work and hope to a point beyond it. To Marx, however, God represented not the guarantor of truth but the inevitable and illusory expression of a false and alienated world. The Christian doctrine of God is true only insofar as it, by its very existence, expresses and protests against the psychological and social confusion which makes it necessary. Marx wrote of the accurate but enfeebled and impotent nature of the Christian protest:

Religious distress is at the same time the *expression* of real distress and the *protest* against real distress. Religion is the sigh of the oppressed creature, the heart of a heartless world, just as it is the spirit of a spiritless situation. It is the *opium* of the people. The abolition of religion as the *illusory* happiness of the people is required for their real happiness. The demand to give up the illusions about its condition is the *demand to give up a condition which needs illusions*.[13]

Through Marx's eyes, then, Christianity serves merely as an anodyne against distress, a reflective rather than effective protest against suffering. The analogy to opium in this context may be understood as a less than diabolical statement of the merciful function Christianity performs on behalf of society. Marx did not indicate that he wished to withdraw that source of relief until conditions are such that it is possible for people to live without it.

Marx's analogy, however, was based on a historical and doctrinal misunderstanding of Christianity. Historically, in the form of sects, monastic reform orders, and political organizations—in movements as diverse as the Cathari, the militant Lollards, the Franciscans, the Anabaptists, the Diggers, the Quakers, the Christian Socialists, the Worker Priests, and the Southern Christian Leadership Conference —Christianity has never been satisfied with its relegation to the interior life of the individual but has repeatedly striven to bridge the gap between an otherworldly ideal of the kingdom of God and its earthly realization. Every such attempt has entailed an effective protest against what it saw as the hypocritical coexistence of the church and an unregenerate world. Throughout the centuries Christianity has produced creative and active protests against its own function as an illusory halo above the real world. Inevitably these protests, such as Münzer's, which Communists so highly value, involved an abrupt integration of primitive gospel values in the world and a total reconstitution of society. Their failures, as Engels knew, paved the way for later successes in a secularized form.

In his misunderstanding of Christian doctrine, Marx fell victim to his own tendency to view man in terms of two absolutes: ideally, as *actus purus,* or realistically, as passive negation. The dialectical relationship between the two Marx incorporated into his vision of the future society, in which man will establish his own identity within a social relationship of noncoercive dependence. Marx looked to the future, however, without recognizing the Christian source and contemporary validity of this dialectic as it is worked out in the life of the church. But Marx read *all* forms of dependence as debasement, and did not realize that Christianity has within itself the balm of resignation, which bears otherwise unbearable burdens, and also the resources of transformation for the overcoming of transient oppression. In this context Teilhard's great attempt at synthesis again comes to our attention. For in his view the Christian's protest against the world takes the shape of resignation, not in the sense of consigning the world to the devil, but by participating in the dynamics of the world for the sake of God's presence in them. Christianity, in fact, never separates itself from the realities of the world or takes refuge in an illusory ideal. The only ideal Christianity knows is that which was historically realized in the person of Christ. His cross is the poignant and universal *expression* of human suffering, and his resurrection is the *protest* against it.[14] He is the soul of resignation and revolution.

THE REJECTION OF FEUERBACH'S PSYCHOLOGY OF RELIGION

In the Paris Manuscripts Marx hailed Feuerbach as the founder of "genuine materialism" but then quickly reversed himself in later publications and attacked Feuerbach's "idealism." To lay the charge of idealism against a man whose preoccupation with food chemistry led him to coin the expression "Man is what he eats" seems at first unfair. But Marx objected to the idealism which abstracts the species-being "Man" from the struggles of historical people. Having abstracted man from his environment, Feuerbach isolated the religious sentiment and, by subjecting it to rational analysis, thought he had solved the riddle of God, man, and society. One would suspect that Marx was never comfortable with the Feuerbachian man who possesses an innate and universal tendency to project the finite nature of his species into a heavenly God, for his structural desire for God which is antecedent to social and productive life reduces the human essence to that of a nonhistorical seeker of God.

The scholarship of many disciplines has, generally speaking, substantiated one aspect of Feuerbach's portrait of man. Otto, Jung, Tillich, Malinowski, and Eliade have in their own ways shown that, in Tillich's words, "Man is immediately aware of something unconditioned which is the prius of the separation and interaction of subject and object."[15] In *The Idea of the Holy* Rudolf Otto distinguished himself from Schleiermacher and all subjective approaches to religion by beginning with the objective reality of the numinous. He emphasized that, although the numinous is analogous to many other feelings, it is not derived from them and is therefore in its content sui generis. Although all people do not possess the spiritual maturity necessary even for the experience of nonrational awe, all are on the ladder of awareness and are moving toward that experience. Beyond the experience of this a priori category we encounter the rational necessity of the absolute, which Teilhard identified on the psychological and the cosmological planes. Now, these and many other positions which characterize man as *homo religiosus* do so not necessarily on the basis of man's successful experience of the divine, but on the ground of his innate and universal *need* to find God. And any discussion of needs returns us to the heart of a vexing Marxian problem.

In the name of the social and economic causes of Christianity, that is, in the name of history, Marx rejected as a false abstraction Feuerbach's *homo religiosus*. But why, having situated man in a historical context, did Marx reject Feuerbach's seemingly harmless theory of projection? Such mass neurosis surely does not prove the existence of God! Feuerbach's work in fact guards against all attempts to ground the reality of God in man's emotional needs and demonstrates even to Christians the unverifiability of the true God. In doing so, however, it also throws into question Marx's reliance upon social needs as indicators of a higher human essence. Marx could not accept the reality of this universal need for God in the Feuerbachian man because such a need might possibly attest to the reality of its object.[16] Needs, as Marx showed in *The Holy Family* (p. 52), are the only indication of a true but nonempirical essence of man based on the heretofore unknown qualities of absolute self-determination and cooperation. Hence Marx was forced to reject the Feuerbachian man's innate need for God. Nevertheless, he usurped Feuerbach's method by transferring it to the sphere of political economy and, to complicate matters, endorsed the atheistic *results* of Feuerbach's thesis. Thus, when in *Capital* we hear Marx call religion "the reflex of the real world" (p. 35), we are receiving only the results skimmed off the top of the Feuerbachian thesis, the core psychological principle which Marx repudiated.

If man's alienation represents only the false supernaturalization of his best qualities, and if human community truly consists in one's appreciation of his species, then the Feuerbachian way to renewal must follow the moral and social principles of a thoroughly dehusked and secularized Christianity, that is, the way of enlightenment and love. Most abhorrent to Marx the revolutionary was this absolutization of love. Feuerbach's remedy for the illusion appears to be drawn from the central message of the illusion itself. Once man understands his divided self, he will, according to Feuerbach, reject the I-Thou relationship which exists between his limited existence and the infinite possibilities of the species (God) and will turn in love to the Thou of his fellow species-beings. Since love of God is but a projection of the loving self, love between people becomes the axial point of all human relationships, thereby rendering all moral relationships religious. With his psychology of religion and his idea of love Feuerbach ignited a revolution only in the sphere of consciousness. In his neglect of the disjoined, socio-economic *basis* of false consciousness, he fell short of theological as well as revolutionary standards of thought; for, absorbed in his idealist interpretation of society, it did not occur to Feuerbach, wrote Engels, "to investigate the historical role of moral evil." In the final and most famous of his "Theses on Feuerbach," Marx provided a succinct alternative to the psychology of religion: "The philosophers have only *interpreted* the world in various ways; the point, however, is to *change* it."

THE REFLEX OF THE REAL WORLD

In Marx's theoretical alternative to a psychology of religion, the socio-economic essence of man and the theory of economic determinism combine in an effort to explain the origin and nature of religion. Because the human essence has no reality other than that stamped upon it by the forms of economic interchange, religion, like any other mental construction, exists as society's offspring and image. It is in this sense "the reflex of the real world." Except for occasional forays into Judaism, Marx tended to focus his reflexive theory of religion on the Protestantism of his own era, and it was in the individualistic and divided character of Protestantism that he saw reflected "the spirit of bourgeois society, the expression of the separation and the alienation of man from man."[17]

The needs of an alienated society, such as the bourgeois, which have called forth and molded a religious response, testify at the same time to the false, alienated nature of that response. By socializing the Feuerbachian essence of man, Marx did not solve the problem of needs. The economic organism, the new essence of man, produces in itself the need for self-realization with the same inevitability as did the psychological mechanisms of the old Feuerbachian species-being. Conditions within the economic organism, e.g., poverty, competition, and injustice, produce collective needs which, since they will ultimately issue into class consciousness and revolution, are "true needs" and productive of good activity. Marx never explained how the same set of social and economic conditions also produces a different set of needs, and how it is that these needs, issuing into religious longings and religion itself, are always and a priori false and their theological expression counterfeit. Such a question again reminds us of the difficulties of any theory which hopes to explain both true and false consciousness, good and bad action, redemption as well as sin, on the basis of perceived material conditions of need. These inconsistencies—and they have no resolution—can lead only to the dogmatic transformation of limited theories of perception into faulty metaphysical principles.

Nevertheless, claiming to have established religion as the child and image of social alienation, Marx was faced with another problem, that of religion's origins in those communities where the processes of survival and sustenance have escaped the taint of alienation. The existence of religion in precapitalist economic settings Marx attributed to the immaturity of man's development. The precapitalist religious man either failed to distinguish himself from the community or was bound in very primitive and authoritarian relationships with nature. The former stage presumably led to the divinization of the community itself, the latter to the worship of nature. Even the various false conceptions of nature derive ultimately from an economic basis, although Engels admitted that to define the economic necessity behind them would be a pedantic exercise. At a point unspecified by Marx or Engels the nature religions were transformed into the Christian reflex of bourgeois capitalism. Drawing heavily upon Feuerbach, Engels claimed that the attributes of numerous gods were at a "further stage of evolution" transferred to one almighty god, who is but a reflection of the species. Perhaps in fear of the "pedantic," Engels did not reveal the mechanics of this operation, other than to claim that the same process of projection, albeit in an industrialized form, is taking place in bourgeois society. As long as man continues to be dominated by the products of his own labor, the same reflexive process which gives rise to religion, and consequently religion itself, will persist.[18]

I do not intend to fault Marx for having failed to include *Religionsgeschichte* and Christian doctrine in his formidable agenda of scholarly pursuits. At the same time it was not quite fair of him to brandish the Feuerbachian method and to parade Christianity as the prime analogy to the fetishism of commodities without first having shown *how* Christianity came to be "the reflex of the real world." Nor do these most tenuous Marxian theories of religious origins deserve to be translated into criticisms of contemporary Christianity, as if one more sophisticated form of untruth should be evaluated against yet another more primitive version of the same error. In one case, the existence and character of religion is laid to the complicated forms of economic development and, in another case, to the lack of that development. It is indeed curious that an atheist, such as Engels, should have admitted to any kind of advance in religious conceptions, that is, to an evolution from the nature religions to monotheism. Even if this evolution represents only that of the socio-economic reflexion, it must be admitted that it does amount to a forward step beyond ignorance and superstition. In a series of epochs marked by the advance of human science, the corresponding refinement of religion, in its latest form as the most sublime fusion of personalism and universalism ever known to man (Troeltsch), must have grated incongruously upon the sensibilities of many a thinking atheist in the nineteenth century.

The reality of God, however much it makes development possible, is

not itself subject to evolutionary predictions of its vindication or supersession. To set this statement into the context of the history of religions
or economics is to shatter the already forced symmetry of the Marxian
theory of religion. For there is at back of the many geographical and
cultural influences on religion a unified experience of the sacred, which
arises not out of cultural usages but only by their means. Mircea Eliade
provides an illustration of the greater sacrality which is antecedent to its
economic expressions:

It is obvious . . . that the symbolisms and cults of Mother Earth, of human and
agricultural fertility, of the sacrality of woman, and the like, could not develop
and constitute a complex religious system except through the discovery of
agriculture; it is equally obvious that a preagricultural society, devoted to
hunting, could not feel the sacrality of Mother Earth in the same way or with the
same intensity. Hence there are differences in religious experience explained by
differences in economy, culture, and social organization—in short by history.
Nevertheless, between the nomadic hunters and the sedentary cultivators there
is a similarity in behavior that seems to us infinitely more important than their
differences: *both live in a sacralized cosmos.*[19]

Nor do the higher manifestations of religion, such as monotheism, fit
the Marxian pattern of religious evolution. The monotheism that Marx
associated with so-called Jewish egoism or bourgeois Deism is present
also in the "High Gods" of primitive cultures. Moreover, at a later stage
we must inquire after the inevitable genius whose consuming idea about
God inspires a response that transcends and shapes cultural, political,
and economic institutions.

Although Marx claimed that each economic epoch is represented by
its appropriate religious illusion, he attempted only briefly to substantiate this with regard to Christianity in two historical periods: the Middle
Ages and the period of modern capitalism. As early as 1859 an American
newspaper had cited the preponderant influence of the church over all
sectors of medieval life as a refutation of Marx's economic determinism
and theory of ideology. Marx's reply in a footnote to *Capital* (p. 36) that
"the Middle Ages could not live on Catholicism" was, like his dismissal
of the Catholic epoch as "that age of materialized irrationalism," an
indifferent shrug of the shoulders to the incubator of the western mind.
Equally incredible was his application of economic determinism to the
history of Christianity in the Middle Ages: " '*Christianity' has no
history.* . . . The different forms in which it was conceived at various
times were not 'self-determinations' and 'further developments' 'of the
religious spirit,' but were brought about by wholly empirical causes in
no way dependent on any influence of the religious spirit."[20]

Had Marx made such an inquiry into the relationship of Christianity
and the social, economic, and political culture of the West, he would

have known that the totality of medieval life and thought—its art, science, industry, and politics—found its integration in subservience to a spiritual reality. Where Christianity failed to transform the political order, it succeeded in establishing the norm of Christian love and justice by which rulers were judged and institutions informed. The story of *Christian* civilization therefore provides a continuing refutation of Marx's reflexive theory of medieval Christian development. The more elaborate the refutation, however, the greater the danger of obscuring the essence of the gospel, for implied in the argument is a quiet justification of the dominant political, economic, and moral forms which the institutionalization of the gospel has spawned. T. S. Eliot's warning to Christian apologists must never be forgotten: "To justify Christianity because it provides a foundation of morality, instead of showing the necessity of Christian morality from the truth of Christianity, is a very dangerous inversion; . . . it is not enthusiasm, but dogma, that differentiates a Christian from a pagan society."[21]

Bearing in mind this objective inexpediency of Christian truth, we now turn to the second epoch with which Marx more successfully associated a form of Christianity, the period of modern capitalism. In the first volume of *Capital* (p. 358 n.) he alluded to a " 'spirit' of Protestantism" which is the manifestation of the individualism and acquisitive tendencies of the bourgeoisie. Long before Max Weber defined that spirit in terms of a work ethic of asceticism, Marx had exposed a relationship between Calvinism's preoccupation with work and abstinence and capitalism's law of surplus wage labor and accumulation.[22] To Marx's ear the power looms of Lancashire, running day and night by means of the relay system, fairly hum with Protestant paeans to work: "One does not only work in order to live, but one lives for the sake of one's work, and if there is no more work to do one suffers or goes to sleep." "We must exhort all Christians to gain all they can and to save all they can; that is, in effect, to grow rich."[23]

Long before Weber (and Troeltsch, Tawney, Niebuhr, and others after him) discovered the Protestant doctrines of the Calling at the core of modern capitalist ideology, Marx had revealed with lethal playfulness the social implications of those same doctrines. Long before Weber associated Calvinist and Jewish business ethics, Marx had identified the practical Jewish spirit of "huckstering" with the spirit of Protestant economy. In the process he claimed (1) that Judaism is nothing but the outgrowth of egoism, (2) that bourgeois society, with its worship of money, is the secularized expression of Judaism, (3) that Christianity's egoistic doctrine of heavenly bliss is the completion of Judaism, and (4) that when the social organization based on gain, property, and money is dissolved, then also the Jew's "religious consciousness would dissolve like a mist in the real vital air of society."[24] In this pseudodialectical pogrom Marx not only overlooked the endurance of Judaism throughout millennia of economic change, but he attempted to explain the unique religious character of that tenacity by reference to a universal tendency, egoism. Had Marx studied his Old Testament more seriously he would have seen how little the Jewish religious consciousness dissolved in Egypt, Assyria, Syria, and Babylon, to say nothing of subsequent persecution throughout medieval and modern Europe.

Since, when discussing religion and economics, Marx was not consciously defining the relationship of superstructure to base, he occasionally failed to distinguish between effect and cause. His basic theories of economic determinism and ideology, however, required a merely reflexive role for the Protestant (and Jewish) doctrines he so closely associated with bourgeois capitalism. Against this theory of reflexion Weber successfully argued that the rise of economic rationalism was influenced, inter alia, by the intrinsic character of Protestant and especially Calvinist beliefs. It is neither to advocate a spiritual-monist hermeneutic of history nor to justify the capitalist economic order that we endorse both Weber's use of the Marxian intuition and his modification of its cause and effect sequence. Weber's simplification of Calvinism and capitalism does not represent the whole truth of a highly complex relationship. Yet his thesis—and the ensuing controversy it generated—at least exposes the fatuity of the dogmatic epithet, "reflex of the real world," when applied to modern Protestantism.

THE DIVERGENCE OF THEORY AND PRACTICE

Rather than define a cogent theory of religious consciousness, Marx preferred to chip away at the inconsistencies of Christianity by citing the historical and structural divergence of its theories and practices. To one who equated essence with historical performance, it is no good attempting to justify Christianity by appealing to an essential truth in it, be it the Jesus of the Gospels, the Spirit, or a social principle, which somehow retains its purity throughout centuries of historical defilement. To Marx the nineteenth-century ecclesial posturing and verbose indifference to the poor *is* Christianity. For an institution as ancient as the church to appeal to the discrepancy between theory and practice as an explanation of its apparent failure was, to Marx's mind, an argument worthy of scorn.

It is important to understand that Marx did not simply repudiate Christianity for its failure to put into practice the lofty truths of the Gospel. Those who interpret him in this light are conversing with the Feuerbachian Marx, with the Marx whose sole aim is the Pauline unity of faith active in love. But Marx's opposition to Christianity drove much deeper than this. When he asked, "Does not every minute of your practical life give the lie to your theory?" Marx was repudiating Christianity not only because it has failed historically to unite faith and works, but, more importantly, because the doctrinal and ethical formulations given it by the conditions in which it arose render any such unification impossible. The individual Christian quite naturally therefore falls prey to the impracticability and inevitable hypocrisy attending a religion in which the doctrine of original sin is seasoned with demands of moral perfection.

At no level of its existence is Christianity able to remove the logical contradictions from its doctrines and practices. The religion of the *logos,* for example, has, in Marx's understanding, bred a spirit of irrationality. *Verum est, quia absurdum est.* When the church proclaims creation and resurrection, Marxism hears only the *fuga saeculi* and denigration of human nature. In response to the church's doctrine of the Mystical Body, he exposed the proliferation of sects, fanatical hatreds between Protestants and Catholics and controversies between high, low, and broad churchmen. Although Christianity is aware of the God-given dominion of man over nature, it suffers work as a curse and a remedy for temptation. Where the church preaches universal love and brotherhood, Marx observed Christian colonialism and the oppression of minorities. Most repugnant to Marx was the cleft between Christian ethics and the laissez-faire practices of Christian business men. He despised a religion which produces of its own inconsistency justifications of economic success as well as ethical afterthoughts, such as philanthropy, which are intended as palliatives for the harsh means and consequences of that success. Whereas Renaissance Catholicism suffered "the dilemma presented by a form of enterprise at once perilous to the soul and essential to society,"[25] bourgeois Protestantism managed to harmonize spiritual and economic enterprise at the expense of yet another Christian principle, love. Christianity's disregard of its own principles is typified in "Parson" Malthus's celebrated statement: "As the population unceasingly tends to overstep the means of subsistence, benevolence is folly, a public encouragement to poverty. The State can therefore do nothing more than leave poverty to its fate and at the most soften death for the poor."[26] Where the implications of Malthus's theory were not followed to their comfortless conclusion, charity was used as the bridge between Christian economic rationalism and the overarching gospel ethic of love. Marx felt, however, that Christian charity—in the form of "concerts, balls, plays . . . for the poor"—serves more to salve the consciences of the rich than the wounds of the poor and that, regardless of motive, it cannot take the place of social reorganization.

Of the Christians who attempted, even amid the countercurrents of industrialization and individualism, to effect a unity of theory and practice, Marx said nothing. He would have undoubtedly pointed with satisfaction not to the attempt of nineteenth-century Christian Socialism in England, but rather to its short-lived and limited success and the church's repudiation of the movement's leader. Marx and Engels, in fact, ruled out the possibility of a coalition between Christianity and communism, stating in a heated passage in the *Manifesto*, "Christian Socialism is but the holy water with which the priest consecrates the heartburnings of the aristocrats" (p. 430). At any event, it was only by carefully selecting illustrations, omitting an entire tradition of protest, and turning a blind eye to the courageous attempts at Christian renewal in his own century, that Marx was able to unmask the schizophrenic character of Christianity and the civilization nurtured by it.

THE IDEOLOGICAL USES OF CHRISTIANITY

The religion which society produces not only reflects the nature of that society but also, according to Marx, serves as the ideological tool of its vested interests. By the time any religion has become codified to the extent that it is open to historical and sociological investigation, it has inevitably become an ideology and an agent of domination. The impassable gulf between the rich and the poor is reproduced in Christianity's celebration of the disparity between the holy God and his sinful creatures. In its supernatural character Christianity transcends the physical and psychological misery of its origins and provides an otherworldly justification of the disparity, the gulf, between the ruling class and the proletariat. While Marx did not identify precisely the theological means by which capitalism accomplishes its domination (that work remained for Max Weber), he did identify two general forms of Protestant ideology by which the proletariat is subdued.[27] The two forms are caricatures of the Calvinist and Lutheran understanding of the Christian in society.

Calvinist asceticism is the logical corollary to the myth of the frugal man and the wastrel by which the wealth of one small segment of the population is explained to the poor. In the application of this moralism, economic success was often understood as a signal of divine affirmation. "All the endowments which we possess," wrote Calvin, "are divine deposits intrusted to us for the very purpose of being distributed for the good of our neighbour."[28] In practice, according to Marx, the possessors of the divine deposit merely encourage the proletarian to overcome his own nature by banking a part of his niggardly earnings and by practicing a form of asceticism, the principal thesis of which is the renunciation of human needs: "The less you eat, drink, buy books, go to the theater or to balls, or to the public house, and the less you think, love, theorize, sing, paint, fence, etc., the more you will be able to save and the *greater* will become your treasure which neither moth nor rust will corrupt, . . . your capital. The less you *are*, the less you express your life, the more you *have.*"[29]

Calvinist renunciation is founded on a dynamic conception of the Calling. Its emphasis on work and underconsumption leads to a fusion of economic and spiritual values and often to a callous abuse of those whose work has yielded little return. Pauperism, Marx repeatedly argued, will not be abolished through charity, punishment, or subjection to Calvinist discipline. Fasting is of no benefit to starving men; nor are sentiments such as these, expressed by the Rev. J. Townsend in *A Dissertation on the Poor Laws, by a Well-wisher of Mankind,* and quoted by Marx:

Legal constraint (to labor) is attended with too much trouble, violence, and noise, . . . whereas hunger is not only a peaceable, silent, unremitted pressure, but, as the most natural motive to industry and labour, it calls forth the most powerful exertions. It seems to be a law of nature that the poor should be to a certain degree improvident . . . that there may always be some to fulfill the most servile, the most sordid, and the most ignoble offices in the community.[30]

In addition to Calvinist asceticism, which ultimately integrates work and accumulation in the kingdom of God, Marx was aware of the Lutheran tendency to separate the gospel from the everyday administration of economic justice. "When grace and freedom come into the earth, that is, into the body," Luther warned, "you must say: 'You have no business here among the dirt and filth of this physical life. You belong in heaven.' "[31] In Luther the importance of the inner certitude of faith transcends concern for political or economic arrangements in society. His doctrine of the Calling, therefore, to Marx's mind, led to an empty spiritualization of any kind of work and an overemphasis on the providential character of the status quo. Such a doctrine underlies many of the church's attempts, such as Bishop Paley's notorious *Reasons for Contentment Addressed to the Labouring Part of the British Public,* to slip an ideological Mickey into the Christian's draught of true resignation. Toying with Luther's doctrine of "vocation," Marx suggested that the proletarian, driven by the scourge of a fourteen-hour day and degraded to an article of trade, may justifiably regard the revolutionizing of these conditions and the destruction of the bourgeois system as his holy calling.

The German revolution has not been forthcoming, Marx complained in 1844, because Germany's revolutionary past is but a theoretical one, the Reformation. Luther overcame the bondage of devotion by replacing it with the bondage of conviction. He freed man from the outward forms of religiosity by enshrining them in the heart of the believer. He abolished the priesthood by creating a kingdom of priests. When put to the political test Luther's doctrine of inner freedom served only to unite the bourgeoisie and the princes against the peasants' literal understanding of spiritual truths. "The Peasant War, the most radical fact of German history," said Marx, "came to grief because of theology."[32]

Implicit in Marx's early criticism of Christian ideology was a general advocacy of the separation of church and state. This appears self-contradictory, and indeed it is, in that Marx condemned an acquiescent church which merely justifies the actions of the state, but also opposed a militant church which interferes in state policy. Marx would reject as ideology Luther's submission to the prince: "But when the prince or some other magistrate calls me, then with firm confidence, I can boast against the devil and the enemies of the Gospel that I have been called by the command of God through the voice of a man." Such a doctrine, according to Marx, leads to the investiture of the prince as "lay-pope" and increases the power of the state, while the individual, having been made a "lay-priest," remains in subjective bondage to religion.[33] According to religious principles furnished it by such doctrines as the Priesthood of All Believers, the state then proclaims the equality of all citizens without respect to birth, vocation, and property, but continues in practice to defend the effects which those differences have upon daily life. Thus the proletarian finds himself living in two worlds: one of suffering under the lack of privilege, the other of theoretical religious equality.

Having attacked the church's acquiescence to the state, Marx did not, however, provide a resolution of the problem, but rather opposed any prophetic judgment by the church in state affairs. Since, he said, Christianity teaches submission to all authorities and constitutions and does not judge on their validity, and since constitutions of states differ, there can be no single Christian principle by which to evaluate political systems. Hence Christianity would do well to practice its own doctrines and to refrain from interfering in the business of human society. For whether in a pluralist or established church system, the ultimate source of religious right, as logic and history prove, is the more broadly based system of human rights. The problem which Marx left so obviously unresolved was to find its resolution in his thought not by a modification of the relationship between two belligerent institutions, but in the dissolution of both church and state and the inauguration of a system of universal human rights.

THE TEILHARDIAN RESPONSE

It was the desire for a comprehensive unity of theory and practice which motivated Teilhard's critique of traditional Christianity. In order to protect the reality of evolution and the cosmic dignity of Christ, Teilhard modified all Christian doctrines, such as those of election, original sin, Incarnation, Resurrection, and justification, which derive their validity from a heavenly decree. Such a theology, based on the divine Word's arbitrary insertion into human affairs, induces those who would become Christian to renounce the world and to dissociate themselves from the progressive aims of civilization. Should the Christian whose faith is informed by a pre-evolutionary cosmology and a juridical theology of the Word nevertheless commit himself to the progress of the world, he is thrust into a double life, a condition of *Selbstentfremdung*, in which his religious belief is estranged from his human aspirations.

Living in an age of scientific analysis, the modern Christian is assailed by a religion of miracles in which God is pictured as "a great landowner administering his estates." The emphasis on miracles and magical conceptions of the sacraments tends to confirm Feuerbach's notion of the Christian's alienation from nature. Unlike pantheism's identification of God and nature, miracles represent (to Teilhard) equally offensive interruptions of nature, extrinsic hypotheses for which the world has no further need. In the ancient world miracles played a dominant role in legitimatizing the words of the apostles and prophets. Contemporary Christians, said Teilhard, confess Christianity not *because* of miracles but *in spite* of them. The organic view of miracles, however, intuits the necessity of God in the regularity of natural events and, extending the traditional doctrine of providence, measures that divine activity by means of biological laws.

Another form of religious alienation Teilhard located in the traditional doctrine of Christian charity. Like Marx, Teilhard opposed the juridical imposition of Christ in human relationships, as if human love exists only as a feeble response to the divine initiative. With Marx he also criticized any ethic based solely on the intention to love. Such an ethic tends to reduce the absolute value of action by making the world a mere testing ground for heavenly sentiments, and consequently creates a rift between Christian theory and practice. Marx and Teilhard further opposed the expiatory or negative practice of Christian charity whereby society's wounds are bandaged by individualistic demonstrations of philanthropy. Where Marx, however, violently obliterated love in pursuit of a new world, Teilhard attempted to disalienate Christian love by universalizing its role in the creation of a similar world.

The instrument of universal love, Teilhard argued, is the Christian church. The Christian love that refashions society and completes the plenitude of Christ affects the course of the world because it is itself organized as an objective phylum within evolution. The biological function of the world religions is to give form and direction to the free psychic energy of the world. The church, more than any other phylum or religion, responds to man's collective need to direct his energies toward a supreme form of personality. The Church is therefore the axis around which the organic socialization of man proceeds, and, as such, is infallible.

The Catholic church represents the fullest development of world religion. Like science or civilization itself, religion is directly associated with the increase of psychic activity and has an ontogenesis coextensive with human history. The true religion (Christianity) emerges by means of evolution and in its organization and aspirations reveals itself not as the final stage, but as the only religion capable of continuing development. Where Engels saw the evolution of religion from local gods to monotheism as a preparation for the scientific supersession of God, Teilhard adhered to the same sequence and to the same supersession of the anthropomorphic residue of earlier times, but with a difference. Far from being a stage through which humanity passes in infancy, the adoration of a Savior God is essential to hominization. Primitive needs are not outgrown but refined in the Catholic church until, by its guidance, they are satisfied in the ultimate monotheism, in worship of "the God of Evolution."[34]

When the church, however, denies the organic, that is, historical nature of the Christian phylum, it separates itself from the concerns of history (which Teilhard identified with progress), and makes of God's presence in the world a mere metaphor. Teilhard took up the communist critique of the historical church at a post-Marxian level by agreeing with Engels's contention that the church has too often blocked the path of scientific advancement. Where Marx exposed Christianity's disengagement from the political struggle, Teilhard criticized its estrangement from the larger sphere of natural and historical evolution. Both objected to Christianity's lack of realism in its attitude toward man. Marx said the man to whom the church (and Feuerbach) offered redemption is an abstract soul. Teilhard characterized the Christian man as the "juridical man" who understands himself, his universe, and his God only in terms of fixed, individualistic relationships.[35]

Nevertheless Marx and Teilhard were speaking of different kinds of "Man" when they accused the church of rendering man less human. For Marx's historical analysis revealed social, political, and economic exploitation which has all too often enjoyed the church's sanction. Paying little attention to economic or ecclesiastical history, Teilhard defined the inhumanity of religious alienation by citing the church's contribution to man's case of arrested development.

Never again, please God, may we be able to say of religion that its influence has made men more indolent, more unenterprising, *less human;* never again may its attitude lie open to the dawning suspicion that it seeks to replace science by theology, effort by prayer, battle by resignation, and that its dogmas may well debase the value of the world by limiting in advance the scope of enquiry and the sphere of energy. Never again, I pray, may anyone dare to complain of Rome that it is afraid of anything that moves and thinks.[36]

The truly human, we have noted, lies in the future and will be realized only if man embraces his own evolutionary nature and assumes responsibility for directing the course of noogenesis. Should the church fail to acknowledge the truth of evolution, as Teilhard said it has done in the interests of its "verbal theology, . . . quantitative sacramentalism, and over-refined devotion," it will have retarded not only man's scientific understanding but also his knowledge of God, for the two are interdependent. As long as the church acts as a "sect" and defends its own cosmology as "a hierarchy of created realities, from earthly to heavenly, from visible to invisible, some being better than others" whose "inequality is to make possible an existence for them all" (Augustine), no knowledge of the God of cosmogenesis is possible. Moreover, any injunction to build a great civilization, as the highest end that humankind of itself can achieve (again, Augustine), is doomed to be fenced about by so-called natural barriers, such as institutions and class structures (as Marx suggested), in a divinely prearranged universe. When the world and all relations in it are given, then the true doctrine of Christian resignation (to God in human activity), said Teilhard, is in danger of becoming "the supine resignation of the Lutheran who leaves all the work to Christ" or "one of the most dangerous and soporific elements in the opium of the people."[37]

Teilhard knew that, in its essence, Christianity is something other than the reflection of the world or the guardian of reactionary policies. In its doctrines Christianity has reshaped the collective consciousness of western man by imbuing it with radically new and formative ideas. One such idea is that of a love which is not merely the refinement of desire, but which, self-giving and self-discovering, capable of personal as well as universal application, introduces a new stage of consciousness. It is a major plateau in man's evolution toward co-reflection and union with God. Rooted in the personal nature of God and revealed in the Incarnation, Christ's love establishes the absolute value of persons. It offers to each person an apotheosis which in the classical past had been reserved for heroes and supermen. Participation in Christ's love, that is, receiving and giving it, imparts to each person a stability and centricity that cannot be guaranteed in pantheist or materialist forms of collectivity.

If the historical revelation of Christ formulates a new ideal of love and validates the worth of the person, the historical resurrection of Christ gives both direction and *telos* to man's evolutionary development.

Christianity is a religion of unending creation, which does not merely relate God's eternal self-creation, but rather celebrates certain historical occurrences that progressively enhance God's identity. The historical nature of Christianity not only implies a beginning, a building up, and a consummation of God's activity; historicity, if taken at full value, also means that man engages in actual and not merely symbolic cooperation in God's progressive revelation and redemption. Far from inhibiting human progress, Christianity, the "religion of evolution," makes progress, and with it the western way of life, possible. Some Marxist philosophers have appreciated Teilhard's alternative to Marx's reflexive theory of religion: The Omega/God reveals himself to Moses, says Ernst Bloch in *Das Prinzip Hoffnung* (vol. 2, pp. 1456–60), as "Ich werde sein, der ich sein werde" and, by setting his providence over the not-yet as well as the present, introduces messianism and grounds for human hope. "Now *the living logic of this hope*," Teilhard would remind us, *"extends very far"*; it informs western civilization in remission as well as revival and, by virtue of its universality, even lends itself to Marx's critique of the church and the communist hope of the supersession of all religion.

Teilhard did not merely assert the formative influence of Christian ideas without attempting to show how the western mind grasps their validity. As we shall see in Chapter V, Teilhard's model for the communication of all supernatural values, e.g., grace, is the condition of reality which nature has imposed upon finite beings. The supernatural, he assures us, means nothing other than the "supremely real." Although he used this formula in connection with his Christology, it applies also to his understanding of the formative influence of Christian ideas. The success that Christianity has enjoyed in creating a coherent and lasting civilization is due to its intuitive expression and satisfaction of psychological needs common to all (western) people. "What has more influence on our minds," Teilhard wrote, "is the consideration of the astonishing harmony that is constantly to be found, as time goes on, between the Christian God and the most subtle developments of our human ideal."[38] For example, Christian eschatology, when seen in terms of a loving personal union, effects a "psychological revolution" by demonstrating the hope and partial realization of man's latent desire for an absolute personality. Dogma not only realizes fundamental human needs, but is itself shaped by them. Hence the revelation of immortality, at one stage of Teilhard's "dialectic," occurs only because reflective thought demands it. Likewise, "by disclosing a world-peak, evolution makes Christ possible, just as Christ, by giving meaning and direction to the world, makes evolution possible."[39] The only criterion, therefore, for criticizing the church is the degree to which it has made concretely real, expressed, and satisfied man's innate needs for progress and heightened forms of personal union.

By the same token, Teilhard used the historical success of Christianity and the psychological coherence of its doctrines to document the reality of the above-mentioned aspirations. The supernatural is confirmed by the psychological, and the psychological is upheld by the supernatural. Their mutual agreement he then adduced as further proof of his system of evolutionary progress. Lost outside the circle, however, are some vital, nonevolutive truths of Christianity. For example, Teilhard inadvertently disclosed the reduced results of his natural theology when he wrote, "The essential message of Christ, I should say, is not to be sought in the Sermon on the Mount, nor even in the drama of the Cross; it lies wholly in the proclamation of a 'divine fatherhood' or, to translate, in the affirmation that God, a personal being, presents himself to man as the goal of a personal union."[40]

The harsh reality of the faith's decline in the post-Christian era threatens Teilhard's assumptions concerning man's innate desire for progress and absolute personality. For if consciousness of this need is awakening all around us, as Teilhard claimed that it is, it would follow that Christianity, as both the formulator and reflector of this consciousness, should also be growing, and that Christ, the soul of progress, should be increasingly welcome in the hearts of men. In this contradiction Teilhard faulted Christianity itself and not those forces that have swept man away from faith in Christ. He resorted to the common Christian appeal to a divergence of theory and practice (or in this case a divergence of traditional and Teilhardian theory) when he affirmed the truth of human aspirations toward progress and the falsity of Christianity's God *"as in these days He is represented to Man."*[41] Hence the atheism of Marxists, the "best" and "most dangerous" anti-Christians, he somewhat naively attributed to Christianity's lack of nobility and failure to inspire love. Rather than pursue this unsatisfactory explanation, Teilhard, as I have indicated, broadened Christianity to make of it a religion whose futurism, universalism, and personalism coincide with and complement all progressive humanist religions.

Had Teilhard read Feuerbach and Marx together, he would have seen how little the mature Marx regarded the desacralized aspirations of man as suitable bases upon which to build a new society or religion. The problem arising between Marx and Feuerbach also plagues the Teilhardian hope for a complementary relationship between Christianity and Marxism. Which of man's core needs are we to choose as the foundation stone for a new humanity? Marx would have rejected with equal disdain Feuerbachian and Teilhardian suggestions for their insensibility to the most secular needs of all: food, shelter, clothing, and *all* else which makes man's transition from animality to human dignity less a symbolic event in human consciousness and more a reality of social and political life.

Historically, Christianity failed to develop the human aspiration which lay at its core. Teilhard offered little historical substantiation for his sweeping generalization of this failure. In every instance, however, the burden of inhumanity which the church laid upon man, as Teilhard saw it, took the form of the retardation of scientific progress. Teilhard seems never to have considered the terrifying implications of his alternative, the unqualified advocacy of science. Does the church's support of all that is thought to be progress—that is, by its encouraging man, in Teilhard's words "to test every barrier, try every path, plumb every abyss"—always and in all spheres lead to a more complete realization of humanity?

We might look for an answer to the question in the church's relationship to capitalism. Although the church relegated the seemingly irrelevant gospel perfectionism to the category of counsels of perfection, normative only for monastics and ascetics, it by no means freed man to do as he pleased in the economic community. Canon-law prohibitions of usury effectively protected the ordinary man in his business dealings and led only to the toleration of interest among the medieval giants of commerce and finance. When, under the pressure of economic factors and new ethical doctrines, the church's opposition to interest gave way, a gradual transformation of theology as well as finance took place. In theology the new attitude culminated in the misappropriation of Calvinist doctrines in order to justify not only work and interest, but also accumulation, wage-labor exploitation, the imprisonment of the poor, and all the atrocities that serve to reduce Christianity to ideology. Whenever Christianity provides an uncritical imprimatur for any secular endeavor (scientific research or the more efficient accumulation of money), or any worldview (evolutionary progress or bourgeois capitalism), it will always run the risk of producing similar ideological results.

Teilhard's view of religion in particular, with its requisite cosmology and belief in progress, threatens to render modern Christianity as unintelligible to the nonwestern mind as Teilhard said the medieval faith is to a modern man of science. Such a judgment is borne out by a new generation's rejection of the myth of progress. There is a close relationship between this rejection and the growing interest in unhistorical forms of religion, whether Christian biblicism or Oriental mysticism. Teilhard's new version of the old interdependence of faith and cosmology brings with it an ideological exclusiveness which is foreign to the essence of Christianity. Moreover, his scientific work-asceticism, with its aggressive identification of progress and the kingdom of God, is nourished by the Calvinist spirit and is therefore susceptible to its particular ideological temptations. Even if an uncritical relationship between the church and a secular system does not totally ideologize Christianity, we still have history's word that the ambiguous nature of many scientific achievements and socio-economic movements argues against the church's unqualified identification with them. The answer, therefore, to the church's pliancy in the affairs of capitalism and its intransigence in the face of scientific progress does not lie at this time in a Teilhardian religion of science.

GROUNDS FOR UNBELIEF?

A single chapter cannot do justice to the Teilhardian and Marxian analyses of religion. Teilhard's response to the Marxist and modern scientific critique of Christianity amounts to an entire theological and evolutionary system, which, in the context of human knowledge, work, and love, attempts the reconciliation of the Incarnation and evolutionary progress. Likewise Marx's criticism of religion is but a prelude to his equally comprehensive, unified, and religious alternative to Christianity. Before exploring the alternatives I should like to summarize the Marxian basis of communist atheism, and in the process to rule out as valid reasons for atheism (1) the laws of science, (2) the church's ideological pliancy, (3) a religious conspiracy, and (4) the affirmations of socialist humanism.

Changes in theology and the scientific outlook now prohibit the search for God's objective presence in the universe. Nineteenth-century science sought God by investigating the material world and, failing to find God, proclaimed, as Engels did, the need to understand natural forces in order to overcome the primitive nonsense of religion. Engels' scientism, upon which the later communist attitude toward religion is partially based (along with Marx's humanism and Lenin's conspiratorial theory), need remain no more sacrosanct than Marx's erroneous and now discarded belief in advanced industrialization as a prerequisite of revolution. The open and developmental nature of all science, including scientific socialism proscribes the dogmatic hybrid, scientific atheism. When the necessity of a precondition of all truth is recognized, the laws of science are more likely to induce awe than atheism.

The lack of dogma which should mark a scientific movement would similarly take into account the far-reaching changes which have taken place in the church and its theology since 1844, the year in which Marx gave classic expression to the ideological function of Christianity in society. Although the communist criticisms of Christianity as an opiate and an agent of ideology continue, they do so in contradiction to the historical criterion by which Marx claims any institution should be judged. One would think that in the light of such diverse movements as "religionless Christianity," Vatican II, and a leftist priesthood in Latin America, Marxism would maintain a continuing reassessment of Christianity's role in society.[42] The old phrases, used to condemn Christianity's interference with scientific progress and human development, no longer apply to a situation in which Christianity now tends to oppose scientific experimentation (extraterrestrial exploration) in the name and for the sake of human development (the cure of disease and poverty). Although neither Teilhard nor Engels recognized this, it is clear that Christianity enters the lists against otherworldly ideologies, such as scientism and utopian communism, and scrutinizes social man in his present rather than future situation. The only point of this observation is to show that any critique of the church's historical action must remain as current as the church's history itself, or it lapses into a reliance on outdated aphorisms and becomes a rigid theory of religion.

It should be reemphasized here that with regard to the ideological function of Christianity, Marxists as well as Marx himself operate with a very general theory of religion. While taking accurate note of capitalism's prevalent (and fraudulent) use of Calvin and Luther, Marx did not repeat eighteenth-century intimations of an organized conspiracy of priests. The only hint of the conspiratorial nature of Christian ideology lies in the inexplicable necessity with which all religion becomes a reflective protest, a tool of ideology, and finally an agent of domination. The alleged universality of this sequence, plus Marx's refusal to join Engels in an appreciation of the revolutionary aspects of Christianity, testifies to the theory which lies behind Marx's historical exposé of nineteenth-century Christianity.

Marx's theory of religion misleadingly appears to derive from a theory of man. The Promethean humanism of the young Marx objected to man's dependent relationship with an externalized being named God on the grounds that such dependence and objectification render man less human. "The more of himself man attributes to God the less he has left in himself." Yet Marxism cannot condemn dependence per se, since dependence, in the form of needs, first relates man to man. Nor could Marx claim that every objectification produces alienation. He believed that in a communist society production on the basis of ability will be accompanied by *unalienated* forms of objectification, and that distribution on the basis of need will produce a new and organic situation of dependence. In other words, if one really begins with man in community, a Promethean disdain for objectification and dependent relationships seems to lead away from the human reality as it is outlined in

Marxism. Nor in the more empirical science of economics does it follow that one's love and compassion for the suffering of others necessarily lead to the denial of religion, especially a religion whose transforming ethic of love rests upon the historical demonstration of God's participation in and victory over suffering. Neither the humanism of the Paris Manuscripts nor that of *Capital* issues logically into a position of atheism. Indeed, it can be shown that despite the avowedly humanist impetus of his atheism, Marx was an atheist before he was a humanist, a socialist, or a communist. The influence that this atheism exerts upon his followers and epigones has a nonempirical and nonsocialist basis. Although scientific socialism persists in reiterating Engels' and Marx's notion of atheism as the consequence of science or the logical extension of the community's self-affirmation, modern communism is still confronted with the private and individualist character of Marx's own will to atheism, and that atheism's extrinsic position as the unmoved mover of his philosophical socialism.

The reasonable conclusions we have drawn are at once contradicted by the persistence of Marxist atheism. The continuing necessity of communism's hostility toward Christianity is due to Marx's insistence upon a particular kind of unification of theory and practice. Ideology demystified is enlightenment; humanism practiced is love. Neither has the power to transform society. Revolution, however, is a term that admits of no completion or actualization. In its proper meaning, it *is* action and therefore the ultimate unifier of the philosophical theory which interprets the social order and the material force which changes it. One committed to revolution is not a dilettante in political theory but a true believer in the practice of human transformation. Bearing within itself the seeds of universal emancipation, and claiming as it does jurisdiction over all sectors of life, revolution either stands in jealous solitude or relinquishes its own identity and force. Christianity is not so much offended by communist violence, which is inconsistent with the gospel ethic, as it is repulsed by the idolatrous character of the revolutionary movement.

This emphasis on Marx's revolutionary rather than humanist atheism by no means dims the prospects of further Christian-Marxist conversation, but rather illumines its proper terms. The dialogic emphasis on theory and practice reveals to Marxists the extent to which revolutionary politics has become a religion of revolution. For Christians it means that they will not necessarily fix upon aspects of human transcendence, such as creativity and love, as points of contact between Christian theism and Feuerbachian-inspired atheism. For the Christian God is neither the reflexive image of psychological needs, nor is he the likeness of economic configurations. The question of theory and practice allows for a return to the more realistic problem of defining the nature of the Christian witness and the possibilities and limits of its political application. Here Teilhard has an important contribution to make. For in addition to the unity of incarnation and human growth around which he built his entire system, Teilhard indicated in several places a more concrete awareness of the church's need to translate its faith into action. While his program for a realistic unity of theory and practice was essentially apolitical, it nevertheless provides a theological model for Christian action which deserves Marxist as well as Christian scrutiny.

Chapter V

THE TRANSFORMATION OF MAN

The education of the human race, represented by the people of God, has advanced, like that of an individual, through certain epochs, or, as it were, ages, so that it might gradually rise from earthly to heavenly things and from the visible to the invisible.

—St. Augustine

In revolt against a stagnating civilization and religion, Marx and Teilhard predicted and passionately advocated the historical transformation of human nature. I shall use the term "historicism" to describe their systems of prediction inasmuch as each rests its case for the future upon evidence carefully selected and interpreted from the past, that is, upon the so-called laws of evolution and history. There was in both writers, moreover, the attempt to humanize the system of social and natural laws by incorporating the element of decision into humankind's otherwise mechanical self-transformation. At this intimation of freedom, both injected moral and religious values into their scientific predictions, thereby revealing themselves as theoreticians and practitioners of hope. It is the substance of this hope and the means of its realization that we wish to examine in this chapter.

Hope is everywhere in Marx and Teilhard. As several commentators have noted, Marx and Engels discerned in every abortive revolt from 1841 to 1871 a sign of revolutionary transformation and "an earnest of the epoch to come." Likewise, Teilhard, while not claiming to be a prophet, admitted to the same "mystical hope" which he believed to animate all scientific research. In "The Mysticism of Science" he remarked that hope and the vista of a limitless future are the two essentials of any religion. If he was right, the sense of hope which pervades the Marxian estimate of man cannot be read and criticized solely as a secondary consequence of his scientific prediction. For Marx's attitude of hope not only was meant to be representative of the world as it some day will be, but also defined his way of standing up before the world and struggling in it. Such hope may inspire courage, self-sacrifice, or physical violence in people who are unable to define its end or final intent. In addition to the predictive criterion by which both science and prophecy are judged, the authority of prophecy is also measured by its power to inspire commitment before the first rays of its day of fulfillment are visible on the horizon. To this second requirement of prophecy Marx responded on no less a scale than that of the prophetic tradition of Judaism and Christianity.

MARX'S HEGELIAN TEMPTATIONS

An All-Matter Universe

The Hegelian system exercised a twofold influence upon Marx's philosophy of history. The two areas of influence may be termed "temptations" inasmuch as Marx modified their content and did not fully succumb to their implications. The first temptation is crude materialism. It was dealt with in Chapters I and IV where we referred to Hegel's susceptibility, when at the mercy of Feuerbach, to an atheistic and materialistic interpretation. Although we discovered an absolute atheism at the ignition point of Marx's opposition to Christianity, that atheism was not the result of Hegel's despiritualization and the crude reduction of reality to matter in motion. For, despite Engels' sweeping assertion that all philosophy belongs either to idealism or materialism—under which he included Marx and himself—a mediating position between the two is not infrequently assigned to Marx's emphasis on the dynamic relations within the economic organism. While this latter assessment does not take into account the foundation of crude materialism upon which Marx built, and the dogmatically preponderant role given to economics in history, it does indicate a modification and improvement of the abstract atheism and materialism to which Hegel's theodicy had given way.

Dialectical Historicism

The second temptation is dialectical historicism, and this is the greater of the two. Its enduring attraction has produced consequences in most systems of human transformation based, like Marx's and Teilhard's, on the rational schematization and predictability of history. This approach to history is in reality a surrender to it, for it allows no other criteria for the evaluation of human nature and activity, the interpretation of events, and the prediction of the future than history itself—as it is shaped by its own "laws" and inner dynamics.[1] All that remains for the historian is to discover these "laws" of history and evolution, to extrapolate upon their necessity, and to invest both the process and the end of their unfolding with moral value. Once the subtle progression, is →will be →ought to be, is made, the historian is safely beyond academic reproach, for he has assumed the mantle of prophet or seer. For my purpose in discussing Marx and Teilhard these general observations provide a provisional yet working definition of historicism, a term which, as mentioned in the introduction, may be applied to both men.

Marx's historicism, like that of so many in his century, represented a failure to escape Hegelian patterns of thought. When Marx turned Hegel "right side up," he not only repudiated idealism, but he also subverted a dialectic designed to glorify the existing state of things. *"What is actual,"* wrote Hegel in the preface to *The Philosophy of Right*, *"is rational."* Hegel possessed both the good sense to adopt a contemporary boundary for his inquiry *and* the curious arrogance to identify the Prussian despotism of his day with the culmination of the spirit's evolutionary flight to freedom. In tacit opposition to his own conservatism, however, he also said, *"What is rational is actual"*; that is to say, whatever may be shown to be rationally valid must ultimately be realized. On this hopeful principle Marx set out to explain the rationale of capitalism's self-destruction by replacing the absolute Idea with the data of economic empiricism and, more importantly, by attempting to deny all rest to the dialectical process. In supplying a new, economic content to Hegelian philosophy, Marx did not seem to be aware of his own failure to abrogate the possibility of an eternal, unchanging principle of historical interpretation. By retaining the formal methodology of Hegelianism, he merely recognized the pointlessness of borrowing only a principle of becoming without also taking over the inner mechanism by which the now materialized dialectic may perform a specific historical mission.

That mechanism was the well-known triad—thesis, antithesis, synthesis—and the mission was the abolishment of the capitalist economic and social order. The question before us in this section is the extent to which Marx allowed the Hegelian mechanism to determine the character and outcome not only of the immediate mission of destruction but also of the positive transformation of human nature. The answers most frequently given suggest that Marx relied upon a suprahistorical rational process or a logic immanent in the progression of history itself. The former confuses Engels's all-purpose dialectic (good for history, agriculture, geology, and mathematics) with Marx's more selective and descriptive use of dialectics. While there is much to say for the latter interpretation, as the ultimate ground of Marxian hope, it too is false, for it fails to distinguish between ordered historical development in which people are mere actors and the genuine historical initiative by which man creates and finally transforms his own nature.

The dialectic which permeated all Marx's thought was based upon three principles from Hegel's *Science of Logic*: (1) the transformation of quantity into quality and vice versa; (2) the interpenetration of opposites; and (3) the negation of the negation.[2] In all areas of life and consciousness, thesis and antithesis are equally real, for they are aspects of the Idea in the process of becoming. Although science generally cannot tolerate a "true" contradiction, Hegel asserted that the creative possibility contained in the contradiction of elements is of the greatest importance for scientific progress. For the negative implies not only exclusion and limitation, but also dynamic antagonism between a thing and the specific negation of its content, which itself must finally be negated in order to achieve a higher and qualitatively different unity. This unity or synthesis results from the sublation *(Aufhebung)* of the old contradiction, whereby certain of its elements are preserved, while others are eliminated. As preserved being and discarded nothingness, or "coming-to-be" and "ceasing-to-be," Hegel added, these terms are meaningless, for their true significance and reality lies in their synthetic unity.[3] It is the historical realization of this union which Hegel assigned to the activity of spirit in the guise of man's progressive organization of the world.

The prescient and arbitrary nature of Hegel's *Philosophy of History* should have revealed to Marx the impossibility of doing a legitimate historical study according to the moments of becoming and the rules of dialectical logic; for whole epochs are generalized and marshalled according to a set pattern whose unfolding and final outcome are already known. Nevertheless, in the face of this obvious danger to scientific empiricism, Marx consciously used the despiritualized Hegelian method in an effort to rationalize the whole of capitalist society. We may pass over Marx's more abstract formulation of the dialectics of capital in the Paris Manuscripts and turn to his more comprehensive discovery and analysis of those laws of capitalism which work "with iron necessity toward inevitable results." At the outset we see that Marx, like Teilhard, was not satisfied with piecemeal "social engineering," to use Popper's term, or the mere analysis of existing institutions, but rather hoped "to lay bare the economic law of motion of modern society." And because Marx gave to his discovery the status of "law" it would seem that the only recourse to his readers (bourgeois and proletarian alike) is conformity to its precepts. For the essential contradictions within capitalism—production by the masses and consumption by the few, poverty and wealth, stagnation and crises—constitute capitalism's inbred tendency toward dissolution. The *objective* expression of the Hegelian dialectic, which alone concerns us in this section, Marx applied on a holistic scale to the death and birth of economic systems:

The capitalist mode of appropriation, the result of the capitalist mode of production, produces capitalist private property. This is the first negation of individual private property, as founded on the labour of the proprietor. But capitalist production begets, with the inexorability of a law of nature, its own negation. It is the negation of negation. This does not re-establish private property for the producer, but gives him individual property based on the acquisitions of the capitalist era, i.e., on cooperation and the possession in common of land and of the means of production.[4]

In Marx's words, the "immanent aim" of this process cannot be deflected by "bold leaps" or "legal enactments." All that a nation's (and an economist's) understanding can do is to "shorten and lessen the birth-pangs" of that which must occur.

This then is the substance of Marx's hope in historical inevitability. The hope in man for whom history is the progressive transformation of his own nature appears to have given place to the metaphysics of a mechanically redemptive process. Yet despite the temptation to solve the riddle of history in this way, Marx, very unlike Engels, resisted his Hegelian heritage and claimed to have neither superimposed a dialectical scheme upon his empiricism nor dealt with history as a metaphysical entity independent of human activity. While admitting in his preface to *Capital* to a flirtation with the Hegelian dialectic, Marx insisted that the apparent a priori construction of his economic system merely reflects the dialectical pattern of reality discovered through scientific means. In *The Poverty of Philosophy* he criticized Proudhon for attempting to inject a phony dialectic into economics, as though every fact were possessed of a morally good and bad side. "Apply this method to the categories of political economy," Marx said, "and you have the logic and metaphysics of political economy" (p. 121).

That Marx did not totally rely on the logic of history may be substantiated more conclusively in his willingness to ally with certain forms of political liberalism. He rejected both the social paralysis of mere philosophical radicalism, as typified by Max Stirner, the Bauers, Proudhon, and Feuerbach, *and* the social chaos of anarchism, as represented by the Bakuninists. Had Marx trusted entirely in the inevitable ripening of historical contradictions, he would not have encouraged trade unionism; nor would he have applauded the parliamentary measures which helped alleviate those very conditions of suffering upon which his revolutionary dialectic seemed to depend. In a similar vein, he maintained that his division of history into periods, or his characterization of it as class struggle does not imply the Hegelian notions of "germ," "destiny," "goal," or "idea," whereby a later period is made to appear the dialectical goal of an earlier one. " 'History,' " Marx concluded, "does not use man as a means for *its* purposes as though it were a person apart; it is *nothing* but the activity of man pursuing his ends."[5] In summary then, Marx uncritically accepted the Hegelian dialectic as the formal basis of reality.[6] He then claimed that he was not a Hegelian inasmuch as he had not *imposed* the dialectical logic upon history but had rather *discovered* it in the economic activity by which man has shaped the events of his own history.

The dilemma of Marx's ambiguous relationship to Hegel boils down to a conflict between science and belief. Sociology and economics, each within its proper sphere of inquiry, measure identifiable causes and effects. Marx, however, transposed the substance of his analysis of capitalist society, namely its progressively antagonistic character, and made it normative for his interpretation of history—past and future. All history is seen as an ascending series of dialectical conflicts and resolutions, whose ultimate goal is the absolute revolution which destroys the basis of the conflict itself. Dialectical history has as its immanent aim the abolition of dialectics and an eternal period of resolution. Now, this transposition of a controlled economic observation onto the plane of world history—with its multiplicity of subjective and objective *possibilities* rather than *neccessities*—represents a leap from science to belief. Marx's interpretation of historical necessity becomes even more suspect when we realize that its impetus, that is, the original discovery of an economic dialectic supposedly made through empirical study, was itself shaped by inherited metaphysical categories. For it was no more psychologically possible for Marx the economist to divest himself of his Hegelian background than it was for Teilhard the paleontologist to suspend his Christian faith for the purpose of unbiased scientific investigation. In either case such a suspension of belief would have been possible only on the limited planes of their respective disciplines. Once they addressed themselves to the whole, Marx and Teilhard were obliged to interpret and attempt to change it according to the "laws" of the tradition each had received.

The Marxian interpretation of history on the basis of a single, unifying principle (conflict and resolution) derives from the methodology of the Christian philosophy of history. For the great Christian interpretations of history—whether eschatological, universal, providential, or periodic—isolate one portion or event of history, make it the norm of interpretation, and allow its form to give structure to the whole. The Christ-event not only exercises the absolute authority of belief among the faithful, but it is also made to impart its particular character to the realm of history which lies outside the individual Christian and the church. Far from being content with the certitude of faith in him who is Alpha and Omega, the Christian philosophy of history has used an abundance of theological metaphors to superimpose the history of Christ, the doctrine of God, or the perennial experience of Christians upon the facts of world history. Hence it conceives history in the image of a dialectical struggle between the two cities, or the periodization of epochs according to the persons of the Trinity; or it inflates the *justitia* and *peccantia* resident in each Christian into an undialectical view of sacred and secular history, of (*Heils*) *Geschichte* and *Historie*.

All this is to say that Marx's indebtedness to the Christian philosophy of history is more profound than a mutual rejection of cyclicism and an insistence upon the historicity of man's struggle with and victory over evil. Nor is their correspondence limited to belief in the power of a historical *kairos* to create a new thing which the circularity of nature cannot erase. For Marx also received—from his heritage of Judaism as well as Hegel's theodicy—the dialectical *form* which humankind's historical odyssey is destined to take. It is the dialectic of God's promise, which is always sure, and its attendant negation, the faithless contingency of his highest creature. Because both elements are real, a resolution of their antagonism must come from beyond the terms of the conflict. The solution is prefigured in a covenant whose conditions are dictated by a faithful God to a repeatedly faithless people; it pre-exists in the promised sublation of the absolute antagonism between Jew and Gentile and in the sacrificial means by which that unity is achieved. It is only fulfilled, however, in Christ, who mediates between the realities of God's absolute perfection and man's sinfulness. Christ's conflict with the powers of sin, death, and Satan results in a higher, qualitatively new, and absolute resolution by which (1) the powers of sin and death are eliminated and (2) man's essential humanity—as intended in the Image of God—is preserved. Man now lays claim to this humanity only insofar as he is "in Christ" and aware of the dialectics of Christian existence: "I am crucified with Christ; nevertheless I live; yet not I, but Christ liveth in me." Long before it had given the world a Hegelian or a Marxian dialectic, therefore, the church was able to sing its "O Felix Culpa" in recognition of the mysterious and dialectical method by which God saves in history.

REVOLUTION

The displacement of the absolute Spirit, with which Marx had identified the Christian God, by its free and self-creative successor, man, represented the first theoretical step toward a philosophy of revolution. In his creative interaction with nature, man now exhibits (ideally) the pure activity formerly attributed to God. In the Paris Manuscripts Marx said that man is what he does and does what he is. His labor, therefore, is not the negation of an ideal state of rest (as Adam Smith said), nor is it an ascetic sacrifice of contemplation. It is rather an "exercise in liberty" which is the direct negation not of rest but of the negation of rest, that is, bondage, laziness, or unhappiness. Hence, according to this dialectical formula, true work equals the negation of the negation. In his empirical analysis of work, however, Marx discovered the systematic violence and repression by which capitalism degrades man's work and robs him of his humanity. On more than one occasion he protested against "the grossest acts of violence to persons" by means of which capitalism was formed and now functions. The violence of this system Marx translated into *objective*, economic laws, which, as necessary preconditions, set the stage for man's recognition of his negated labor and his decision to transform it. The *subjective* side of this dialectical ripeness is the universal frustration, dissatisfaction, poverty, and hatred within the proletarian class which must eventually ignite a revolution. As a transformer of human nature, the proletarian revolution is *the work* par excellence, for it catastrophically realizes the human goal implicit in the slow and tortuous evolution of labor.

Given the social, productive nature of man, the "alteration of men on a mass scale" which Marx promised has nothing to do with the investiture of man with a new, individual unit of identity, nor is it accomplished by a preternatural psychic combustion. To Marxism the change is more radical, for, transforming more than the attitude of the inner man, the behavior of the individual, or the policy of an existing government, it refashions the entire human organism. "In the revolutionary activity," Marx argued against Stirner, "the changing of oneself coincides with the changing of circumstances." Only in the crucible of this total change can it be said that man has ceased to be " 'as of old.' "[7]

In the fullness of time the proletariat, as the universal representative of the dispossessed, seizes power and sets in motion the disintegration of the old society. Should the proletariat overthrow bourgeois political power without disturbing its source, the capitalist mode of production, it would soon realize that it had merely reshuffled the wealth in what remains a capitalist society. The revolution itself, said Marx in "Social Reform," requires the political act of destruction in order to realize its social goal. Only after the initial work of revolution is completed will it be possible for social evolution to take place without political revolution.

Although Marx never planned or participated in a specific revolution, his comments on the subject exhibit a certain progress in sophistication from the early naiveté of the Paris Manuscripts and the *Manifesto*, where he tended to look for a sudden and almost magically successful transformation. He realized, for example, in the later "Address" to the Communist League that a temporary alliance between the proletariat and the petty bourgeoisie may be necessary in the first stage of the revolution. The workers will bear the burden of revolutionary fighting, but due to the realities of the state's composition, the petty bourgeoisie, at first reticent to initiate revolt, will seize the victory for itself and call upon the workers to maintain tranquillity and to guard against excess. This the proletariat must resist through continual antagonism and terrorist activities; where the now-powerful petty bourgeoisie enjoins peace and forgiveness, the proletariat, Marx said, must engender strife and excitement in order to press by all means available for communist programs and the overriding objective: "The Revolution in Permanence."[8]

Explicit in this program was Marx's belief in physical violence, not as the creator of revolution nor merely as its regrettable by-product, but as its necessary instrument. At first glance, physical violence appears to constitute an authentically new eruption within the repressive capitalist process, the proletariat's violent escape from economic necessity. In the deed, however, violence is the logical outcome of Marxian historicism. For, having so brilliantly exposed the systematic violence by which capitalism lives and retains its power, and having traced the results of that violence in human alienation, Marx proceeded to embrace violent revolution as a means of liberation. The murderous pattern discovered beneath the surface of the history of ideas was taken as a law applicable to all history: "Force is the midwife of every old society pregnant with a new one"; "between equal rights, force decides"; "revolutions are the locomotives of history."[9] As the aphoristic results of historical demythologizing, these are memorable. As historicist clues to history, however, they serve only to stifle any creative solution to the problem of injustice by enslaving Marxism to its own preconceived categories. The predicted violent revolution, far from being a new philosophical method, is merely another capitulation to historical necessity.

When we verify the presence of violence in the Marxian philosophy of revolution, then, we are showing not only the dispassionate realism, but also the fatalism, of one who studied history and, justifiably, did not expect the bourgeoisie to abdicate its entire socioeconomic existence without a struggle to the death. It is further necessary to prove the key role of violence in revolutionary praxis in order to destroy the wishful thinking and false hopes engendered by one or two mild exceptions to violence in the Marxian texts. (For example, by 1895 Engels' model for social change was Christianity's quiet but pervasive assumption of power in the Roman Empire of the fourth century.)[10] For the proletariat, violence plays a vital role in all three stages of the revolution. Unlike Engels, who held the bourgeoisie would strike first, Marx favored a well-timed seizure of power. At the height of the revolution, violence destroys old modes of production and their corresponding social institutions and makes way for new ones. With this in mind, Marx claimed that the Reign of Terror served a valuable, preparatory function in the

French Revolution: "The anxious and cautious bourgeoisie would have taken decades to perform this work. The bloody action of the people, therefore, prepared the way."[11]

The final task of revolutionary violence occurs after the petty bourgeoisie has taken control of society on the strength of the proletariat's initiative. Then the proletariat must do everything in its power to sustain feelings of public vengeance against the bourgeoisie: "Far from opposing so-called excesses, instances of popular revenge against hated individuals or public buildings that are associated only with hateful recollections, such instances must not be tolerated but the leadership of them taken in hand."[12] With these texts in mind, it is difficult to disagree with Engels' graveside interpretation of his friend's life and vocation: "For Marx was before all else a revolutionist. . . . Fighting was his element."

The unconditional nature of the method in Marx's historicist system—one might say, the undialectical character of violence itself—makes of revolution an autonomous power. As a method of change it becomes independent of its origins in compassion and its goal of cooperative labor. Where work is defined as the creative interaction with nature by which man gradually transforms his own nature, violent revolution ceases to be the first true work of the proletarian. For, where true work is creative, violence only destroys. Where work humanizes man and his environment, violence dehumanizes both agent and victim and reduces man to a state of bestiality. Where the violent revolution is intended as a temporary work, violence transcends the conditions and grievances of its practitioners and mysteriously perpetuates itself with the force of a communicable disease. Violence is a peculiarly human deed which nevertheless separates man from his true humanity.

Marxian violence holds special terror, for it has been rationally welded into the final and exclusive method of determining truth, into revolutionary praxis. And because this is so, the autonomy of revolution holds no promise of a more human order. Instead it generates a morality suited only to its own character and needs. It is pragmatism with a point of view: not "whatever works is good," but "whatever works for the proletarian revolution is good." Marxian praxis tests the "this-sidedness" (*Diesseitigkeit*) of theories about the material world and reserves its approval for whatever practical action contributes to the fulfillment of proletarian destiny. This dynamic aspect of Marxist morality is captured in Engels' "proletarian morality of the future" and in Popper's phrase, "moral futurism."[13] The iron laws of economic determinism which exempted both the exploiters and the exploited from moral responsibility are still at work in Marx's theory of revolution—with the same depersonalizing effect. Hence, the conventional morality by which Marxists are variously labeled "the friends of humanity" (by Abraham Lincoln) or antihumanists does not apply here, for all law must now serve history.[14] Marx and Engels did not therefore oppose what they called the "firebombs" and "death machines" of the professional streetfighters on moral grounds. They would have condemned modern Marxists' penchant for street battles with the police, not as violations of morality, but rather as mindless "plebian" attempts to make an "impromptu revolution" where the conditions of revolution do not exist.

Alongside the cynicism of a morality based on praxis, the autonomy of the revolution also generates its own religious mysticism. For it is one thing to theorize on the maturation of dialectical forces, and quite another to articulate the certainty of that theory to hundreds of workingmen in St. Martin's Hall, London. There the air is charged with evocation, and the philosophy of dialectical materialism is transmuted into a unified vision around which a forsaken man might build his hopes. Revolutionary mysticism is aware of a kingdom which, although submerged beneath the meanness of contemporary political events, gives significance and purpose to them. The submerged but efficacious presence of this kingdom within history distinguishes Marxian "terrenism" (as Teilhard named it) from the superficiality of sixteenth-century millennialism or nineteenth-century liberalism. Although the few are initiated in the kingdom's pattern of growth, the many may *participate* in its truth only when they take it by force. Historical dialectics is as meaningless without revolution as the kingdom of God without the incarnation. Hence the protracted hardships of revolution, well understood by Marx and Engels, were telescoped into a single moment of decision. The revolution therefore has a *kairos,* a "decisive hour," at which time the whole of society splits in two in a cataclysm of the most "violent, glaring character."[15]

Once begun, the revolutionary movement continues irreversibly in perfect rapport with the needs of the proletariat: "The consequences of its own deeds drive it on."[16] "The Times" of its birth are prophesied in documents which claim reliability (a secularized inspiration) by virtue of the historical fulfillment of earlier prophecies: "Brothers! We told you as early as 1848 that the German liberal bourgeois would soon come to power and would immediately turn their newly acquired power against the workers. You have seen how this has been fulfilled." The same document (an address to the Communist League) sees a revolution "near at hand" which may be called forth by an attack of the Holy Alliance against Paris, "the revolutionary Babylon." This is followed by a warning against false Communists, who "call themselves Republicans or Reds," but who are only the petty bourgeoisie in sheepskins.[17]

Aside from the remarkably eschatological phrasing of these passages, our attention is also arrested by the religious logic which informed the substance of Marx's revolutionary hope. The defeat of the 1848 revolutions, for example, does not spell defeat for the true revolution, but rather creates the counter-revolutionary conditions necessary for the emergence of liberation; the proletarian blood of the three thousand Parisian martyrs makes ready the ground for the coming revolution. The religious logic of Marxian hope transcends optimism in the face of defeat by discerning *in* defeat itself the evidence of victory. This hope intones, "The revolution is dead! Long live the revolution!" and sings its sacred hymn:

> . . . No more tradition's chains shall bind us
> Arise, you slaves; no more in thrall!
> The earth shall rise on new foundations,
> We have been naught, we shall be all.

THE NATURE AND DESTINY OF THE PROLETARIAT

Christianity and Marxism announce the advent of a new order of life in the saving action of a Man or a corporate representative of man in history. But in neither system does the saving agent emerge as merely a logical or natural consequence of the complex of human needs and material conditions. In both instances that which introduces a change in human nature and a new order of life is itself something new. Christianity expresses the force of this new thing in many ways—as the Rod from the stump of Jesse, in the doctrine of the Virgin Birth, in the stark contrast between Logos and flesh—in short, in the divine initiative of Christ's redemption of human nature. For Marxism the new thing is the proletariat's seizure of initiative. Out of the slough of passivity, the proletariat has emerged and shaken free from the material conditions and ideologies which have held its body and mind in chains. With respect to the proletariat of old which Marx said experiences "activity as suffering," Eliot's words have fresh significance:

> They know and do not know, that acting is suffering
> And suffering is action. Neither does the actor suffer
> Nor the patient act. But both are fixed
> In an eternal action, an eternal patience
> To which all must consent that it may be willed,
> And which all must suffer that they may will it
> That the pattern may subsist . . . .[18]

It is the "pattern," which, by a leap from suffering to acting, the proletariat destroys.

The Problem of Freedom

To Marx, the proletariat's act is more than a reflection or an outgrowth of the dialectical pattern. Its passion represents something other than the Hegelian "cunning of reason" which manipulates the special interest of a world historical figure in order to channel its energy toward the desired end. Nor does it represent what Engels so much as designated the transformation of quantity into quality: increasing industrialization + poverty = revolutionary consciousness. Against this "algebra of revolution" (as Herzen called it), Marx held that ripeness is not quite all, that an abyss lies between the men who chafe under the maturation of economic laws and the men who take the decision to revolt. He knew, for example, that in the England of his day industrialization had created the conditions of revolution, but that the proletariat lacked "revolutionary ardor." In apparent contradiction to his doctrine of economic determinism, he asserted that "the materialist doctrine that men are products of circumstances and upbringing . . . forgets that it is men who change circumstances and that the educator himself needs educating."[19]

But what is the origin of this freedom to act? This mysterious initiative, it seems, comes about when the proletariat crosses a second threshold of consciousness, this time at a higher, collective level, and becomes aware not only of its need (consciousness) but of the possibilities of its own being (self-consciousness). In attempting to discover how unfree people can create the conditions of freedom, we are confronted by a regression of long duration until we arrive at the primal man whose only claim to humanity lies not in language, consciousness, or religion, but in productive activity. Consciousness, Marx asserted repeatedly, is the product of life, of what man does. Thus we have not and probably will not put our finger on the button which triggers a new collective consciousness in the proletariat. We cannot nor could Marx single out the factor or set of factors in an alienated environment of machinery, poverty, and ideology that spark the new, positive revolutionary idea. (Nor can we explain the privileged position of Marx's own bourgeois consciousness above and at the vanguard of the proletarian revolution.) Man cannot *be* what he *does*, for he must bring to that action a plan or at least an idea if, to use a communist example, the occasional, frustration-born destruction of machinery is to blossom into not just a *coup d'etat*, but a thoroughgoing and finally rational social revolution. This means also that proletarians do not change their nature through revolutionary praxis because the formative role of consciousness dictates that "the slaves must be *free for* their liberation before they can become free, and that the end must be operative in the means to attain it."[20]

Since Marx assumed that human action depends upon a higher form of consciousness, that is, the collective insight requisite to decision, we may ask a further question: How does the proletariat comprehend the true nature of its own limitations and the potential for freedom which lies within its grasp? Marx's attempt to give a coherent explanation lacks conviction. In *The Holy Family* he linked consciousness of need—"that practical expresssion of necessity"—with the proletariat's self-liberation (p. 52). In a blunter fashion Engels recited his Hegel verbatim and equated freedom with knowledge, that is, more specifically, the knowledge of necessity. Now, more is involved in this formulation of Marxian implications than a simple description of the interplay of freedom and necessity as it operates at the inception of the revolutionary act. When not only the deed itself but also its *character* and *direction* are dictated by collective consciousness, and consciousness by necessary external forces, sociological explanations of freedom have strayed into moral and theological ones. For the obligation to recognize dialectical necessity and to act at its behest, which is Engels' version of freedom, was presented by Marx (by implication) and Engels in unmistakably moral tones. As a form of morality, however, this version of freedom has little to do with the internally constant freedom which makes the person's acknowledgment of his own accountability possible or meaningful.

This loss of personal responsibility occurs in the literary creation of a class by means of abstraction. Marx began by researching the suffering of real people whose misery he determined to alleviate through revolutionary action. But the proletarian messenger of revolution displayed such recalcitrance toward the role appointed him that Marx was forced to create a stylized abstraction of what he felt the proletariat ought to be. In the *Manifesto* he falsely claimed for it a majority in Germany and, finally, a real universality in which all people participate. In *The Holy Family* he called it "the abstraction of all humanity" (p. 52) and wildly idealized its dissatisfaction: "One must be acquainted with the studiousness, the craving for knowledge, the moral energy and the unceasing urge for development of the French and English workers to be able to form an idea of the *human* nobleness of that movement" (p. 113). Despite his early warning against the subsuming of individuals under a class, Marx did just that, with the result that the nature of man is rendered so abstract as to become impredicable of moral responsibility. In his desire to enhance the multiform possibilities of human development Marx was forced into a uniform, class-bound abstraction from which he could not return.

Christianity is of course aware of the collectivities (class, race, nation) to which man belongs and recognizes the web of determinism these spin around man's freedom to do as he would like. But it also presents a more constant, theological freedom (*libertas*) which, completely foreign to Marxism, is not determined by the economic and social interplay of freedom and necesity, a freedom which lives and thrives equally well under conditions of exploitation, class action, and revolution. It is a freedom, moreover, whose exercise is not restricted to the end-time after the drama of necessity has been played out. Theological freedom lies in the love of Christ that determines the Christian's being and action. Because Christ liberates man from legal, moral, and ultimately physical necessity, the Christian is free, servant to none. The other side of Luther's dictum also holds, in that Christ's love establishes itself as a totality in the Christian life. Under the freely accepted totality of love, with its living basis in Christ's sacrifice, the Christian is slave, bonded to all. "Our freedom then," said St. Augustine, "consists in submission to the truth," which is God. This is the divine limit or necessity beyond or against which every act of freedom so-called is meaningless caprice.

In this broad sense, Christians and Marxists have to face the smirk of the existentialist who claims unconditional freedom. But here the similarity of limitations ends. For the Christian God is not a constellation of historical conditions, which, once decoded and acted upon, produces freedom, but is the unconditioned being who imparts his own freedom to man in the form of responsibility. This personal level of freedom was unknown to Marx and Engels. Instead, they relied on an optimistic assumption that Christianity never makes: When a class knows what it ought to do, it does it! Such a naive cause-effect sequence in Marxian epistemology (and morality) renders man a mechancial creature, robs him of the power to contradict the flow of history, and, as formulated, does not serve as an adequate intellectual tool of revolution. Christian doctrine, I believe, is closer to the truth of human nature when it portrays human beings who daily oppose and abuse that which they know to be true. If one can imagine it, Christianity, with its doctrine of freedom from the law, sin, and the power of death, is more revolutionary than Marxism, in that it proclaims God's *action* and not human knowledge as the bridge to freedom. Knowledge of God, as St. Paul's dilemma over what he knows and what he does demonstrates (Rom. 7), will not suffice to rescue man from the doldrums of bondage to self. Theological freedom exists in action, or as St. Paul says, in faith active in love (Gal. 5:6). For this reason we may never equate knowledge or even revelation with freedom by assuming a Marxian-like epistemological cause-effect sequence. God did not merely demonstrate his existence in the incarnation in order to further our knowledge of him, but rather Christ suffered, died, and was raised in specific actions designed to transform the necessity of sin and death and to create in man certain decisions and modes of behavior for which he is accounted responsible.

For the *religious* man, then, the recognition of necessity continues to signify bondage to sin until he apprehends the love of God in Christ, which enters the mundane processes of necessity from without and brings with it the freedom of detachment, peace, obedience, and love. For the Marxist, however, it would seem that the recognition of necessity remains what it is—a clearer view of bondage—even if it is in the nature of that necessity, as Engels taught, to transcend itself in freedom. Against Marx's Prometheanism, which demanded freedom, his own system stood firm, allowing no room for a free human act from within or a divine act from without.

Praxis: Hegel's Incarnational Model

An enumeration of the revolution's component parts has not produced a cogent explanation of its decisive and free character. A gulf still exists between objective conditions and laws on the one hand and subjective need and indignation on the other. Marx's desire to solve the problem led him away from rational analysis toward the language of religious mysticism in which subject and object merge. As a living function of the economic process, the proletariat does not reflect as a class upon its experience but acts as the conscious expression of it. It resolves all metaphysical and moral questions of its identity into self-conscious action; hence the slogan of the early communist association, "All Men Are Brothers," is streamlined under Marx's influence to "Workers of all Countries, Unite!"

Marx's methodological model for the union of subject and object in praxis had a direct bearing on the persona he finally bestowed upon his abstracted block of humanity. Hegel's philosophical theology provided a model in the Incarnate Word's speculative unification of spirit and world, rational and real, theory and praxis.[21] As long as self-consciousness remains estranged from the Absolute Self-consciousness, Hegel taught that it is "unhappy" and incomplete. When the human subject defines itself sufficiently (as the proletariat must do) to be aware of an Other as object outside itself, the human first knows itself as a nullity and is afraid. As a kind of symbolic figure of what is to occur in absolute knowledge, the Absolute Idea (God) concentrates his perfection into a single representative of human nature. Just as the proletariat must subjectively recognize its essence in the objective situation and commodities around it, so human nature can unify itself only by recognizing its own subjectivity in its divine Creator. But man's first knowledge of God as "Other" produces only fear and an awareness of his great distance from God. The distance, however, is overcome from the divine side in the Incarnation. Christ is the mediating term between human knowledge and the divine object of knowledge.

Although we see that, as a class coming to consciousness, the proletariat occupies a similar mid-ground, we have not yet discovered the Hegelian model for action. This Hegel provided when he located the universal expression of the Spirit's death and rebirth in the death and resurrection of Christ. The revolutionary aspect of Christ's death, "by means of which the world is given a totally new form," is evident in its symbolic reversal of private interests and personal desires. Christ's death dissolves the social values which made that death necessary and exalts their antitheses. It exercises the same destructive effect on the individual's "particular self-existence" and fills it with the "universal self-consciousness" of the negative's part in all reality, including God. What Hegel says of Christ's death applies with equal validity to Marx's stylization of the proletariat, "the general representative" of humanity whose acceptance of the "notorious crime" of the ruling class transforms and liberates the whole social structure. Hegel said in Christ's death "the subject is itself drawn into the process; it feels the pain of evil and of its own alienation, which Christ has taken upon Himself by putting on humanity, while at the same time destroying it by his death." Thus in the proletariat the realities of objective need and awakening consciousness meet, and, through its suffering, death, and resurrection, the whole is transformed.

Hegel taught that from the human point of view the Christian copies the Object's (God's) tendency to destroy and unite, as revealed in Christ, by participating in the divine praxis, worship. From the human side, Christian worship annuls the difference between subject and object. Hegel understood the rhythm of worship as a going out into the world and a reshaping of it. The result of Marx's secularization of Hegel's theory of worship was not only the subject-object unity of class consciousness, but also the mystical fusion of thought and action. The mysticism of both worship and revolution ultimately confers participation in the inaccessible Other.

Suffering: The Judaic Persona

One of the ironies of Marx's work on class is his claim that the proletarian revolution would not "draw its poetry from the past, but only from the future." History, Marx claimed, occurs once as tragedy, the second time as farce. Revolutions occur, as it were, in historical costume; thus Luther played St. Paul, and the French revolutionaries wore the Roman togas of the Republic and the Empire. Having demythologized its past, the proletariat will not be satisfied with historical repetition. It will achieve the world's first pure, nonimitative revolution.[22]

Closely associated with the Hegelian methodology, however, and more profoundly rooted in Marx's religious heritage, is the literary persona of the proletariat. One suspects that *because* Marx placed his hope in man rather than the dialectic, he refrained from analyzing the proletariat too closely and limited the terms of its description to the poetry of the Old Testament. In the proletariat Yahweh's Suffering Servant re-emerges in all the stolen splendor of its vicarious suffering, universality, exclusivity, poverty, and long-deferred hope. One class, said Marx, must be acknowledged as the representative of the whole society. In it the defects of the whole society are concentrated, so that its suffering purges itself and all others of "the muck of the ages." The proletariat represents an exclusively chosen instrument of salvation *and* the final beneficiary of its world-historical mission, man. Its sacrificial act foreshadows universal peace and brotherhood, to the end that "the alliance of the working classes of all countries will ultimately kill war" and inaugurate a new and brighter day.

Marx's distortions of this powerful religious idea, however, were manifold. Unlike the Servant of Yahweh, the proletariat bitterly despises its suffering and is motivated as a class only for the purpose of abolishing its own condition of servitude. Whereas the Servant's suffering is the means whereby he accomplishes his work and becomes effective in the salvation of others, the proletariat accomplishes its task of redemption by violently ridding itself of its own suffering degradation. Marx claimed that the proletariat represents man, but its revolutionary seizure of the means of production guarantees improvement only for one class. Furthermore, the desire for vengeance which motivates the class struggle and which endures in the indeterminate period of the proletarian dictatorship reveals but a perverted relationship to the serenity of the Servant's victory hinted at in Isaiah 53:10, 12:

> He shall prolong his days,
> and the pleasure of the Lord
> shall prosper in his hand. . . .
> Therefore will I divide him a portion with the great,
> and he shall divide the spoil with the strong.

In his secularization of Christ's prophetic forbear, Marx meant to re-create freedom. Within the essential being of the proletariat he fused the will to suffer and the will to act. What escaped his revolutionary poetry, however, was the living Christ, whose death and resurrection were more than methodological models and whose demand upon the world cannot be escaped within the refuge and sanctuary of class. When social conditions and the radical means of their improvement threaten to efface or stylize the responsible character of man, the living Christ summons us to return and to be conformed to his image of true personhood. At any point in life one must be able to pause and evaluate his being and behavior not merely in relation to an ideal human nature which lies in the future, but on the basis of one's stance in the present scheme of things. But if he is unable, as the proletarian is unable, to assess the meaning of the struggle within himself, he is bound to lose his soul to a mass movement whose horizon is ever receding.

TEILHARD'S HEGELIAN TEMPTATIONS

An All-Spirit Universe

One of the factors contributing to Hegel's enduring influence is his system's uncanny tendency to spawn antithetical views of life: from it sprang conservatism and revolutionism, romanticism and realism, theism and atheism, idealism and materialism. In terms of the last antithesis, Marx and Teilhard represent two possible lines of development implicit in Hegelian philosophy. Where Marx chose the road to materialism, Teilhard for a brief period in his career held that "to explain the shape of the world means to explain the genesis of Spirit."[23] The first Hegelian temptation is the spiritualization of the world. For Hegel and Teilhard the Spirit both pre-exists as the ground of all thought and freedom and also undergoes development by way of the universe's experimental organization. To the "transcendent aspect of Omega," which exists independent of evolution, Teilhard gave the name "God." Emphasis on the otherness of God, however, tends to petrify the duality of matter and spirit, which Teilhard, like Hegel, wished to dissolve into a spiritual and cosmic process of becoming. Where spirit, mind, and thought are given the status of the physically real, there the duality has been absorbed in monism.

Teilhard established the primacy of spirit (=mind=consciousness) by showing that evolution follows a direct line of cerebralization which leads to man. Spirit-monism conceives the birth of self-consciousness and subsequent history as the Spirit's emergence from its past into its self-conscious present. As we might expect, the Hegelian tendency to neglect the intrinsic character of historical events reoccurs in Teilhard's doctrine of spiritualization. Social upheavals are read off as manifestations of emerging consciousness, and universal history is reduced to an "immense psychic exercise" in which "Life on earth is in some ways more interesting than real lives."[24] With Marx, Teilhard transcended the sense of self-satisfied completion in Hegel, so that the end of matter and history lies in the Spirit's future when the dual nature of man's knowledge of God and the material world will be absorbed in a higher absolute synthesis of knowing and being.

We have in Chapter III followed the development of Teilhard's metaphysics away from spirit-monism toward the theory of complexity-consciousness. This development in Teilhard paralleled Marx's attempt to escape metaphysical patterns of thought by means of scientific inquiry. The totality of Spirit as the controlling category of thought gave way in both thinkers to the totality of *history*. In Hegel nature remained a nonhistorical and undialectical background for the Spirit's long conflict with itself. In Teilhard, however, the evolution of nature did not signify the alienation of spirit. Matter is more than a principle of individuation as negation. Its individuation, especially in man, is the result of the Spirit's creativity and freedom and follows upon the personal call by which God addresses man as a historical creature. While Teilhard referred to these theological concerns only in devotional works, they were implicit in his rejection of Hegelian notions of a pure spirit.

Evolutionary Historicism

By escaping the temptation of spirit-monism, Teilhard cast himself into the arms of natural history, where he discovered an un-Hegelian and un-Marxian, but equally comprehensive *key* to the whole of reality. At no level, save that of the person's experience of sin and redemption, did Teilhard's discovered law of nature and history (complexity-consciousness) reveal what for Hegel and Marx was the most important phase in the dialectical sequence: the negation of negation. This is true primarily because Teilhard took his cue from natural evolution, whose long progress toward human-self consciousness has not been achieved by the unfolding of the relatively simple laws of Hegelian dialectics. In contrast to this simplicity,

the dialectic that is characteristic of evolution proceeds not so much by position and opposition as by opposition and divergence, composition in convergence, and transformation in emergence. Moreover, the sequence of the phases of divergence, convergence, and emergence can hardly be said to correspond to our mental categories; it is even opposed to them. . . . Contrary to its apparent homogeneity, there is nothing linear in evolution; it is discontinuous. There is no growth except through mutations or transformation points. Seen from close range, everything is continuous; but if one stands back a little, all is discontinuous.[25]

Now, there is some question as to Teilhard's recognition of the disjunctive and regressive character of evolution. For his use of the scientifically discredited term "orthogenesis" suggests not only the teleology of nature but also the smooth rectilinear progress of life. All that concerns us in this scientific controversy, however, is that the negative element in this progress appears not in a struggle between antagonists, but in the stagnations, failures, and dead ends to which the inventiveness of the animal and human effort to sustain life is constantly subject. In this sense Teilhard thoroughly stripped Hegelian negation of its potency and creativity by relegating it in nature as well as human history to the nonstatus of evolutionary wastage. Even where Teilhard spoke of a natural or historical transformation "in which the sum of its earlier properties is partly retained and partly given a new form," this *Aufhebung* is achieved without conflict and destruction. The appearance of reflection in man, for example, was treated more as an emergence from a multiplicity of environmental factors and biological possibilities than as the synthetic result of a conflict between two tribes of anthropoids. In fact, the figure used was that of the child in the course of ontogeny. Likewise, the two energies of evolution, while appearing to contradict one another, are on a scientific level seen to be heading in opposite directions, the radial toward organization and the tangential toward eternal wastage and meaninglessness. Moreover, on the metaphysical level they are understood as one energy radiating from Omega and underlying the material as well as psychic forces in the universe.

What we have uncovered in Teilhard's understanding of evolution is an undialectical (in the Marxian sense) process of unification which pervades every stratum of reality. At the peak of the universe the Holy Trinity, whose union Teilhard claimed as a model for his notions of creative union and personalization, imparts to this process no sense of conflict. The later rapport that Teilhard discovered between spirit and matter, the within and the without, rules out a metaphysical or a sociopolitical doctrine of alienation. Similarly, on a historical plane the proposed reconciliation of faith in God and faith in the world, of Christianity and communism, presumes an underlying and already-existing harmony between the two. "Religion and science," he said, "are the two conjugated faces or phases of one and the same complete act of knowledge."[26]

On the strength of a statement such as this, it might be argued that, despite Teilhard's interest in negation, his vision of the whole nonetheless corresponds to Hegel's; for the negations of the antagonisms in Hegel are always relative to an Absolute Spirit of truth, whose preexistence, permutations, and ultimate destination are known to the philosopher. So in Teilhard the dead ends of evolutionary life are experienced existentially but, more importantly, are transcended in the spiritual assurance of ultimate success. Were we to interpret Marx as a doctrinaire Hegelian, the ultimate relativity of evil in his view would also lead to an understanding of the world as an irreversible process of unification. But we know that Marx absolutized the antitheses in the material world, that is, took evil seriously, and hoped to destroy its independent power by means of a willed act of negation. Creative negation stems from a belief in the positive reality and effectiveness of evil. It therefore champions violent revolution, rather than emergent evolution as the means of human transformation.

By the time nineteenth-century biology confirmed earlier suspicions of nature's so-called historical development, Marx and Engels had already preoccupied themselves with purely economic theories of history. These economic theories, as we have understood them, were greatly influenced by a Hegelian metaphysics whose laws were held inapplicable to nature. Only later did Engels expressly contradict Marx's emphasis on the disjunction of nature and man by superimposing the socioeconomic dialectic upon the whole realm of nature.

From his evolutionary point of departure Teilhard reversed Engels' method by imposing the *evolutionary form of nature* on human history. This he did first by downgrading the importance of the "struggle for life," and then by transferring the more congenial biological laws of association and complexity-consciousness to the history of ideas and institutions. When Teilhard rejected the "crude transference of the mechanical laws of selection to the domain of man," he did not do so on methodological principle. For while he was unwilling to explain "mutual exploitation and destruction" as a law biologically necessary for man, he *was* willing to characterize human society by means of the equally biological concept of convergence. "There is only one real evolution, the *evolution of convergence,* because it alone is positive and creative."[27] In a more straightforward way, the preface to *The Phenomenon of Man* announced the presupposed " 'biological value' attributed to the social fact around us." And in a 1952 essay Teilhard stated outright, " *. . . natural evolution and cultural evolution are one*—to the extent that the latter presents the direct extension and accentuation of the general phenomenon of organic evolution in the humanized world."[28] Although he made much of reflective consciousness, by which man sets himself apart from the brute, that consciousness does not represent—as it does in Marx—an absolutely new event, for it has been prepared for in the psychic content of every granule of matter and every living organism. History, whose essence it is to possess an "outside" of corporeality and an "inside" of thought (to paraphrase Collingwood), has pre-existed in the mere events of nature, and in that pre-existence has compromised its freedom and humanity.

The Myth of Progress

When transferred to the realm of human history, the assurance of biological convergence yields western humanity's most pervasive myth: the belief in progress. Where Marx understood technological improvement and its attendant forms of social organization as the welcomed prerequisites to bourgeois suicide, after which new history will begin, Teilhard incorporated these forms of improvement directly into the saving progress of evolutionary history. With his proclaimed "faith in progress" Teilhard addressed himself to the problems of the twentieth century armed with the sentiment of the nineteenth. The optimism with which the prince consort heralded London's Great Exhibition of 1851 remained undimmed a century later in Teilhard. The prince said, "Nobody who has paid any attention to the peculiar features of our present era will doubt for a moment that we are living at a period of most wonderful transition, which tends rapidly to accomplish that great end to which indeed all history points—*the realization of the unity of mankind.*"[29]

To correlate this hope in human progress with the achievements of natural evolution, as Teilhard did, is to ask at least five related questions: (1) Does the regularity of increasing organization and consciousness establish itself as a law in all of nature? (2) Does this comprehensive pattern occur in human society, so as to establish itself as a universal, socio-natural law? (3) What is the connection between nature and history? (4) If all of nature exhibits a progression toward more complex organization and consciousness, may we assign a higher value to the later stages in this progression? (5) If the linked progression toward organization and consciousness occurs in society, may we assign a higher value to the later stages of human history (the present or the future)?

For the sake of argument we might give a provisionally affirmative answer to numbers 1 and 2. (This would entail acceptance of Teilhard's questionable correlation of organization and consciousness and its application to the most minutely differing organisms in the whole exceptionless realm of nature.) It further presupposes the same correlation in human affairs, so that Ernst Benz's comment—to the effect that global technology is more catholic than the Catholic church and more ecumenical than the ecumenical movement—would necessarily be taken to imply a corresponding universality of awareness.

With these reservations in mind, we may seek the Teilhardian nexus between nature and history. He discovered it only in the most general and highly selective analogies, in poetic metaphor, in his own and the world's postulated need for unity, and finally, as we shall see in the next section, in the conformity of Christian revelation to his evolutionary hypothesis. But none of these tenuous connections establishes progress until we have affirmed numbers 4 and 5. And this we cannot do. Progress in nature exists only in relation to man's understanding of developmental modification as *improvement*. If we accept good will as the one form of value, as Kant did, evolution is progress in that it has led to one who is capable of moral goodness. But it is difficult to discern such value in evolution itself. Is a bird, Collingwood asks, really of more value than its ancestor, the archaeopteryx?[30] When we relate a similar question to the present state of human organization and knowledge throughout the *whole* world, we are certainly able to see vast areas of scientific, social, and even moral improvement. But we do not see the regularity and universality of improvement which would allow us to formulate a law of progress applicable to all human life. For to speak of progress more is required than change, development, or complexification. There must also be, in J.B. Bury's words, a corresponding "increase in happiness," or in Teilhard's, an advance in "the structure of being."[31] To either requirement—the ethical or the ontological—twentieth-century forms of mass organization and ideology have proved notably unsympathetic.

Despite this, Teilhard continued to believe in a universal law of progress; for his true criterion of evolution was not man, mind, personality, or freedom, but rather the destined result of evolutionary transformation—the collective Superman, the ultrahuman, the hyperpersonal—the Man who now awaits his own birth. Wherever the person as he *now* exists is accepted as the criterion of value, the idea of progress evaporates. Hence it is not surprising that Teilhard in several places equated progress with "futurism" and deftly proceeded from biological principles, through historical analogies, to historicist prediction. The predicted "illuminating involution" of humankind upon itself, forshadowed in present social structures, derives ultimately from the curvature of evolution. The irreversibility of this sequence is guaranteed by the provisional success of "world history" (300 million years of it), the indestructibility of Spirit, and the presence of a "prime mover ahead." "Nothing," Teilhard cried, "absolutely nothing . . . can arrest the progress of social Man towards ever greater interdependence and cohesion."[32]

Rarely did Teilhard allude to the human freedom which subverts every system of predictive historicism with the multiple possibilities of creativity, change, and inbred resistance to the familiar dangers of "unanimization." The subjectivity of history has at this stage of Teilhard's methodology, and by his own admission, all but given way to the necessity of objective laws intelligible to those able to see them. The history of human freedom has become little more than the explication of progress. As in Marxian historicism, history's true function is to "provide a sufficient thickness of the present" for science's prediction of the future. But since evolutionary prediction now centers on man's psychic possibilities, history for Teilhard tended to be the opposite of what it was for Marx. Political, cultural, and economic movements constitute phases of what Marx in *The German Ideology* scornfully called "the evolutionary history of consciousness." In this curious consequence of scientific phenomenology, Teilhard's evolutionary historicism came full circle with his earlier spiritualism—in its disregard for the intrinsic character of events and its subservience to a universal pattern—and thereby rearticulated the failures of its Hegelian progenitor.

THE INCARNATION AS UNIVERSAL HISTORY

Teilhard's earliest literary efforts reveal his preoccupation with the unity of the natural and supernatural term of the world. The later essays insist that the progressive convergence of consciousness demands a supremely personal center as well as goal, whose existence Teilhard postulated by means of a scientific affirmation of faith. This faith in the directed nature of consciousness (spirit) toward an upper term constitutes, in a general way, the first phase of Teilhard's apologetic method. The scientific probability of Omega, to Teilhard's mind, established "a correct physics and metaphysics of evolution."

The second phase was the articulation of a Christology proportionate to the dimensions and character of evolution. More than a phase, however, Teilhard's doctrine of Christ incorporated the familiar categories of matter and spirit and became the key to the interpretation and completion of the entire universe. Christ's union with the world of evolution, Teilhard said in "Social Heredity and Progress," "expresses the history of the universe." In what follows I do not wish to dwell on the biblical basis of his realistic conception of the cosmic Christ nor on the feasibility of formulating a Christology commensurate with an evolutionary worldview. Here we are only interested in understanding how the Incarnation functions as the ground and principle of man's historic self-transformation. We shall see that whereas Marx gave to his conception of history the dialectical form of the Messiah's defeat and victory, Teilhard imposed upon his Christ the form of evolutionary history. This Teilhard accomplished by means of an extreme Incarnationalism, which, for purposes of exposition, might be compared to three interrelated teachings of the second-century father, Irenaeus of Lyons: (1) recapitulation, (2) physicalism, (3) accommodation.

1. Because the scientist's hope does not assure the ultimate attainment of Omega, and because forces of dispersal as well as convergence are at work in the universe, the revealed Christ is needed as the spearhead and embodiment of the evolutionary ascent. Like the Christ of Irenaeus, who sums up all the ages of man and the development of the race (*anakephalaiosis*), Teilhard's Christ is the "First," the "Head," the "total man" who recapitulates "in the depth of his consciousness, the consciousness of all men." Having gathered in himself "the totality and the fulness of humanity," Christ now leads it to glory via the process of evolution.[33]

2. Following Irenaeus in his opposition to those who hold matter in contempt, Teilhard portrayed Christ's recapitulation of all human experience in extremely *physical* terms. While totally relinquishing neither the manhood nor the historical individuality of Christ, Teilhard grasped the Incarnate Lord at the point where the intuition of his science discovered Christ's greatest efficacy. Christ is Omega and biologically fulfills the attractive, personalizing, unitive, and loving functions previously attributed to it.[34] We may impose on Teilhard's theology the traditional distinctions between Christ's universal presence in the created world and his gracious unity with the faithful in church and sacrament, but for all practical purposes of interpretation Teilhard's "pan-Christism" dissolved these distinctions. We find him early in his career struggling with the natural relationship between all being and Christ, a relationship for which his later christological term, "physical center," was to provide little clarification. In an evolutionary view of creation which consistently stresses the immanent rather than the transcendent, the Incarnation assumes, in addition to its localized character, the form of an incomplete process. Teilhard wrote, "Of the cosmic Christ, we may say both that he is and that he is entering into fuller being."[35]

Here we approach the transition from the Christ who unites himself with his church to the Christ who fills all things. Of the former it is correct to speak of an incomplete body awaiting the complete unity of the elect. Concerning the latter, Teilhard observed and extended the perfect continuity between Christ and church, head and body, of which Irenaeus and the Fathers wrote, to include "the whole range of human works, of material determinisms and cosmic evolutions." Even this was not a departure from early Christian theology. In his massive study, *The Whole Christ*, Emile Mersch writes, "The idea that the Incarnate Word is in Himself the unity and harmony not only of men, but also of the entire universe and even of material things was to remain a favorite theme for the Fathers of the Church."[36] Teilhard placed this theme in an evolutionary perspective when he wrote,

Already co-extensive with space and co-extensive with duration, Christ is also automatically, in virtue of his position at the central point of the world, co-extensive with the scale of values which are spaced out between the peaks of spirit and the depths of matter. Projected, then, on the screen of evolution, Christ, in an exact, physical, unvarnished sense, is seen to possess those most awesome properties which St. Paul lavishly attributes to him.[37]

We are at first taken aback not by the affirmation of this pan-Christic unity, which is perfectly orthodox, but by the order and mode of Teilhard's presentation. For what is true by virtue of Christ's presence in history, his unity with God, and his cosmic dominion, is accepted and celebrated by Teilhard on inordinate grounds. The mystery of Christ's relationship to the world has been desacralized to the extent that Teilhard's phenomenology claims to *see* in the extended laws of biological evolution the divine repletion of all things and the unity for which Jesus prayed in the upper room.

The physical unity between Christ and all "human works," "material determinisms," and "cosmic evolutions" is effected by the Eucharist. What Teilhard more prosaically termed the "secondary and generalized sense" of the Eucharist's efficacy he gives magnificent expression in "The Mass on the World":

Since once again Lord—though this time not in the forests of the Aisne but in the steppes of Asia—I have neither bread, nor wine, nor altar, I will raise myself beyond these symbols, up to the pure majesty of the real itself. I, your priest, will make the whole earth my altar and on it will offer you all the labours and sufferings of the world.[38]

When the priest says *Hoc est corpus meum*, his words transform the bread into the reality of Christ. Although these actions reflect a historical death and are repeated at regular intervals in time, Teilhard taught that they signify a single communion that has been in progress since the beginning of messianic preparations. Once we understand this in the context of man's dynamic and ever-expanding relationship with other men and the material world, the way is opened for the eucharistic consecration of the entire cosmos. On a universal scale, then, Christ sanctifies *ex opere operato* everything material, everything spiritual, and every graded interfusion of the two.

3. When St. Irenaeus was faced with explaining why God did not render man perfect from the beginning rather than imposing upon him a long process of growth, he said, "As then the Mother is able indeed to bestow nourishment on her babe, but the babe is as yet incapable of receiving the nourishment which is too old for itself; so God also was indeed able Himself to bestow on man perfection from the beginning, but man was incapable of receiving it: for he was a babe."[39] What Irenaeus was introducing is God's *accommodation* of his means of salvation to the physical, intellectual, and cultural capability of its recipients. This is the "soteriological argument," first systematized in Irenaeus, and subsequently used by the Fathers to infer from the nature of man the nature of Christ and the necessary form of his saving action. Emile Mersch further demonstrates the close relationship between the soteriological argument (accommodation) and doctrines of the physical solidarity of man and Christ.[40] Teilhard's Christology, too, must be understood in terms of this relationship. Only when man has understood himself as the agent of an increasingly convergent evolution can he comprehend the immense and dynamic presence of Christ. More than this, however, the position of man in the cosmos *requires* an evolutive

Christ, one who is capable of satisfying the aspirations of humankind insofar as these aspirations are integrally related to evolutionary human nature.

Teilhard, however, exceeded the traditional argument when he said that "Christ must be universal because our ideal demands his universality," or that "by disclosing a world-peak, evolution makes Christ possible."[41] On this principle it is at least possible for man to abuse the privilege of the divine accommodation and, by his perverse determination of his own destiny, to draw up the blueprints for God's saving plan. God's accommodation, in Teilhard's understanding of it, sheds more light on nature than it does on Christ's grace. Teilhard claimed merely to have transposed the ancient message of Christ's cosmic dominion into an evolutionary worldview. But, unlike St. Paul and the Fathers, he so thoroughly fused Christ and cosmology, Christogenesis and cosmogenesis, that Christ's vehicle is made to share in his grace and glory. The nature of Christ must conform to human nature in order to save it, for what is not assumed is not redeemed. We have shown in Chapter III how Teilhard equated human nature with evolution become conscious of itself and how this effectively transfers original sin to the process of evolution. In the recreation of this human nature, evolution again becomes the indispensable agent of the divine economy. Where it was stigmatized as the source of unavoidable by-products, such as sin and failure, evolution is now considered in its physical unity with Christ and is exalted as "the way out towards something that escapes total death, . . . the hand of God gathering us back to himself."[42]

The second phase of the Incarnation is Christ's death and resurrection. Although Irenaeus held that Christ did not come to die—but to destroy sin and give life to man—he nevertheless laid emphasis on Christ's death as "the condemnation of those who crucified Him . . . and the salvation of such as believe in Him." Despite his self-avowed adherence to an Irenaean form of "progress," Teilhard at this point severed his mooring in the tradition by assimilating the work of Christ's death and resurrection into a pattern of natural development. In his doctrine of redemption the emphasis on physical union rather than the sacrificial event mirrors his understanding of evil and history. Although he hoped to reaffirm the immensity of the cosmic Christ by picturing the entire universe's participation in the ascent from multiplicity toward unity, the effect was to disparage the tenacity of moral evil and Christ's victory over it. In this theology of evolution the cross becomes a symbol of human growth, and the lamb of God comes to signify the progress of the world. As a "law common to all life," the crucifixion in Teilhard's thought appears to function as a theological substantiation of his evolutionary hypothesis: "The cross is the symbol of *the arduous labour of Evolution*—rather than the symbol of expiation." Through it man learns "that the most effective means of progress is to make use of suffering."[43]

In this there is a great similarity to Hegel's understanding of the Incarnation as a frozen pictorial illustration of a more real and dynamic process of truth. When the redemption is so closely associated with the condition of existence itself, and when the recognition and adherence to the ascendent tendency of this condition is invested with the highest value, then participation in the event of Christ's death and new life is reduced to a moralistic imitation of nature. This association also serves to remove the element of conflict from the redemption as it was achieved by Christ and copied in a socio-economic form by Marx. By relegating the expiatory nature of Christ's redemption to second place in his system, thereby de-emphasizing the conflict and victory involved in the divinely-willed suffering, Teilhard evinced an undialectical view of historical evil as that which is to be outgrown or discarded, but not borne, contested, conquered, and destroyed. His doctrine of the Incarnation and redemption therefore proposes a transformation of man that conforms in every way to the substance of his evolutionary hope.

Before elaborating the three historical moments of the Incarnation by which man—as evolution and in Christ—transforms his own nature, I ought to indicate several of the difficulties involved in arriving at what appears to be so straightforward a diagnosis of Teilhard's Christology. The difficulties involve authentic tensions within the Christian message as well as outright contradictions in Teilhard's thought. The first difficulty has to do with the place of the historical and eternal humanity of Christ in the process of evolutive recapitulation. The New Testament affirms the humanity of Christ as a matter of fact and as a matter of polemic; it also ascribes to him a physical dominion whose cosmic dimensions are ascribable to human nature only with the greatest difficulties of the imagination. Nevertheless, redemption, the eucharistic presence, and the cosmic dominion of Christ derive from the permanency of his manhood. "But this man, because he continueth ever, hath an unchangeable priesthood" (Heb. 7:24 KJV), which, it must be added, functions as a continuation of his historical ministry of reconciliation. The communication of the divine and human properties of Christ may be extended on a lesser scale according to traditional theology, so that whatever Christ was and continues to be becomes the property of his Church. This is the continuing basis of the mystical body and the Eucharist, even in the latter's material and cosmic extensions.

Here enters a Teilhardian contradiction. On the one hand, Teilhard insisted that his (and St. Paul's) universal Christ rests upon the historical Jesus of the Gospels. "To be the alpha and omega," Teilhard wrote in "Sketch of a Personalistic Universe," "Christ must, without losing his precise humanity, become co-extensive with the physical expanse of time and space."[44] On the other hand, it is just this "precise humanity" that seems to be absent at the foundation of Teilhard's cosmic Christology. Teilhard struggled with the idea of a particular and in any way final revelation of Christ to one historical situation; he found the notion of a Christ-universal more attractive than the contested reality of the historical Jesus, from whose life radiates the mystical energy of two thousand years.[45] In order to emphasize this universality, he experimented with a "third nature of Christ," "Christ total and totalizing," in which, "through the transforming effect of the Resurrection, the individual human element born of Mary, finds himself left not only at the stage of a cosmic element . . . but at the ultimate psychic center of an assembling universe."[46] But if Teilhard hoped to demonstrate the immensity of the Incarnation, especially by means of the socio-material extension of the Eucharist, more than a mere allusion to the humanity of Christ is needed. It is not enough to retain it in a third nature as a symbol of psychic convergence. Rather, the human nature's historic *character* as a death and resurrection ought expressly to be linked with the eucharistic consecration of the world—not first in the symbolism of work—but with a realism which has its roots in the intrinsic value of Christ's saving actions.

Second, Teilhard maintained the scriptural tensions between the present and the future tense of salvation only in an analogical sense. The analogy—and source of contradiction—is the relation of Christ and Omega. His identification of the two seems to indicate, despite scattered objections, a kind of development in Christ, to the end that the Christian's salvation, which is closely linked with the progress of the Incarnation, lies almost wholly in the future. The universe, Teilhard wrote, "must necessarily reach its fullfillment, ahead of us, in some pole of superconsciousness in which all the personalized grains of consciousness survive and 'superlive.' It culminates in an Omega Point. This he identified with "Super-Christ" or "Christ the evolver."[47] Moreover, Omega governs not only as a center still in formation but also as a real center which gives cohesion to "those elementary advances by which the fabric of evolution is empirically taking shape." Only in this attenuated sense does Teilhard's evolutionary Christology (as distinct from devotional works) proclaim the realization of Christ's redemption of the world. He instead presented an analogy drawn from science's requirement of an Omega "*already in existence* and operative at the very core of the thinking mass." From this analogy Teilhard did not and indeed could not develop the sense of Christ's newness, which, in a secular setting, Marx attempted to impart to proletarian initiative. The Incarnation does not merely facilitate with greater certainty the convergent ascent of history toward the peak of its cone; it begins history anew by signaling the judgment and defeat of the forces that had held it in bondage. The *kairos* has occurred, and eternal life has begun. Christians now, therefore, being justified by God's grace, may enjoy a supernatural unity in Christ to which the heightened consciousness of future generations can add nothing.

The third and final difficulty has to do with the divine accommodation. This accommodation, based on John 16:12 ("I have yet many things to say to you, but you cannot bear them now"), becomes in Teilhard's exposition a human method of preparing and restricting the means by which God may effect salvation. Because his futuristic ideal of manhood considerably eclipsed that which Christ established once and for all, Teilhard was able to write, "Christ needs to find a world-peak for his consummation, just as he needed to find a woman for his conception."[48] Here the preparation for God's *kairos* is seen as a condition of existence open to scientific investigation and manipulation. This led Teilhard to merge the valid notion of the Christian's developing sanctification and preparation for the parousia with the doctrine of God's justifying grace. And from man's establishment of the necessary conditions of salvation it is but a short step to his self-redemptive transformation.

THE MOMENTS OF THE INCARNATION

Having established man as conscious evolution and having situated the entirety of that evolution beneath the physical aegis of the incarnate Word, we are now enabled to trace the Incarnation's historical moments in which man transforms his own nature. It is possible to speak of knowledge, work, and love as *moments* inasmuch as they contribute to the greater unity of the whole creation and its Lord. We may do this remembering that every decision and action takes place in the context of the Incarnation and that the moments are only conceptually divisible; for their transforming effectiveness depends upon their union.

Knowledge

Teilhard's hope for the ultimate transformation of man in God was built upon the value of knowledge. With the appearance of thought the tandem-like evolution of material complexity and psychism crossed its first critical threshold. Not only is man now able to reflect upon his own supersession of nature; he is also initiated into the value of enhanced being, which is given him as the promise of evolution. But he must *see* it: "Union increases only through an increase in consciousness, that is to say in vision . . . It is so vital and blessed to *know* . . ." "To *be* more is in the first place to *know* more."[49]

In three aspects Teilhard's approach to knowing resembles that of Marx. Human knowledge, first of all, is reflective and accurately reproduces its external environment. With Hegel also Teilhard confessed that "this duality of the cognitive order and the real order has since seemed to me arbitrary and false. We have no serious reason for thinking that things are not made in the same pattern as that in which our experience unfolds them."[50] While Marx and Teilhard both wished to relate the concrete and the cognitive, Marx attempted a theoretical explanation of false consciousness and Teilhard, as we have noted, did not.

Second, when it came to defining this relation Marx and Teilhard emphasized the constructive aspect of knowledge. However different their secondary motives, Teilhard and Marx wished to do away with the distinctions between knowing and being by demonstrating their interdependence. The epistemological skepticism of the Paris Manuscripts and the "Theses on Feuerbach" reappears in Teilhard's dubious attitude toward science's attempt to penetrate the "phenomena in themselves, as they would take place in our absence." In Teilhard, knowing (for the sake of action) therefore consists in the dialectical interaction of man and nature. The following sentence written by Teilhard might well have appeared in the *Economic and Philosophical Manuscripts*: "Object and subject marry and mutually transform each other in the act of knowledge; and from now on man willy-nilly finds his own image stamped on all that he looks at."[51] Teilhard would agree that the reality and shape of the material world's "this-sidedness" (*Diesseitigkeit*), as Marx called it, can be tested only by a constructive and participatory act of knowing, so that the convergent character of evolution is known only as it is enacted by its leading shoot.

Third, but not of least importance, this knowledge is possible for the individual "seer" or "mystic." Although knowledge as construction is a collective act, it is preceded by the single visionary whose intuition of the unifying pattern within the multiple helps chart the course of the masses.

Teilhard's emphasis on knowing has led his detractors to characterize his system as a modern form of gnosis. It has, among other factors, led us to a comparison of his historicism with that of Marx. Up until this point even Teilhard's Christology appears to have fallen victim to the seer's evolutionary historicism. But here at the moment of human knowledge we encounter an unexpected emphasis on decision which, as in Marx, appears to disrupt the neat pattern of dialectical, evolutionary, or christological historicism and robs it of its inevitability. Repeatedly and in a variety of ways Teilhard stressed the necessity of choice in "auto-evolution." The growth of consciousness Teilhard steadfastly likened to freedom, so that to his mind the provisional success of evolution, to which the burgeoning of consciousness witnesses, indicated not only the necessity of choice but also a nisus toward being which is immanent in the structure of conscious freedom. Nevertheless, man can never fall back on the recognition of necessity but at every stage of his evolution, he (as the species) must somehow choose to continue. Where the philosophical and practical difficulties involved in the classical formulation of class consciousness are only partially relieved in revolutionary mysticism, Teilhard's expanded notion of collective decision is assailed by even greater difficulties. For in it there is no practical hint as to the identity of the decision makers, the concrete options before them, or the mechanism by which their decision might be executed. Indeed, if the noosphere is now approaching this crucial point of decision, as Teilhard said that it is, it seems that national, racial, and societal fragmentation may force humankind to choose negatively in default of its ability to choose at all.

Because the choices he offered were most often in terms of orthoelection or selection, socialization or individualism, optimism or pessimism, the specifically Christian value of the decision was obscured. Yet in an early text Teilhard explicitly cojoined man's decision for evolution and his faith in the physical operation of the Incarnation. In "Forma Christi" he wrote, "If we are effectively to fall under the domination of Christ, the centre of the world, . . . we must of our own free will open our hearts to him. If we are really to enter into the chosen universe that is marked off all around the incarnate Word, we must *choose* to form part of it."[52] The urgency of this choice reproduces something of the biblical spirit of the "now," the "acceptable time" or the "vertical today" of which von Balthasar speaks with great force.[53] In consideration of Teilhard's later writings one might ask if it is possible to translate effectively the urgency of conversion, partially conditioned by the imminence of Christ's return, into an equally urgent advocacy of evolutionary progress as the vehicle of humankind's incorporation into Christ. Does, following Teilhard, the contemporary Christian's reluctance to pray *marana tha* diminish his knowledge of the true God or the conviction of his decision for the explicit Christ? The sanctity of Teilhard's life and the breadth of his incarnational theology answer no; our answer can be given only tentatively after an examination of the last two moments of the Incarnation.

Work

The second term of Teilhard's progression, "To know more in order to be capable of more, in order to be more," finds its concrete expression in human work. Among the many factors that differentiate Teilhard's view of work from that of Marx we may isolate three formal affinities. Through work, first of all, man creates and ultimately transforms his own nature. This work, secondly, constitutes the embodiment of knowledge and must never be separated from it. Finally, this synthesis of knowing and doing is effected through a form of mystical detachment not unrelated to Christian worship.

1. In words which, but for their incarnational orientation, might have found their way into the Paris Manuscripts or *Capital*, Teilhard announced the human moment of man's transformation in Christ: the *"fashioning of our own self."*[54] The consummation of Christ and the construction of human nature occurs not so much by man's intended fidelity and obedience to Christ as it does in the material content of human work. Teilhard's remarks on work, therefore, bear great resemblance to those statements of Marx in which the active, social, and physically real characteristics of human nature receive emphasis. If it were possible to detach the Teilhardian worker from his supernatural organism and to omit violent revolution from the Marxian man's working agenda, the two positions would be virtually indistinguishable.

But where Teilhard celebrated the "genetic links" between the kingdom of God and human effort, Marx rejected the progressive and transformative power of work and equated the alienation of labor with the loss of the human essence. Dominating his philosophy, therefore, is the search for an effective method of restoring work, and with it human nature, to its proper position. In the Marxian system of dialectics, this method entails the raising of work to its most redemptive—and destructive—power, to the work of revolution.

Unlike the Marxian system, Teilhard's neither teaches nor implies the necessity of a social revolution. In fact he acknowledged that his "possibilities and tendencies are not exactly to start any definite social movement, but to help to create a kind of spiritual atmosphere in which the whole of life should be enlightened and transformed."[55] Indeed, impervious to Marxian ideas of revolution and alienation stands Teilhard's belief in the unfallen power of human work to express Christ's transformation of the world. The culmination of work in Teilhard therefore was not violence but, as we shall see in the following section, the appearance of a new form of love, whose vast energies will unite humankind in its work of evolution.

In anticipation of this there was in Teilhard an almost Lutheran preoccupation with the holiness of everyday labor—not in Luther's strict sense of sanctification but in that of man's partnership with God in the redemption of the world. Teilhard's confidence in the unlimited possibilities of work, once extended to its universal term of synergy, is reflected not only in his agreement with Luther's sanctification of vocation, but also in a Calvinist-like enthusiasm for reshaping the world to the glory of God. Is this to say that Teilhard had no sensitivity to the forces that interfere in man's desire, with Marx, to work his way to a human essence, or, with Paul, to "do all in the name of the Lord Jesus"? The answer returns us to Teilhard's doctrines of sin and redemption. Where Marx and St. Paul, each in his own way, looked to an objective event by which their respective universes are set right, Teilhard emphasized the subjective elements of pain and renunciation in human work. The expiation formerly associated with the cross (and proletarian redemption) now coincides with human creativity's "painful pangs of birth" by which the laborious advance of evolution continues.

2. There was in Marx and Teilhard a desire to establish perfect continuity between thought and action, to the effect that once the crucial decision to revolt or to converge is taken, the active consequences of that decision gain their own momentum independent of further intentions or other subjective factors. In other words the Marxian and Teilhardian man must lose himself in the self-transformative work (be it revolution or research) in which he is engaged. The Marxian loss of self occurs in the individual's subsumption beneath a class abstraction and his participation in a revolutionary work whose violence destroys all personal identity. It is this "mystique of destruction" for which Teilhard professed no understanding and from which he wished to differentiate his own doctrine of detachment through action.

Teilhard's notion of the renunciation of self rests upon the uneradicable identity of the person who exists in Christ Jesus. *"First and foremost,"* he wrote, "I am in Christo Jesu; it is only *afterwards* that I am acting, or suffering, or contemplating."[56] Because it is in the nature of Christ the Evolver to be eternally active in the progressive consummation of his Body, the Christian adheres to this momentum toward consummation and sacrifices his own desires to it. Unlike the pagan who adheres to the world in order to transform it, the Teilhardian Christian "pre-adheres" to Christ in order to achieve the same transformation at a more profound level.

On the collective plane, however, it would seem that Teilhard's notions of personal identity and transformation cannot be derived from preadherence to Christ, but that the process must be reversed. Where the Christ of the Gospels is not confessed as Lord—and this is the case for most participants in noogenesis—consciousness of his presence and, in a sense, his physical reality itself must be developed by means of participation in evolution. By losing oneself in convergent evolution, the individual and the species ultimately discover the personalization and unitive transformation that have always existed in those individuals who, as the ecclesial phylum (the church), have preadhered to the explicit Christ. Here it must be re-emphasized that the detachment practiced on a noogenetic scale, however, takes the circuitous route of first conquering the world, of testing every barrier to progress, in order finally to discover God's presence in and at the term of evolution. Also, unlike the individual Christian's and the Church's co-creative work, the collective effort enjoys no supernatural means of escape should it fail to realize its mission of unification. Even in defeat, *precisely* in defeat, the Christian's faith calls upon the grace of Christ. The noogenetic route, however, offers supernatural transformation only at the end of the line, and only to the extent that human nature is able to change and modify its own consciousness. What is most remarkable about this latter route is that despite its inspiration in Teilhard's preadherence in Christ, it claims to deduce quasi-Christian benefits and finally Christ himself from a non-Christian form of self-abnegation and work-righteousness.

The strongest reaction to this route occurred early in Teilhard's career when he incurred the fatherly disapproval of Maurice Blondel. "We should remember," said Blondel, "that we do not have to conquer the universe, or to find Christ in nature. We have to give up the whole of creation for the precious Pearl, to die in the world to be nourished by a new life. Hence, the dark night which the soul must cross, without a smooth transit from matter to spirit, from the physical to the hyper-physical Christ."[57] The differences between Blondel and Teilhard amounted to more than their variant perspectives on mysticism. For Blondel had detected yet another biblical tension, that of love for Christ and conformity to the world, with which Teilhard's mysticism of achievement had failed to deal on any but the superficial level of synthetic formulas.

3. Teilhard's answer to Blondel and to all who have accused him of concordism with the world relied upon a definition of human work as sacrificial worship. His action-mysticism, especially as it is applied to the whole of humankind, contained a subtle restatement of the means by which man solidifies his personality in God. The man of noogenesis does not first realize his true identity in union with God and, following that, proceed to the business of evolution; rather he first realizes his own being through evolution *in order* to find unification in God. According to Teilhard's view, one does not properly empty himself of all material and intellectual achievement and then offer his empty husk as a sweet-smelling sacrifice to God. Nor does he embrace the contemplative life before he has reached the limits of his power to act in conformity with God's unification of the world. The Teilhardian Christian, as a member of Christ's body and a representative of noogenesis, attempts to intensify his own being and to extend it as far as possible along the axis given by the complementary sources of evolution and revelation. With each successful step along this axis the Christian both renounces the previous stage and retains, by transforming the given area of experience, God's presence in it. Each step, it must be remembered, represents a concrete way of operating on the material world. Only when the Christian's or the race's efforts have brought them to the limits of their being (we have

noted their radically different boundaries), does the combination of their laborious achievement and its implied renunciation manifest itself as a fitting sacrifice to God.

Formally, then, worship for Teilhard as for Marx consisted in the collective unification of man's knowing and doing into one continuous and self-justifying action. Where the Marxian secularization of worship denied Christ and issued into a method by which non-Christian action transforms the world, Teilhard's extension of the same concept "Christified" everything and achieved a similar result—but by universalizing the hated (by Marx) tradition of work as the sacrifice of human energy to a higher being. As far as Marx was concerned, the formal contribution to his method of destruction all but exhausted his interest in the uses of Christian worship.

What use he did make of it, however, is enough to suggest a criticism of Teilhard's pan-Christism and its tendency to provide a minimal definition of Christian worship by equating it with scientific research.[58] It is not that research cannot be worship, for indeed all creaturely activity, by its very existence and especially in its groping toward unity, participates in a natural act of worship. Further than this, by virtue of the Incarnation it may be said of all human work that it in some implicit way relates to the eternal humanity of Christ. What Teilhard did not always clarify, however, is the profound difference in *quality* between those whose so-called "worship" remains wholly unconscious and those whose participation in the great Body of Christ flows from a conscious identification with him. Given his entire philosophy of consciousness and his personal devotion to the church's primary symbols and media of worship, the neglect of this explicitly Christian threshold of consciousness remains an inconsistent feature in his pan-Christic vision of human transformation.

Love

Were we to adapt a Marxist formula and show that for Teilhard human transformation is effected by the recognition, choice, and working out of necessity, we still would have overlooked the equally naturalistic and Christian factor that differentiates Teilhardian luxuriance from what is so often Marxian aridity: man, in order to succeed, must *love* his own evolution. Subjectively, this *"ardor* for life" penetrates and exhausts the marrow of all matter and experience in order to enter a more intimate communion with God. This will be obvious from portions of the "Hymn to Matter" and "The Mass on the World" from which I have quoted elsewhere in this study. Yet because Teilhard understood the Incarnation as coextensive with the whole span of evolution, he resisted the traditional injunction to *use* the world as a means of rising to God.

Because he could speak, however imprecisely, of "Christ in the World of Matter," Teilhard was able to risk the dangers of unordered love and to *enjoy* the world for its own sake: "It is you, matter, that I bless . . . as you reveal yourself to me today, *in your totality and your true nature*."[59]

The *objective* place of love in Teilhard's system helps to explain the scientific rather than ethical, sentimental, or biblicist basis of his opposition to Marxist violence. "Love is by definition the word we use for attractions of a personal nature. Since once the universe has become a thinking one everything in the last result moves in and toward personality; it is necessarily love, a kind of love, which forms . . . the material of human energy."[60] This metaphysics of love holds at all levels of the Teilhardian universe: in the substratum of "feeling" for personal and cosmic unity, in the universal efficacy of the Eucharist, and in the fundamental "physico-moral energy" of the universe. Man reaches the limits of experience when he transcends the love of individuals and humanity and attains in his own mind what will eventually become a reality of every other mind and being: a universal sympathy with the actual movement of reality.

By using the love of Christ as a model for a higher synthesis, Teilhard rapidly takes us up the ladder of created things and persons to a vision of the whole movement of evolution. The fuller our vision of that whole, the greater is our obligation to love it for Christ's increasingly enlarged presence in it. Christ is most realistically loved as a world. As mysticism, Teilhard's love for the whole evolutionary embodiment of Christ secures him a place among twentieth-century Christian thinkers. As ethics, however, this physicalism of love had better been arrested at the level of the person, where its cosmic tendency might have tarried over the nascently political mandate to love the oppressed. When he announced that Christian love has exhibited "too much gentleness and not enough force," he was merely reinforcing his black-and-white antithesis between individualist sentiment and cosmic participation without acknowledging the political and social gradations of Christian love that lie between. Likewise, in dismissing St. James's brand of religion as "*passé*,"[61] that is, as superseded, Teilhard failed to explore the realist basis of this religion and the possibilities it offers of participation, not in the Lord of progress, but in the Christ who resides in all who suffer: "As you did it to one of the least of these my brethren, you did it to me."

There is, it seems to me, a great danger in establishing an ethic—even in the name of love—on the basis of one man's privileged intuition of the whole movement of reality. Marx and Teilhard assumed such privileged positions outside the processes they surveyed, and both evaluated all action according to its contribution to the end of those processes. Communist "morality of the future" has its distinct echoes in Teilhard's insupportable belief that "technical progress necessarily and function-ally adds moral progress to itself."[62] Hence, whenever one contributes to the progress by which the world is completed, he is practicing a higher "morality of movement . . . which is only defined by relation to a state or object to be reached," and whose justification lies not in its good intention but its materio-spiritual success.[63]

The triple orientation of praxis, the future, and success further resem-bles Marxian ethics in its apotheosis of an ideal of man unverified by historical experience and removed from human nature as we know it. Teilhard's reduced definition of contemporary man, that "function of a cosmic stream," coupled with his belief in this man's *obligation* to love (via participation) every form of progress, exposes his philosophy to the great danger of Hegelianism and Marxism: the sacrifice of persons to the future.

This danger is at once minimized when we realize to our great relief that Teilhardianism lacks the sociological foundation necessary to a political movement. More importantly, its ethical principle, however aligned with the Marxian, is unalterably opposed by the essential categories of revelation from which he began, in one sense, and with which he completed, in another, his grand synthesis of theology and evolution. For however attenuated his portrayal of biblical tensions, and however impersonal his doctrines of personalization, amorization, and Christogenesis, the essentials of these categories nevertheless retain the associations of nearly two thousand years of Christian tradition. Where Marx, as I have shown, was totally bereft of an ethical ideal by which the integrity of the person is preserved, Teilhard clung to so much of the church's life and vocabulary that, despite the dangers of innovation and experimentation, such words as "Christ," "love," and "person" still have meaning for evolutionary ethics.

THE SIGN OF JONAH

The dialectical and evolutionary forms of historicism examined in this chapter have in common a fundamental dependence upon Christian ideas of history. Dialectics creates a law of conflict, evolution a law of progress. As interpretive patterns both motifs may claim a basis in tradition as well as Scripture. But a philosophy of human transformation cannot satisfy its audacious hope unless it penetrates the motifs and appreciates the continuity between the Christian philosophy of history, even in its secularized forms, and the church's historical embodiment of the living Christ. One does not plunder the basis of such an organ-ism, codify its form, and imagine that, once that form's historical and doctrinal basis is discredited, it will neverless serve as a suitable framework for redemption. The dialectical form of suffering, conflict, and victory *works* only when it is taken with its content, which is Christ. Similarly, the figure of organic growth which Teilhard imposed as a law upon Christ and his church leads to a supernatural transformation only when it recognizes in its origin and continuing vitality the transcendent spirit of Christ. The transformative power of Christ rests upon its resistance rather than its adherence to the laws, schemes, and diagrammatics of history. Freedom from the law in its broadest sense means freedom from the necessary laws of history, such as violence, conflict, growth, and progress, which, precisely *because* they claim to be necessary to humankind's salvation, must be excluded from it.

The incompatibility of historicism and Christianity is in no way mitigated by the element of decision which Marx and Teilhard incorporated into their systems. For, despite the urgency which surrounds this decision, neither writer made serious provision for man's failure to choose or his wrong decision. One suspects that the dramatic moment of choice constitutes another mythic temporalization of what both writers, having selectively interpreted their data, saw as the inevitable consequence of the economic or evolutionary conditions of existence. Behind the contingency of decision in both lies the comforting shadow of certainty: the provisional coherence of evolutionary and dialectical laws, and for Teilhard (as well as Engels), the indestructibility of spirit (= mind). Hence the decision in both amounts to an acceptance and confirmation of already-established laws of natural, social, and historical movement; it is, even in Teilhard's cosmic Christianity, a matter of siding with a winner.

Christians are susceptible to this kind of thinking and often discern in repentance, humility, sacrifice, or "victorious living" not only the key to personal happiness but also the clue to universal history. But this is to be resisted. The only clue Jesus deigned to give was the sign of Jonah, and even as he gave it he castigated those who sought it. Christianity, it is said, generates a philosophy of history, but only insofar as it first enables Christians to participate fully in the sign of Jonah and to share in the fellowship of Christ's death and resurrection. The first and essential step in a Christian philosophy of history has nothing to do with the establishment of a worldview based on the social uses of suffering or on the necessity of planetary success. The Christian philosophy which hopes rightly to interpret man's historical transformation needs to begin not with homogenous laws of transformation but with the unique event which puts other laws, whether Mosaic or thermodynamic, in their proper place. By putting man in touch with this freedom in Christ, the philosophy of history begins from the inside, the within of history, and tentatively works its way outward, explicating the too-often brutal facts by means of the inner freedom experienced by successive generations of Christians. Paradoxically, whenever the explication of freedom becomes so clear and concrete as to be amenable to codification, its essence is obscured, and the historian must begin anew. Theology's continuing failure to identify human achievement with the divine confirms the great mystery which surrounds God's integration of the within and the without of history. That God has and will continue to rule the within and the without of history until the two form a glorious unity remains, after all, the substance of things hoped for and the evidence of things not seen.

Chapter VI

THE NEW COMMUNITIES AND THE END OF HISTORY

It has been the custom hitherto for men to hold us as their own property, which is pitiable enough, considering that Christ has delivered and redeemed us all, without exception, by the shedding of his precious blood, the lowly as well as the great. Accordingly, it is consistent with Scripture that we should be free and under no authority.

—The Twelve Articles of the Peasants (1525)

"Revelation," writes Wolfhart Pannenberg, "is not comprehended completely in the beginning, but at the end of the revealing history."[1] The same principle, if applied to the meaning of history itself, conveys something of the great investment Marx and Teilhard held in the future of humanity. Its perfection provides an eschatological epiphany of man and God and alone justifies the historical development that has been necessary to its attainment. In principle, at least, this eschatological epiphany accords with Christianity's teaching that the history of faith is subject to its "author and finisher," who alone justifies man's hope and effort. Marx's preoccupation was with a temporal, and Teilhard's with an atemporal end of history. This is wholly consistent with their disinterest in the possibilities of that end's realization in or disruption of necessary historical laws. Nevertheless, the conclusion of history in both writers introduces a fundamental change in the uniform pattern of history and evolution, with the result that dialectical conflict passes away, and smooth orthogenetic progress culminates in the death and resurrection of the noosphere.

The new man who appears at history's end is in reality the new community, in which the relationship between the individual and his social environment has been perfected. For both writers Teilhard's phrase, "union differentiates," seems to capsulize the working principle of man-in-community. As we survey the stages of these communities, one of the issues is the extent to which Marx and Teilhard, on the basis of all that has gone before in their systems, can justify a final

146

epiphany of the ultrapersonal. Is it, after all, a utopian device or the natural fruition of humanist and Christian beliefs?

REIGN OF LAW: THE PROLETARIAN DICTATORSHIP

The dialectical mysticism of Marxian revolution leads us to the "community of revolutionary proletarians" in which the self-indulgence of violence and revenge has given way to the less appetitive qualities of discipline, authority, and organization. Between the essential freedom of man, from which Marx began, and the perfect union of person and community, toward which he tended in hope, lies a period in which the tutelage of the law prepares the whole human race for the ultimate gift of freedom. The features of this intermediate community are well known. The most notable are (1) its centralization of the means of production and key services, such as commerce, communication, transportation, and education, in the hands of the state; (2) the repressiveness by which the proletariat, now "organized as the ruling class," makes its "despotic inroads on the rights of property and on the conditions of bourgeois production"; and (3) this period's indeterminate length, traceable to Marx's belief that true communism will begin only on a worldwide scale.[2]

Save for its increase in detail, the dictatorship of the proletariat, as described by Marx in private correspondence and intraparty communiqués, differs little from the "crude communism" that he had disparaged in the *Economic and Philosophical Manuscripts* (pp. 125–26). Crude communism represents an arrested stage of negation in which anticapitalism has satisfied itself not only with a social antithesis but also a social reflection of its greatest enemy. By forming only the antipodes, as it were, of capitalism, crude communism either totally abolishes or imitatively universalizes capitalist principles without transforming them. In the former case, everything which proves incapable of common ownership, such as artistic and intellectual ability, is forcibly abolished in a regressive drive toward a "pre-conceived minimum." This development, based on envy and the desire for security, Marx deplored. In the latter case, this negative mentality merely inflates capitalist principles without purifying their sinful character. Hence the bourgeois institution of marriage—puritanically caricatured in the *Manifesto* as a facade for seduction and wife-swapping—is not improved upon by the formation of a community of women, for this would amount to exchanging the sin of sexual hypocrisy for that of prostitution. In either case, Marx emphasized, the *personality* of human beings is deformed. On the same principle, he added, any demand for equal wages that does not attack the mode of production, distribution, and consumption, will produce only a better remuneration of slaves. This "universal prostitution with the community" does nothing to transform the alienated character of work and, in the end, makes of society the abstract and universal capitalist. Thus Marx himself provided the best commentary on the aims and achievements of the dictatorship of the proletariat, a conception which, but for its contemporary relevance, might well have been forgotten.

The idea of proletarian rule unites antiutopian and utopian elements which together shed light on the limitations as well as the open possibilities of human nature. Although Marx attempted to shake the foundations of the bourgeois legal system, his dictatorship of the proletariat exists as a concession to law against the anarchy of human nature. With Luther, he knew that the only freedom man is capable of receiving is that of inner spirituality, which, because of his metaphysical presuppositions and the predominance of method, Marx historified and identified with the end-time of the class struggle. As historical periods, then, we find the reign of law preceding rather than coexisting with the reign of freedom, the former serving as a kind of dialectically-determined *paidagogos* unto the latter. The tutelage of the law emerges in the need for rational organization of the proletarian community. Although Marx's biographer recalled that he "relied exclusively on the intellectual development of the working class,"[3] there are in his writings scattered intimations of the organization destined to become the final arbiter of communist policy. As the revolutionary ardor of the workers began to cool, Marx grew to trust in the insight of the few to change the consciousness of the many: "The only way to bring about this change is to act in the capacity of the General Council of the International Association. As the General Council we can initiate measures . . . which later, in the public execution of their tasks, appear as spontaneous movements of the English working class."[4]

When this need for *Marxian* organization is appreciated, one better understands Marx's initial opposition to the Paris Commune, for, despite Engels' later association of its petty reforms with the dictatorship of the proletariat, it represented only the solidarity of good intentions and opposition to the provisional government.[5] Although Marx calculatedly annexed the Commune to his own social movement, he later catalogued its faults, especially its decentralization, and admitted that it was never, nor could it ever have been, a working form of socialism.[6] Nowhere is Marxian antiutopian realism more evident than in these words: "With a modicum of common sense, however, it could have reached a compromise with Versailles useful to the whole mass of the people. . . ."[7] Instead, it pursued an ideal community for which history was unprepared.

The very distrust of human freedom and speculative socialism that defined Marx's antiutopianism and made a dictatorship necessary evaporated into utopianism when Marx laid down the principles of proletarian rule. It must be noted that he never got beyond *principles* (with a few illustrations from the Commune), for, paradoxically, all experimental attempts to establish socialist communities, that is, to move from theory to practice, were condemned by Marx as "utopian." Experiments such as Cabet's Little Icaria were utopian, according to Marx's definition, not only because they wished to restore old property relations, but also because their nonviolent posture relied ultimately on the good will of the ruling class.[8]

If we substitute "working" for "ruling" in the last phrase, we have uncovered the utopian strain in Marx's own dictatorship of the proletariat. He initially rejected any possibility of the state's intervention in society on behalf of its citizens and never dreamed of the many ways a creative democracy may exercise its authority to promote the well-being of its people. In rejecting the expediency of constitutional safeguards, and with them formal or legal guarantees of freedom, Marx meant to stress material or economic freedom. Despite his distrust of legal power, he then proceeded to cast the proletariat in the role of legal guarantor of this broader freedom and assumed that, since the mode of production is changing and state officials now earn the equivalent of workers' wages (as in the Paris Commune), there would be no abuse of power. He did not seem to realize that, compared to fame, prestige, and sheer joy in the exercise of power, the desire for money sometimes offers the least incentive to unscrupulous political ambitions. This misreading of human nature carries over into some of the specific points of the communist program in the *Manifesto*. One thinks particularly of the intended centralization of the means of communication and envisions the alienation produced by new, self-justifying ideologies in a press controlled by the state. How ironic such developments have proved to be—in the light of Marx's early struggle, while editor of the *Rheinische Zeitung*, to overcome the restrictions of Prussian censorship! In these and other reservations one might harbor concerning the proletarian dictatorship, the basic questions revolve around the nature of man. In the following section we shall investigate the consequences of violence and the interminable exercise of despotism for Marx's hope in the liberation of the human community.

THE KINGDOM OF FREEDOM

Marxian hope corresponds to the most profoundly human aspirations, not for new political structures, but for new selves. When the dictatorship of the proletariat finally ends and man emerges from his prehistory into the realization of his true essence, he will live in freedom from the law—in the widest application of that term's theological meaning. Such freedom will consist in (1) the realization of the human essence in unalienated forms of production as well as in an open-ended sphere of freedom that lies outside the realm of work; (2) the fulfillment of individual potentialities in a cooperative society; and (3) man's direct assumption of responsibilities previously administered by the state, religion, and other economically-based institutions.

1. The cessation of the division of labor will yield a cooperative noncompetitive mode of production in which society produces only to fulfill its own needs. Where labor has ceased to be a human form of capital, man will finally be free to express his social essence in all its diversity. Whatever the new man creates or helps to create, his labor will not have purchased for him ownership of another product but a specific share of the communal production; for this reason he will have no special product to exchange. Where the division of labor led to the exchange of exchange values, an equally rational organization of labor according to *human* values will result in the individual's participation in communal consumption.[9]

Marx departed only briefly from these generalities in order to combat the Lassallean idea of the "undiminished proceeds of labor." Against this rival socialist group, Marx cited necessary deductions for the replacement and expansion of the means of production, for health and accident insurance, for general costs of administration and education, and relief for those unable to work.[10] Outside scattered remarks that indicate a preference for universal suffrage and the communal sponsorship of those performing specialized duties, these few stipulations against Lassalle exhaust Marx's so-called program for the future. Even the new ideology, "From each according to his abilities to each according to his needs," presents a dilemma; for the equal value to which each person is traditionally entitled does not solve the problem of functional inequalities that will persist even in the most egalitarian society. To this as well as to other economic or administrative queries concerning the new society Marx replied with the too-familiar device: "The scope of this exposition does not permit of developing the subject further."[11]

Thus, in Marx (as in Teilhard) the anticipation, prophecy, and advocacy of massive transformation yields little insight into the working order of the thing transformed. Instead Marx generalized upon a new kind of transcendence, which both builds upon and surpasses the now disalienated necessities of labor, beyond which, he promised, "begins that development of human power which is its own end, the true realm of freedom."[12] Only in the light of this economic freedom, derived from the shortening of the working day, will people live to develop their own artistic, educational, and scientific powers as ends in themselves. This "new frontier of hominization" or "pacification of existence" of which Marxian scholars sing, has its inspiration in Marx's own dream of the amalgamation of all natural and social sciences into a single science of man.[13]

2. Most critical views (including Teilhard's) of Marx's prediction of the new humanity accuse him of a disregard for personal freedom and a tendency toward collectivism. But these charges are unfounded. The many Marxian predictions of the personalistic qualities of communist society were never meant to describe the dictatorship of the proletariat. So personalistic was this "all-round development of individuals" to be that many commentators have attributed to the new society the creative and intensely individualistic properties of the artist seeking self-expression in a community of artists. The major question, then, is not whether or not Marx proclaimed personal freedom, but whether his philosophy of man can deliver it.

In the Paris Manuscripts the ideal of interpersonal cooperation functions as a definition of the human essence and as a principle of verification. Only in the empiricism of later works did Marxian compassion discover the *value* of the individual person. Marx's goal of the "social-individual," whose personal identity depends upon his participation in creative union with his fellows, represents a fusion of Marx's early naturalism and later ethical concerns. In words that formally anticipated Teilhardian theories, Marx wrote, "Only in community with others has each individual the means of cultivating his gifts in all directions; only in community, therefore, is personal freedom possible."[14]

The methodological necessity of violence, however, destroys any illusion of the intrinsic character of personal values in Marx's social philosophy. In his version of creative union the naturalistic terms of man's wholly determined functions in society will not by their very definition tolerate the predication of ethical values. The Marxian thesis is that man becomes what he does, that he changes his nature in accordance with the creative and revolutionary actions he performs. According to the logic of this axiom the new society must be an extension of the violent activities that brought it about, especially when we recall the law of conflict that governs the course of all history, the depersonalizing effects of violence, and violence's amenability to institutionalization—whether at the hands of a capitalist or proletarian dictatorship. Normally one would reject out of hand the simplistic notion that any country that has experienced a successful violent revolution must necessarily retain the chaos of that upheaval as a part of its national character. But according to the Marxian theory of consciousness—that views persons, institutions, and values as effects of economically-determined social interaction—we would be led to such an absurdity. With his own philosophy in mind, therefore, we must question Marx's prediction of the cooperative and person-oriented society that is to evolve from the hateful deed of revolution and the rigid uniformity of the proletarian dictatorship. At best, a new society with such an undistinguished pedigree might hope for guarantees of freedom under constitutional law. But, as we are about to see, Marx absorbed the theological structure of freedom from the law and prophesied the dissolution of all legal and religious absolutes.

3. The perfect relation of person and community inaugurates a dialectics of unprecedented human development, or so claim Marx, Engels, and most Marxist scholars. Perhaps, in comparison with the rest that remains for the people of God, or St. Augustine's principle of peace and inner coherence, or even Teilhard's vision of the race's ecstatic participation in Omega, the Marxian terrestrial future appears to throb with the dynamism of human discovery. But according to Marx's theory of history, the dialectic has no existence, no movement, outside the class struggle that propels man forward and develops his sense of need and historical initiative. Communism restores the quality of old relationships, summarily strips production and creation of their alienating necessity, and adds a new quality of interpersonal cooperation that precludes the possibility of rupture and alienation. By this preclusion it also removes man from historical existence, in any Marxian sense, and makes of him a static "man without attributes" (Moltmann) in a technologically advanced condition of *non posse peccare*. Neither Marx nor Engels seems to have accepted the implications of Engels's remark, "But if all contradictions are once and for all disposed of, we shall have arrived at so-called absolute truth—world history will be at an end."[15] It is for this reason that the development of the future society suffers a curious reversal and proceeds according to a principle of atrophy rather than creative dialectics. What Engels said of the state, then, may be applied to all institutions and to Marxian history itself: *er stirbt ab* (it dies away).

Those things that die, strictly speaking, are the various agencies of mediation between the individual and the community. Man affirms his "individuality and its uniqueness" in production while at the same time, by satisfying another's need, he verifies the organic interdependence of human nature. "Thus," wrote Marx, "I will have received the confirmation of my own existence in your thinking and in your love. . . . Our acts of producing would have been like so many mirrors, reflecting for each other our own existence."[16] In the new society, what Marx calls the intermediary "third thing," be it class, duty, law, or religion, is abolished, so that the individual participates directly in the life of the community, unhindered by external means disguised as ends. When he has come to love, as it were, that which had formerly been commanded, the new man will enjoy the righteousness accorded to those who have abolished laws by internalizing them. This is the significance of the withering away of the state. For the state, as well as religion, has in the past presented a dichotomous morality that both threatened and supported humankind. With the unification of private and public morality communist society will, in the words of Marx's Inaugural Address, "vindicate the simple laws of morals and justice which ought to govern the relations of private individuals, as the laws paramount of the intercourse of nations."[17] In this new morality the state's imposition of duties without rights, its distinction between the political and the social spheres of life and, most of all, its armed vindication of private property, will render it useless as an instrument of communism.

In the case of Christianity, which has also functioned as threat and support—with the emphasis on the feeble and misleading nature of that support—Marx foresaw the gradual disappearance of the faith, as the alienating conditions which made it psychologically and politically necessary also disappear. Religion disappears, while all other forms of civilized life are being reconstituted, because communism itself is the secularized reconstitution of the Christian religion. If the first (and contemporary) stage of this *Aufhebung* conveys something of the "new intolerance" of which Proudhon warned Marx in 1846, this crude persecution of Christianity, Marx promised, will itself be transformed into "self-originating *positive* humanism."[18]

The secularism that will have been perfected in the new age, however, will not necessarily provide a more coherent view of reality. This is especially true in a nonhistorical society in which personal relationships and the meaning of individuals will need to be defined by criteria other than revolutionary, party, and class loyalties. In such a period of stasis, when the worker and his class have withdrawn from the dialectics of historical struggle, the individual will need a new absolute, transcending the old historicist worldview, in order to make sense of his own life and death. At the close of history, after the struggle has been won—then, more than at any other time—the Marxian man will seek renewal, meaning, and completion in an Omega God.

ANOTHER TOTALITARIAN FUTURE: THE PENULTIMATE NOOSPHERE

The penultimate phase of the noosphere, predicted by Teilhard de Chardin, corresponds in principle and detail with the communist society of the future. The socialization of consciousness that Marx predicated of the new man (in *The German Ideology*) was extended by Teilhard and visualized as a *"new psychological stage"* whose capacity for co-reflection facilitates "the direct inter-communication of brains through the mysterious power of telepathy."[19] The crossing of this threshold, as in Marx, will occur only when the pattern of necessity is first recognized and then rationally organized by human freedom. Just as economic freedom will enhance human cocreativity, so the penultimate noosphere will see the variously-determined burdens of habit give way to man's psychic effectiveness and a "freedom we have never dreamt of." With this in mind, Teilhard set great store in the liberating powers of tele-communications, mechanization, and computer technology—all of which were seen as harbingers of a hominized world. The socialization of consciousness breaks down the differences between physical and mental labor, allowing the Marxian man to hunt in the morning and to philosophize after dinner and the Teilhardian "man in the street" to do research in physics or biology. Such freedom of diversification for the sake of the community leads to the confluence of all sciences into "a single natural science centred on man the knower and man the object of knowledge." In the new communities the profit motive and the quest for security will have been forgotten, as the Marxian and Teilhardian man strides toward fuller-being rather than well-being. Only when humanity has emerged from its adolescent prehistory and reached the maturity of socialization, wrote Teilhard, will "this consciousness be truly adult and of age."

The geopolitical expression of this social consciousness bears a poverty of definition comparable to Marx's vague program for the future. While Teilhard presented no political blueprint for "unanimization," his entire philosophy of convergence and his aversion to bourgeois individualism undoubtedly favor some form of socialism. Throughout his life, confidence in the principle of socialization, or, as he called it, totalization, continued in tension with an equally firm distrust of empirical communism. Of Teilhard's two dozen or so direct references to communism, many of which have appeared in this study, none offers an in-depth analysis of Marxist philosophy or political developments. His most important contribution to the subject is the essay, "The Heart of the Problem," in *The Future of Man* (pp. 260–69), in which he overlooked his usual criticisms of communism and understood it as a terrestrial complement to Christian transcendence. His most frequent criticisms of communism deplored the suppression of its own vision of a "universal vibrant humanity," the depersonalizing effect of its collectivism, and its lack of the most important dimension in life, the spiritual. When he was not privately discoursing on "the only means of overcoming communism," he was publicly praising socialization and laying down the superficial outline of a Christian-Marxist synthesis. This tension between political reality and universal ideal was heightened in Teilhard's lifetime by the appearance of phenomena with which Marx never had to come to terms: regimes claiming to be proletarian dictatorships. In face of these, Teilhard's enduring confidence in the principle of totalization represented a victory for the ideal and led him away from socio-political analysis to geopolitical prediction.

The prophet in him held to many Marxian principles, such as the supranational unity of all people, a world language, the abolishment of war, racial synthesis, and eugenics. This "pan-organized world," moreover, will hold to the same morality and ideology, so that humankind may one day find itself thinking the same thoughts and unanimously ratifying a single set of values. But what will the common denominator be: scientific law or Christian principles?

Oliver Rabut suggests "the general acceptance of science and its consequences" as the single value around which the world will be organized.[20] Although it is the necessary basis of the future, science is not in itself the supreme value in Teilhard's system. For science, in its method and scope, is impersonal and finite. As a means of organizing nature, however, it prepares humankind for the reception of the personal and the infinite, whose dynamic process of unification constitutes the spiritual principle within all forms of human development. With Marx, Teilhard would agree that man—as he unifies himself—is the highest essence for man, and that any attempt to insert a form of mediation, such as science, between man and his essence or man and his God retards his growth toward the upper limits of his humanity.

Yet Teilhard, like Marx before him, entrusted the leadership of socialization to an elite. As a young man Teilhard doubted the feasibility of a philosophy of collectivism. "It seems to me," he wrote in 1915, "that once you pass from individual consciousness to collective phenomena you fall back into the inevitable, into blindness."[21] To avert the onset of blindness Teilhard envisioned an elite of seers, composed of all races, classes, and nationalities, whose mission it would be to consolidate universal belief in the grandeur of humanity's future. Two Teilhardian assumptions made these vanguards necessary: One is the inferiority of a disorganized and socially unaware humanity; the other is the functional, and possibly biological, inequality of the races. The former led him to disparage the "mass of humanity" as "profoundly inferior and repulsive," needing "to be kept on leading strings."[22] Here it is necessary to add that Teilhard's approval of the fascist principle of organized elites—like his admiration for the personalistic and social attributes of democracy and communism respectively—should not be magnified into a political credo. His "politics" goes no further than the superficial prediction of a synthesis comprising the best elements of the three ideologies dominant in 1936.[23]

It is nonetheless apparent that the naturalistic fallacy involved in Teilhard's moral futurism, that is, the confusion of evolutionary development and ethics, applies *only* to the future. For the unique particularity of persons, as well as their biological brotherhood—facts more scientifically certain than any disputed notion of progress—do *not* at present imply the equal political rights of self-determination. The organic relation of all people does not, Teilhard claimed, dissolve the hierarchic structure of nature.[24]

The latter belief in the inferiority of certain peoples led him to advocate some form of eugenics to deal with "unprogressive ethnical groups." Teilhard concluded that the mandate of progress and true charity will require society to give priority to those who demonstrate a capacity for development rather than to "life's rejects."[25]

It is difficult to reconcile this presumably rhetorical commendation of progress-at-any-price with either the gospel or his own prediction of a loving "conspiration" of humankind. It should go without saying that Christian love finds its most significant vocation among life's outsiders, the poor, the brokenhearted, the captive, and the blind. Similarly, any great civil society, and especially one claiming a basis in Christian love, can measure its greatness only by its willingness and ability to care for its least productive members. Otherwise it will be neither civilized nor Christian, and surely less than great.

Thus it appears that Marx and Teilhard relied upon totalitarian and elitist principles to guide the way toward a higher quality of personal life. In *The Phenomenon of Man* Teilhard wrote, "It is, in point of fact, only by following the ascension and spread of the whole in its main lines that we are able, after a long detour, to determine the part reserved for individual hopes in the total success. We thus reach the personalization of the individual by the 'hominization' of the whole group" (p. 174). In consideration of the Marxist means of "hominization" we have concluded that the detour is too long. Can Teilhard's belief in the individual's right to develop his personal qualities via democracy be reconciled with his equally firm belief in the principle of totalization? Or does the totalitarian detour, questioned in Chapter II, bypass man's destination of personal freedom?

The answer may lie in the strength of Teilhard's Christian presuppositions. Although the principle of creative union, by which the person enhances his own identity through unification with another, seems to reign in both conceptions of the future, Teilhard's belief in personalization is organic to his system and Marx's is not. Teilhard began his theology with a trinitarian model of the interrelationship of persons and, only on that basis, proceeded to apply his dictum "union differentiates" to the whole spectrum of organic life. While Teilhard's later naturalistic definition of humanity (as a function of evolution) threatened human freedom and responsibility, his fundamental concern for persons never allowed him to acquiesce in the violence that necessarily accompanies any process of totalization. Because he did not realize that only coercion causes *all* people to think and act in uniformity, he believed that the "bourgeois spirit" of comfort and security could be abolished without hatred or violence. This trust in the power of collectivism to evolve toward the personal sounds as naive in Teilhard as it does in Marx. But theologically Teilhard prepared for personalization and did not allow the neutral idea of evolutionary success, which is admittedly strong in his thought, to override the specifically Christian idea of personal union in love. Teilhard's belief in totalization without coercion may indeed be naive, but his understanding of the bankruptcy of violence (as a means of personalization) made him, in this respect, wiser than all the Marxists.

Teilhard's renunciation of the traditional means of socialization led him to a theological vision of the future in which the noosphere does not succumb to a Marxian-like process of atrophy and dehistoricization. Communism will appear as the denouement of history, but the development of the noosphere, *because* it is essentially Christian, retains its motive principle; for even in its extreme phase, the noosphere's perfection lies ahead of it. The revelation of Omega's grace instills in humanity the appetite for more-being and thus draws the race ever forward. Awareness of this divine action will increase until the noosphere, without being consummated, will have evolved into what Teilhard called the theosphere. In that time, "there will be little to separate life in the cloister from the life of the world. And only then will the action of the children of heaven (at the same time as the action of the children of the world) have attained the intended plenitude of its humanity."[26]

The *Aufhebung* of religion that Teilhard envisioned bears a close resemblance to Marxian notions of secularization. In both conceptions the inclination to worship an Other is absorbed by the noblest and therefore most religious aspirations of humanity, with the result that the imposition of religion as a "third thing" between the individual and the possibilities of his self-perfection is abolished. Just as Hegel predicted the *Aufhebung* of religion by philosophy, and Marx by a new society, so Teilhard absorbed Christianity into a new science of man and a new religion of science. Such a synthesis will not spell the end of religion but, as Tillich imagined it, the end of religious alienation. "There will be no secular realm, and for this very reason there will be no religious realm. Religion will be again what it is essentially, the all-determining ground and substance of man's spiritual life."[27]

Hence Marx and Teilhard agree in their prediction of a unifying totality, but differ in their attitudes toward the role of Christianity in its ultimate achievement. The totality in Marxism is achieved by society's reconstitution of Christianity; in Teilhard the same alienation of the secular from the sacred is overcome, and the same totality is erected —but by *extending* the influence of Christianity into all sciences, social movements (including communism), and other agencies of human perfection. If there is no provision for the church's opposition to technological excess, it is because, in Teilhard's vision, humankind's advanced psychic sympathy will have made such abuses impossible. Nor will it any longer be incumbent upon the church to guard against becoming an ideological spokesman for science, for science, as the agent of hominization, will have entered into a synthesis with all else that contributes to human spirituality. In a world in which uniformity will reign in all areas of life and thought, the church, as *mediator* between science and belief, history and revelation, and ultimately between man and God, will no longer be necessary. For having discovered and developed the "plenitude of its humanity" humankind will have come to the brink of omega and the end of history.

POINT OMEGA

The rubble of man's exhausted powers of self-transcendence, including his ability to project himself into the future, must eventually form the walls of his new prison. No amount of bravado concerning humanity's absolute future—e.g., the Marxist kingdom of freedom—can satisfy the individual's and the race's desire to escape total death. The appetizing prospect of an open future may leave a comfortlessly bitter aftertaste unless it is understood as God's absolute future, whose perfection cannot be identified with or transcended by another social, political, or scientific project. Unlike the Marxian future, as represented by the vacuous "Noch-Nicht-Sein" of Ernst Bloch, the absolute future in Teilhard de Chardin possesses an already existing reality whose personal character influences every phase of human development. The Teilhardian man neither strives toward the absolute future (God) as an unknown form of human transcendence, nor does he build it in the way the Marxian man "makes history." He is united with it in love. Teilhard's principle of creative union demands an I-Thou relationship at all levels of existence. Although Marx and his followers use this principle as a basis for social and economic interdependence, they reject its applicability to the ultimate question of humanity's relationship to God. Instead the Marxian man suddenly finds himself called by a mysterious vacuum or related to the exigency of his own needs and possibilities rather than to another Person. Teilhard, on the other hand, was consistent in his use of creative union and personalization, to the end that he was able to speak of the completion of personality in a supremely personal God.

Just as creative union has produced a greater definition of the terms united, so the final involution of human consciousness will have brought humankind to its natural acme of personalization. Teilhard made it clear, however, that, without the presence of another personal being, God, this human perfection would not endure as a utopian realm of freedom, but would yield to the psycho-physical compression that formed it and disintegrate "in self-disgust." Even the attraction of

Omega does not override man's freedom to reject the ultrapersonal. Teilhard sounds a biblical note when he admits the possibility of a gigantic rift in the noosphere between believers in Omega and those who refuse to prepare for the reception of higher being. Those who refuse to cross the threshold will presumably join those who in their lifetimes rejected life and death in communion with Christ.[28]

In general, however, Teilhard depreciated the crises and the utter lack of human sympathy which, according to apocalyptic literature, will characterize the end, in order to integrate convergent evolution into the gracious salvation of God. Man's inability to sustain a self-transcending organism and the possibility, at least, of eschatological dissidence, prove that Teilhard did not share Marx's ultimate reliance upon the good will and social cooperation of man. Hence at no stage in his system did Teilhard hope in a nontheistic golden age to which the Christian might add, as icing on the cake, the eternal governance of God.

Theologically, the development of human potential will prove rather to be a massive cooperation in divine grace. That development prepares for the gift of absolute grace, without which the earth, even at the apex of its self-illumination, would die, never to rise again. Just as each individual must arrive at his nadir of exhausted possibilities, at which point of death he is united to God, so also that portion of the human race which has achieved its historical limit must now find death and new life in an ecstatic moment of self-forgetfulness. This Teilhard subsumes under the great symbols of the end of history: Parousia, Resurrection, Judgment. As Parousia, the end-point of history uncovers him who has been present throughout its course of convergence. At the Parousia, Teilhard wrote, "the universal Christ will blaze out like a flash of lightning" to establish the organic complex of God and the world, the Pleroma. While using little of the traditional language of Resurrection and Judgment, Teilhard's figure of an ecstasy in the noosphere retains two essential elements in the doctrine of the Resurrection of the Body. The first is the emphasis on the indestructible individuality of each member of the Pleroma. The second is the physical interdependence of all flesh, which enables him to dwell upon the organic significance of salvation (and damnation) in him who will have manifestly filled all things: "Within a now tranquil ocean, each drop of which, nevertheless, will be conscious of remaining itself, the astonishing adventure of the world will have ended," and God-Omega will be all in all.[29]

THE ABSOLUTE FUTURE

The apocalyptic tradition insists upon the continuity between temporal actions and their eternal consequences. But it also grasps the meaning of history only in the cataclysm of its end. The end of human history, according to Marx and Teilhard, will be revealed as a protraction and a reversal of the whole pattern of historical development. The former emphasis on continuity accords with that biblical tradition which stresses the eschatological judgment and transfiguration of historical persons, rather than the creation *ex nihilo* of demigods fit for paradise. It is a safe assumption that Marx and Teilhard would therefore criticize any last-minute reversal of the universal laws that have paved the way toward the realization of humanity. Yet each in his own way tolerates such a reversal. In Marx the law of dialectical conflict atrophies in an unintroduced period of static harmony; and in Teilhard, cooperation in grace turns to absolute reliance upon God's power to sustain and perfect that which has been germinating in the noosphere. The Marxian reversal betrays an attempt to escape the reality of death. For Teilhard, the noosphere's death in union with Omega represents his belated acceptance of that which he had consistently rejected as an evolutionary and historical principle.

In both cases, whether by the gradual withering of the law or the Resurrection of the Body, the reversals claim to have set free the highest quality of personal life. Only Teilhard's claim is justified, however, because he, first of all, recognized man's need for an absolute, and, second, understood why man cannot be an absolute for himself. It is in the nature of an absolute, Teilhard taught, to perfect in man that which he is unable to accomplish for himself. Equipped with a belief in God as humanity's absolute future, Teilhard did not need to maintain a nervous silence with respect to the bogy of all finite, historical, and therefore false absolutes: death. An open future leaves personal death and natural entropy untouched and fails to protect man from the tedium as well as the possible terror of history. In a future which closes upon God, death is the last historical act of the individual and the noosphere. As such it takes its place alongside the rest of historical experience and awaits its transfiguration in One who has put all things, including death, under his feet. An open future holds up the illusion of an eternal dialectic of knowledge and action. A closed future, however, in which the subject is vouchsafed a vision of its Object "face to face," offers the contemplative repose that has traditionally followed upon man's active and frustration-ridden search for completion.

When we question the validity of all utopias, and especially Marx's kingdom of freedom, we do not do so in order to celebrate original sin or to revel in the "human condition." For, as Teilhard's work proves, just as integral to the Christian human condition is the believer's creativity and hope in an absolute future. By criticizing a premature absolute, such as communism, Christianity does not mean to dampen the spirit of its aspirations and achievements, but rather to avoid the petrification that hinders the *further* development of love, justice, and personal expression. A Christian witness to God, then, is vital to every utopia, for it must shatter the complacent self-deception of those who would erect upon some preconceived human possibility an absolute system of values.

NOTES

Chapter I   Introduction: Ideas and Postulates

1. *The Poverty of Historicism* (London: Routledge and Kegan Paul, 1957), p. 134.

2. *Economic and Philosophical Manuscripts*, trans. T. B. Bottomore, in Erich Fromm, *Marx's Concept of Man* (New York: Ungar, 1961), p. 137.

3. Karl Marx and Frederick Engels, *Werke* (Berlin: Dietz Verlag, 1961), 1:51.

4. *The Philosophy of History*, trans. J. Sibree, *Great Books of the Western World*, ed. R. M. Hutchins, vol. 46 (Chicago: Encyclopaedia Britannica, 1952), Introd., pp. 161–62.

5. Marx and Engels, *On Religion* (New York: Schocken, 1964), reprinted from 1957 Moscow ed., p. 50.

6. Gal. 1:15; 2:20.

7. Marx, *Capital*, vol. 1, ed. Frederick Engels, trans. Samuel Moore and Edward Aveling, *Great Books*, vol. 50, p. 85.

8. *MSS.*, p. 129.

9. Fromm, *Marx's Concept of Man*, p. 32; Giulio Girardi, *Marxism and Christianity*, trans. Kevin Traynor (Dublin: Gill, 1968), p. 52.

10. *Capt.* I, p. 85.

11. See *Capt.* I, pp. 15, 27–30, 42, and Herbert Marcuse, *Reason and Revolution* (London: Routledge and Kegan Paul, 1955), pp. 281, 297.

12. *Science and Christ*, trans. René Hague (London: Collins, 1968), pp. 39–40.

13. *SC*, p. 40.

14. Ibid.

15. St. Thomas Aquinas, *Summa contra Gentiles*, III, 22, cited in Emil Rideau, *Teilhard de Chardin: A Guide to His Thought*, trans. René Hague (London: Collins, 1967), p. 428, n.

16. Marx and Engels, *Selected Correspondence* (Moscow: Foreign Languages Publishing House, n.d.), p. 151. See R. G. Collingwood, *The Idea of Nature* (Oxford: Clarendon, 1945), pp. 15–16, and Ernst Benz, *Evolution and Christian Hope*, trans. Heinz G. Frank (London: Gollancz, 1967), p. 85.

17. *SC*, p. 43.

18. See the essay "Science and Christ or Analysis and Synthesis," *SC*, pp. 21–36. Teilhard assumes that "essentially, all energy is psychic in nature; but . . . that in each particular element this fundamental energy is divided into two distinct components: a *tangential* energy which links the elements with all others of the same order . . . as itself in the universe; and a *radial* energy which draws it toward "even greater complexity and centricity—in other words,

forwards.'' The tangential represents energy as it is generally understood by science. The radial is internal, spiritual, and detachable from the force of entropy (*The Phenomenon of Man*, trans. Bernard Wall, London: Collins, 1959, pp. 64–65, 72–73, 88, 272, and passim).

19. *Le milieu divin*, trans. Bernard Wall et al. (London: Collins, 1960), pp. 29–34.

20. The "soul" in the first sentence is the spiritual entity which enjoys immediacy to God by reason of its creation. In the second sentence it is the "sensitive soul," which operates in man's perception of the universe around him (St. Thomas Aquinas, *Summa Theologica*, trans. Fathers of the English Dominican Province, *Great Books*, Vols. 19 and 20, I, q. 78, a. 1).

21. W. David Stacey, *The Pauline View of Man* (London: Macmillan, 1956), p. 222.

22. *S. Theol.* I, q. 91, a.1; I, q. 81, a. 3, ad. 2, and I, q. 82, a. 4, ad. 1; I, q. 90, a. 4; and I, q. 76, a. 7.

23. *Human Energy*, trans. J. M. Cohen (London: Collins, 1969), pp. 72–77.

24. *SC*, pp. 41–42.

25. *PM*, p. 309, *MD*, pp. 56–57; *HE*, p. 46. On God's separateness from nature, man, and history, see *Writings in Time of War*, trans. René Hague (London: Collins, 1967), p. 159; *The Appearance of Man*, trans. J. M. Cohen (London: Collins, 1965), p. 271; *Man's Place in Nature*, trans. René Hague (London: Collins, 1966), p. 121; *The Future of Man*, trans. Norman Denny (London: Collins, 1964), p. 265; "Comment je vois," unpublished, 1948, Archives of the Teilhard Centre for the Future of Man, London, p. 13; *PM*, p. 298 n. Teilhard expresses the relation between immanence and transcendence with the awkward phrase, "God (the transcendent aspect of Omega) . . ." (*Activation of Energy*, trans. René Hague, London: Collins, 1970, p. 146). He would have approved of this definition in Gerhard von Rad, *Old Testament Theology*, trans. D. M. G. Stalker (New York: Harper and Row, 1962), 1:180: The name of God, Yahweh, represents "not what he is, but what he will show himself to be to Israel; . . . 'I will be there (for you).' ''

26. *PM*, p. 294; see "Le coeur de la matière," unpublished, 1950, Archives of the Teilhard Centre for the Future of Man, London; and *Letters to Leontine Zanta*, trans. Bernard Wall (London: Collins, 1969), pp. 87–88. See also, Popper, *Poverty of Historicism*, p. 135.

27. *WTW*, p. 285.

28. *SC*, p. 42.

29. *FM*, p. 188.

30. "Comment je vois," p. 18.

31. *PM*, p. 261

32. *MSS.*, pp. 119–20.

33. *Relig.*, p. 50.

Chapter II   The Shapes of Evil

1. The two words are used interchangeably; see *Werke, Ergänzungsband*, i. 512, 521. Marx publicly ridiculed and discarded the term "alienation" in the Manifesto of 1848.

2. Paul Tillich, *Systematic Theology* (London: Nisbet, 1957), 2:61.

3. Ibid., 2:53.

4. *Lecture on Romans*, trans. and ed. Wilhelm Pauck, *The Library of Christian Classics*, vol. 15 (London: SCM, 1961), pp. 167–68.

5. *Systematic Theology*, 2:60.

6. One such essay is preserved: "Die Vereinigung der Gläubigen mit Christo nach Joh. 15, 1–14 . . ." (1835) (*Werke, Ergänzungsband,* i. pp. 598–601). In *Capt.* I, Marx quotes Luther four times—on exploitation, monopolies and usury—all approvingly (pp. 93, 150, 293, 373).

7. R. H. Tawney, *Religion and the Rise of Capitalism* (London: Penguin, 1938), p. 48.

8. Marcuse, *Soviet Marxism* (London: Routledge and Kegan Paul, 1958), pp. 200–201, and Hans Urs von Balthasar, *Man in History* (London and Sydney: Sheed and Ward, 1968), pp. 57–58.

9. Luther, *The Bondage of the Will*, trans. J. I. Packer and O. R. Johnston (Westwood, New Jersey: Revell, 1957), pp. 103–4.

10. Marx and Engels, *The Holy Family or Critique of Critical Critique*, trans. R. Dixon (Moscow: Foreign Languages Publishing House, 1956), p. 52. See Helmut Thielicke, *Theological Ethics*, ed. William H. Lazareth (London: Black, 1968), 1: 167–70.

11. *Capt.* I, p. 307; cf. p. 31; *MSS.*, p. 95.

12. Marx, *Selected Essays*, trans H. J. Stenning (London: Parsons, 1926), p. 92.

13. *Capt.* I, p. 105.

14. Ibid., p. 89.

15. Ibid., p. 88.

16. Ibid., pp. 171, 176, 211.

17. Marx and Engels, *Manifesto of the Communist Party*, ed. Frederick Engels, trans. Samuel Moore, *Great Books*, vol. 50, p. 422.

18. *Capt.* I, pp. 176–77.

19. Marx and Engels, *Selected Works* (Moscow: Foreign Languages Publishing House, 1951), 1: 325–26.

20. *Lecture on Romans*, p. 159.

21. *Holy*, pp. 162–63; cf. *Manif.*, pp. 420–21.

22. *MSS.*, pp. 140–41.

23. On ideology, see Marx and Engels, *The German Ideology*, pts. I and III, ed. R. Pascal (New York: International, 1947), pp. 24, 39, 40–42, and *Capital*, vol. III, ed. Frederick Engels, trans. Ernest Untermann (Chicago: Kerr, 1915), pp. 705–6.

24. *Essays*, p. 76.

25. Marcuse, *Reason and Revolution*, employs the term "reification" (*Verdinglichung*) as a synonym for alienation (p. 279). The concept was originally developed at length by Georg Lukacs, *History and Class Consciousness*, trans. Rodney Livingstone (London: Merlin, 1971), especially pp. 83–222.

26. *Corres.*, pp. 224, 228.

27. *Letters from a Traveller*, ed. Claude Aragonnes, trans. René Hague et al., with a memoir, "The Man" by Pierre Leroy (London: Collins, 1962), p. 207; cf. *The Vision of the Past*, trans. J. M. Cohen (London: Collins, 1966), p. 191.

28. *Germ.*, p. 37.

29. *PM*, p. 249.

30. *LT*, pp. 100–01.

31. *LLZ*, p. 80; *FM*, pp. 272–81, and Robert Speaight, *Teilhard de Chardin* (London: Collins, 1967), pp. 289–90.

32. *FM*, p. 283.

33. *FM*, p. 140; *LT*, p. 328; *FM*, pp. 194, 240–41.

34. *FM*, p. 195.

35. *FM*, p. 230.

36. *SC*, p. 101; cf. *AE*, p. 160.

37. *FM*, pp.171–72.

38. *WTW*, pp. 56, 283; cf. *Letters from Paris 1912–1914*, trans. Michael Mazzarese (New York: Herder and Herder, 1967), p. 152, and *The Making of a Mind: Letters from a Soldier-Priest 1914–1919*, trans. René Hague (London: Collins, 1965), p. 183.

39. Speaight, *Teilhard*, p. 269.

40. *PM*, p. 159.

41. *PM*, pp. 238, 244.

42. *PM*, pp. 256–57; cf. *MPN*, pp. 100–101.

43. In "Le coeur de la matière," unpub., Teilhard recorded his first longing for the "uniquely sufficient and uniquely necessary," and the important trauma produced by the appearance of change in the "absolute" nature of his rock and metals collection (pp. 2–6). These childhood anxieties were to continue to the end of his life (*LT*, p. 338). In 1916 we hear him speaking of his vulnerability to depersonalization and ennui (*MM*, pp. 100–07); isolated and sentenced to silence in China at the beginning of World War II, Teilhard was "at times prostrated by fits of weeping, and . . . appeared to be on the verge of despair." It was overcome, Fr. Leroy recalls, by the strength of his own will and the depth of his Christian resources (*LT*, p. 36). For one of Marx's rare introspective allusions to his own sense of isolation, see *Letters to Dr. Kugelmann* (London: Lawrence, 1934), p. 138.

44. *PM*, p. 230. Christopher F. Mooney, *Teilhard de Chardin and the Mystery of Christ* (London: Collins, 1966), has called attention to the importance of the word "issue" as a fundamental orientation of Teilhard's psychology (p. 17).

45. *LT*, p. 269.

46. *MM*, p. 145; cf. *FM*, p. 237.

47. *MD*, p. 73; cf. pp. 58–63, and *Hymn of the Universe*, trans. Simon Bartholomew (London: Collins, 1965), p. 31.

48. "Explanations of the Disputation Concerning the Value of Indulgences," quoted in Heinrich Bornkamm, *Luther's World of Thought*, trans. Martin H. Bertram (St. Louis: Concordia, 1958), p. 170.

49. *HE*, p. 50.

50. *MD*, p. 87.

51. *WTW*, p. 230; cf. *PM*, p. 245; *HE*, p. 88.

52. *MD*, p. 68.

53. *MD*, pp. 69–70.

54. *LT*, p. 353; cf. pp. 350, 352, 359.

55. *MSS*, p. 131.

56. *MM*, p. 144.

57. Josef Pieper, *Hope and History*, trans. Richard and Clara Winston (London: Burns and Oates, 1969), p. 69. The first to ask a similar question of Teilhard was Maurice Blondel in their *Correspondence* (with Auguste Valensin), trans. William Whitman (New York: Herder and Herder, 1967), p. 44.

58. *MPN*, p. 117, and Engels, *Dialectics of Nature*, trans. C. Dutt (Moscow: Foreign Languages Publishing House, 1954), p. 54; cf. pp. 49–50, 387–88.

59. *HE*, p. 40; *PM* p. 231; *FM*, pp. 41–42, 296; *SC*, pp. 42–43.

Chapter III   The Origin and Nature of Evil

1. *Capt*. I, p. 80; cf. p. 253.

2. Ibid., p. 354.

3. *The City of God*, IV, 4, quoted in Luther, *Lecture on Romans*, p. 38. The great pioneer in the quest for the cause of sin was Augustine of Hippo. His struggle with a variety of explanations of the first evil will shaped and limited theological options for centuries. Augustine vacillated between two basic positions: pride and the inherent weakness of free creatures. Augustine's answer, which established pride as the queen of the sins, is one to which most theological traditions continue to pay homage. Among those anti-theists, such as Marx, who developed other explanations of evil, the Augustinian influence endured in tattered remnants. See Robert F. Brown, "The First Evil Will Must Be Incomprehensible: A Critique of Augustine," *Journal of the American Academy of Religion* 46, no. 3 (September 1978):316–17.

4. *Germ.*, p. 92.

5. Marx, *Pre-Capitalist Economic Formations*, ed. E. J. Hobsbawm, trans. Jack Cohen (London: Lawrence and Wishart, 1964), p. 81; cf. pp. 71–72. As in Teilhard de Chardin, primitive man is always a tribe or family. There is no question of a first couple. See *Capt*. I, pp. 171–72, n.

6. *Pre-Capt.*, pp. 71–73; cf. *Capt*. I, pp. 171–72.

7. *The Poverty of Philosophy* (Moscow: Foreign Languages Publishing House, n.d.), p. 36. Some of the Fathers, e.g., St. John Chrysostum and St. Basil, also described private property as a direct result of the Fall, but it remained for the proto-Marxist Digger Gerrard Winstanley to describe the Fall as the result of "particular property." See Reinhold Niebuhr, *The Children of Light and the Children of Darkness* (New York: Scribner's, 1944), pp. 91–92, 96, and *The Works of Gerrard Winstanley*, ed. George Sabine (Ithaca, N.Y.: Cornell University Press, 1941), p. 270.

8. *Capt*. I, p. 293 n.

9. Ibid., pp. 293–94.

10. *Religion within the Limits of Reason Alone*, trans. T. M. Greene and H. H. Hudson (New York: Harper, 1960), pp. 34–36.

11. *Sel. Wks*. II, p. 153.

12. *Germ.*, pp. 7, 15–19; *Capt*. I, pp. 171–72 n.

13. *Pov. Phil.*, p. 144.

14. *Germ.*, p. 29.

15. *Corres.*, p. 40.

16. *Capt*. I, p. 7.

17. Nicholas Berdyaev, *Christianity and the Class War*, trans. Donald Attwater (London: Sheed and Ward, 1933), p. 109.

18. *The Convergent Spirit* (London: Routledge and Kegan Paul, 1963), pp. 166–67.

19. *Werke, Ergänzungsband*, i, p. 608.

Kant and Fichte sail the sky,
Seeking there a distant land,
While my experience on the street
Is all that I can understand!

20. *Novum Organum*, II, 40, *Great Books*, vol. 30.

21. Marx could only associate the greatness of Aeschylus and Shakespeare (arising as it did from primitive economic milieux) with the artless truth of childhood. Their present appeal in a completely different economic situation reflects man's need and inability to reproduce the truth of childhood on a more sophisticated plane (*Grundrisse*, ed. and trans. David McLellan, London: Macmillan, 1971, pp. 44–46). Marx should have realized that it is precisely those qualities most distantly removed from the infantile or the simple for which Aeschylus and Shakespeare are today revered.

22. M. M. Bober, *Karl Marx's Interpretation of History*, 2nd ed. revised, Harvard Economic Studies 41 (Cambridge, Mass.: Harvard University Press, 1948), p. 318; cf. pp. 321–23.

23. *PM*, p. 64.

24. *An Essay on Man* (New York: Doubleday, 1954), p. 119.

25. *Corres*., pp. 498–500. My italics.

26. *PM*, p. 120.

27. *AM*, p. 32; cf. *HE*, p. 60 n. and *Christianity and Evolution*, trans. René Hague (New York: Harcourt, Brace Jovanovich, 1971): "Adam and Eve are images of mankind pressing on toward God" (p. 52).

28. *VP*, p. 154; *PM*, pp. 97–99.

29. *VP*, p. 135; cf. p. 131.

30. *CE*, pp. 50, 191–93.

31. *Perspectives de l'homme*, 2nd ed. (Paris: Presses Universitaires de France, 1960), p. 184. Cf. *PM*, pp. 97–99, and Engels, *Dialectics of Nature*, p. 339.

32. *Dialectics of Nature*, pp. 268–69.

33. *SC*, p. 180.

34. *CE*, p. 47. In *CE* see the essays, "Note on Some Possible Historical Representations of Original Sin" (pp. 45–55) and "Reflections on Original Sin" (pp. 187–98).

35. Teilhard adds in a footnote, "Accordingly one can say that there is room *in this interval* for anything that a trans-experimental source of knowledge might demand" (*PM*, p. 186 and n.).

36. *CE*, p. 210. This is probably an unconscious reaction to the gross and speculative exaggerations of Adam's prelapsarian mental and physical prowess which are scattered throughout western theology.

37. *CE*, pp. 209–10. Cf. *PM*, pp. 187–89 n. The race Teilhard called "type X of

humanity," which "took over" from its nonhuman neighbors, the Australopithecines. The place he believed to be central or southern Africa, and the time, the early Quaternary Age (*AM*, pp. 198–204).

38. C.S. Lewis, "Poem for Psychoanalysts and/or Theologians," *Poems*, ed. W. Hooper (London: Bless, 1964), p. 113.

39. *The Confessions*, trans. E. B. Pusey, *Great Books*, vol. 18, XII, 4–6, and *WTW*, p. 95; cf. p. 63.

40. *HU*, pp. 68–69.

41. *HE*, p. 57.

42. P. B. Medawar, *The Art of the Soluble* (Harmondsworth, England: Penguin, 1969), raises this and many other objections to Teilhard's use of anthropomorphism and analogy (pp. 88–89).

43. *Hominisation*, trans. W. T. O'Hara (Freiburg: Herder, 1965), p. 47.

44. Oliver Rabut, *Dialogue with Teilhard de Chardin* (London: Sheed and Ward, 1961), p. 36–39.

45. *PM*, pp. 168–69.

46. *Hominisation*, p. 50.

47. "Comment je vois," unpub., p. 18.

48. Ibid., p. 19. Note the resemblances between Teilhard's and the Eastern church's doctrine of creation. See the remarks of Paul Evodokimov, *L'Orthodoxie*, quoted in John Hick, *Evil and the God of Love* (London: Collins, 1968), pp. 223–24.

49. Ibid., p. 19, and *CE*, p. 51.

50. *SC*, p. 128.

51. *FM*, p. 134.

52. Ibid., p. 253 n.

53. *WTW*, p. 71; cf. *CE*, p. 53, and *PM*, p. 312.

54. *CE*, p. 51.

55. Ibid., p. 84 and n.

56. The "infrahuman," e.g., deformity, pain, illness, is to be distinguished from the evil which proceeds directly from the person (Piet Schoonenberg, *Man and Sin*, trans. Joseph Donceel, London; Sheed and Ward, 1965, p. 41). In Teilhard there are physical modalities of sin. See *HE*, pp. 85–88; *MD*, p. 61.

57. *CE*, pp. 39–40.

58. *HE*, p. 87.

59. *S. Theol.* I, q. 93, a. 8.

60. Luther, *The Smalcald Articles*, I, *The Book of Concord*, ed. T. G. Tappert, trans. T. G. Tappert et al. (Philadelphia: Fortress, 1959); Søren Kierkegaard, *The Concept of Dread*, trans. Walter Lowrie (Princeton: Princeton University Press, 1957), pp. 84–85; Emil Brunner, *Man in Revolt*, trans. Olive Wyon (London: Lutterworth, 1939), p. 421.

61. *On Free Choice of the Will*, trans. A. S. Benjamin and L. H. Hackstaff (Indianapolis: Bobbs-Merrill, 1964), I, 15. On the neutrality of hierarchical systems before man's corruption of them see *S. Theol.* I, q. 96, a. 4.

62. This is also Schoonenberg's approach in *Man and Sin*, pp. 45–46, 195.

63. *MD*, p. 142.

64. *Germ.*, p. 29.

65. *PM*, p. 221, and *SC*, p. 94.

Chapter IV   Against Christianity

1. Leslie Dewart, *The Future of Belief* (New York: Herder and Herder, 1966), pp. 55–57; Rahner, "The Teaching of the Second Vatican Council on Atheism," *Concilium* 3 (March 1967): 5–13; Fromm, *Marx's Concept of Man*, p. 64; Garaudy, *From Anathema to Dialogue*, trans. Luke O'Neill (New York: Herder and Herder, 1966), pp. 90–92; Teilhard, *FM*, pp. 266–67.

2. N. Lobkowicz, "Karl Marx's Attitude Toward Religion," *The Review of Politics* 26, no. 3 (July 1964): 329–30. On the expediency of Herschel (later Heinrich) Marx's conversion, see the authoritative biography by David McLellan, *Karl Marx* (New York: Harper & Row, 1973), pp. 4–5, against the defense of the elder Marx's motives in Franz Mehring, *Karl Marx*, trans. Edward Fitzgerald (London: Bodley Head, 1936), pp. 2–4.

3. Cited in Mehring, *Karl Marx*, p. 46.

4. *MSS.*, p. 140.

5. *Relig.*, p. 41.

6. Ludwig Feuerbach, *The Essence of Christianity*, trans. George Eliot (Marian Evans) with an Introductory Essay by Karl Barth, trans. James Luther Adams (New York: Harper & Row, 1957), p. 33.

7. Barth, "Introductory Essay," p. xxxviii.

8. Nathan Rotenstreich, *Basic Problems of Marx's Philosophy* (Indianapolis: Bobbs-Merrill, 1965), provides a brief etymological and theological sketch of the positive meanings of *alienatio* (pp. 144–49).

9. *Lecture on Romans*, pp. 25–26.

10. *Werke*, I, pp. 26–27. Marx's uncritical acceptance of Feuerbach surfaces in his many terse, if not crude, restatements and applications of the Feuerbachian criticism of religion: *Relig.*, p. 41; *MSS.*, pp. 99, 146, 165–66; *Germ.*, p. 1; *Holy*, pp. 230–33; *The German Ideology*, pt. II, trans. Clemens Dutt (Moscow: Progress, 1964), pp. 201, 275–76; *Capt.* I, p. 31.

11. *Essays*, p. 62.

12. *Theology of Culture*, ed. Robert C. Kimball (New York: Oxford University Press, 1959), p. 10.

13. *Relig.*, p. 42. The source of this passage's language as well as its content is Feuerbach's discussion of prayer in *The Essence of Christianity*, p. 122.

14. Jürgen Moltmann, "Toward a Political Hermeneutics of the Gospel," *New Theology No. 6*, ed. Martin E. Marty and Dean G. Peerman (London: Macmillan, 1969), p. 69. On the cross as protest, see J. G. Davies, *Christians, Politics, and Violent Revolution* (Maryknoll, N.Y.: Orbis Books, 1976), pp. 157–58.

15. *Theology of Culture*, p. 22 (all italicized).

16. Nor did Marx show appreciation for Engels's explanation of the "universality of religion" based on the universal "urge to personify" (*Anti-Dühring*, Moscow: Foreign Languages Publishing House, 1954, p. 480). In *Dialectics of Nature* Engels also said that needs cannot be taken as proof of God or an absolute (p. 269). Yet in that same work Engels revealed his own need for an absolute by his obstinate belief in the everlasting nature of mind (p. 54). As a young man Engels confessed an enthusiastic admiration of Schleiermacher's

religion of the heart (*Werke, Ergänzungsband*, ii, pp. 403–9).

17. *Essays*, pp. 59, 66–67.

18. *Anti-Dühring*, pp. 438–39; *Corres.*, p. 505; also *Dialectics of Nature*, p. 238. Following Bruno Bauer, the young Marx saw Christianity as a direct descendant of Platonism (*Werke, Ergänzungsband*, i, p. 223), but he soon revealed more interest in the material rather than philosophical origins of Christianity.

19. *The Sacred and the Profane*, trans. Willard H. Trask (New York and Evanston: Harper & Row, 1961), p. 17.

20. *Germ.* II, p. 162.

21. "The Idea of a Christian Society" in *Christianity and Culture* (New York: Harcourt Brace, 1940), pp. 46–47.

22. *Capt.* I, pp. 111, 113, 237, 293, 295–96, 301, 381, and Max Weber, *The Protestant Ethic and the Spirit of Capitalism*, trans. Talcott Parsons (London: Allen & Unwin, 1930), pp. 157–59, 172.

23. Zinzendorf, quoted by Weber, p. 264 n., and John Wesley, quoted by Weber, p. 175.

24. *Essays*, pp. 88, 92–96. Cf. Weber, p. 165.

25. Tawney, *Religion and the Rise of Capitalism*, p. 47.

26. Quoted in *Essays*, p. 110. See A. F. Young and E. T. Ashton, *British Social Work in the Nineteenth Century* (London: Routledge and Kegan Paul, 1956), pp. 29–30, and J. L. and Barbara Hammond, *The Town Labourer, 1760–1832* (London: Longmans, 1966), pp. 220–21.

27. This in addition to Marx's charge that the Roman Catholic church justified out of self-interest the slavery of antiquity and the serfdom of the Middle Ages (*Relig.*, p. 83).

28. *Institutes of the Christian Religion*, 2 vols., trans. Henry Beveridge (London: Clarke, 1962), Bk. III, ch. vii, 5; cf. Bk. III, ch. vii, 9.

29. *MSS.*, p. 144.

30. Quoted in *Capt.* I, p. 320.

31. *Lectures on Galatians* (1535), trans. Jaroslav Pelikan, *Luther's Works*, vol. 26, ed. Jaroslav Pelikan (St. Louis: Concordia, 1963), p. 116.

32. *Relig.*, p. 41.

33. *Relig.*, p. 51. Cf. Luther, *Lectures on Galatians*, p. 18.

34. *CE*, p. 119 n. Cf. pp. 119–208, 237–43.

35. See *CE*, pp . 125–26.

36. *WTW*, p. 90.

37. *WTW*, p. 244, and *MD*, p. 71.

38. *SC*, p. 109.

39. *CE*, p. 128.

40. *HE*, p. 156.

41. *FM*, p. 260.

42. How would Marx react to José P. Miranda, *Marx and the Bible*, trans. John Eagleson (Maryknoll, N.Y.: Orbis Books, 1974), an exegetical *tour de force* which implicates Israel's Yahweh in the struggle for liberation? Or Gustavo Gutiérrez, *A Theology of Liberation*, trans. and ed. Caridad Inda and John Eagleson (Maryknoll, N.Y.: Orbis Books, 1973)?

Chapter V   The Transformation of Man

1. A law is a theoretical statement concerning the ordering of particular phenomena which, so far as known, is invariable under given conditions. The unavoidable subjective elements of historiography plus the unrepeatable nature of history itself rule out the possibility of historical laws. No one has made this point more vigorously than Sir Karl Popper, especially in *The Poverty of Historicism*.

2. This is Engels's summary in *Dialectics of Nature*, p. 83.

3. Hegel, *Science of Logic*, trans. A. V. Miller (London: Allen and Unwin, 1969), pp. 54, 107–8, 129–32.

4. *Capt.* I, p. 378. Engels's historical application of dialectics is even more grandiose. He begins with primitive communism, which is negated in all forms of private property, which phase is finally sublated in a qualitatively higher form of common ownership (*Anti-Dühring*, p. 191).

5. *Holy*, p. 125; cf. *Germ.*, pp. 18–19, 38–39, 42–43.

6. Marx to Kugelmann: "He [Dühring] knows very well that my method of development is *not* Hegelian, since I am a materialist and Hegel is an idealist. *Hegel's dialectics is the basic form of all dialectics*, but only *after* it has been stripped of its mystical form . . ." (*Corres.*, p. 240, my emphasis).

7. *Germ.*, II, pp. 229–30, 412, 414.

8. *Sel. Wks.* II, pp. 102–8.

9. *Capt.* I, p. 372; *Capt.* I, p. 113; *Sel. Wks.* I, p. 198.

10. *Sel. Wks.* I, p. 109. In a speech before the Hague Congress of the International, Marx cited England and the U.S.A. as possible exceptions to the need for violence in the proletarian revolution (*On Britain*, 2nd ed., Moscow: Foreign Languages Publishing House, 1962, pp. 494–95).

11. *Essays*, p. 137.

12. *Sel. Wks.* I, pp. 103–4.

13. *Anti-Dühring*, p. 131, and Popper, *The Open Society and Its Enemies*, 3rd ed. rev. (London: Routledge and Kegan Paul, 1957), 2:206.

14. See *The Civil War in the United States*, ed. Richard Enmale (London: Lawrence and Wishart, n.d.), p. 282. On Marx's rebuttal of love and the general interest see *Germ.* II, p. 267. His discourse on ethics was brief: " . . . I do not give a damn for 'intentions' " (*Corres.*, p. 376). On the Christian's participation in violent revolution, see Thielicke, *Theological Ethics*, II, *Politics*, 333–46, and J. G. Davies, *Christians, Politics and Violent Revolution*, pp. 143–44, 166–80.

15. *Manif.*, p. 424.

16. *Sel. Wks.* I, p. 136.

17. *Sel. Wks.* I, pp. 99–100.

18. T. S. Eliot, *Murder in the Cathedral* (London: Faber and Faber, 1935), Pt. I, p. 40.

19. *Sel. Wks.* II, pp. 365–66.

20. Marcuse, *One-Dimensional Man* (London: Routledge and Kegan Paul, 1964), p. 41.

21. For what follows see the *Lectures on the Philosophy of Religion*, trans. E. B. Speirs and J. Burdon Sanderson, ed. E. B. Speirs (London: Kegan Paul,

Trench, Trübner, 1895), 1: 66–70; 3: 71–75, 81–98, and *The Phenomenology of Mind*, trans. J. B. Baillie, 2nd ed. rev. (London: Allen and Unwin, 1949), pp. 251, 759–61, 780–81.

22. *Sel. Wks.* I, pp. 225–27.

23. *WTW*, p. 154. For other Hegelian expressions, see *WTW*, p. 41, 168; *VP*, pp. 133–34, 232; *HE*, pp. 22–24, 95–99; *LLZ*, pp. 86–87; *LT*, pp. 150–51. Like Hegel, Teilhard used the word "spirit" interchangeably with "mind" (=Geist=Consciousness).

24. *HE*, pp. 23, 39.

25. F. G. Elliott, "The World-Vision of Teilhard de Chardin," *International Philosophical Quarterly* 1, no. 4 (December 1961): 627–28.

26. *PM*, p. 285.

27. *CE*, p. 87; cf. *VP*, p. 213; *PM*, p. 109; *FM*, pp. 28ff.

28. *VP*, p. 263. The young Marx said almost precisely the same thing, but later reversed himself (*MSS.*, p. 137).

29. The prince goes on to substantiate his belief in progress by means of the same examples Teilhard offers, e.g., modern transportation, rapidity of communication, the growth of science and industry (quoted in J. B. Bury, *The Idea of Progress*, London: Macmillan, 1920, p. 330). In his list of great philosophers Teilhard included Herbert Spencer in the company of Aristotle, Spinoza, Leibnitz, and Hegel (*AE*, p. 99).

30. Collingwood, *The Idea of History* (Oxford: Clarendon, 1946), p. 322.

31. Bury, *The Idea of Progress*, p. 336; *PM*, p. 286 n.

32. *FM*, p. 228.

33. *SC*, pp. 62, 164; *CE*, p. 88; and St. Irenaeus, *Five Books Against Heresies*, trans. John Keble, *A Library of Fathers of the Holy Catholic Church* (London, Oxford, and Cambridge: Parker and Rivingtons, 1872), II, 22, iv; III, 18, i; cf. Eph. 1:9–10 and Rom. 5:12–21.

34. *SC*, pp. 54–66.

35. *WTW*, p. 298.

36. Emile Mersch, *The Whole Christ*, trans. John R. Kelly (London: Dobson, 1938), p. 265. See *SC*, p. 58.

37. *CE*, p. 88.

38. *HU*, p. 19.

39. *Against Heresies*, IV, 38, i.

40. Mersch, pp. 241, 317.

41. *SC*, p. 55 n.; *CE*, p. 128.

42. *SC*, p. 213; in a similar context he wrote, "Evolution is holy" (*WTW*, p. 59). See also *SC*, p. 190, and *CE*, p. 129.

43. On the cross, see *MD*, p. 87; *WTW*, pp. 68, 71; and *SC*, p. 36. In "Christ the Evolver," *CE*, pp. 146–48, he aligned the kingdom of God with progress and Christian rebirth with biological becoming.

44. *HE*, p. 91.

45. *CE*, pp. 44, 158–59.

46. "Comment je vois," unpub., p. 21. Cf. *CE*, p. 236.

47. *SC*, pp. 163, 167; *HE*, p. 149; *SC*, p. 148.

48. *CE*, p. 128 n.

49. *PM*, p. 31; *FM*, p. 19.

50. *WTW*, p. 162; *PM*, p. 33.

51. *PM*, p. 233.

52. *WTW*, p. 257.

53. von Balthasar, *Man in History*, p. 35. Cf. Heb. 3:7; 4:7; 2 Cor. 4:2; Isa. 49:8.

54. *MD*, p. 43.

55. *Letters to Two Friends*, trans. Helen Weaver (New York: New American Library, 1968), p. 128.

56. *SC*, p. 75.

57. *B-T*, p. 26.

58. *WTW*, pp. 88, 187–88; *SC*, pp. 214 ff.; *LT*, p. 344.

59. *HU*, p. 69. On Augustine's use of *uti* and *frui*, and ordered and disordered love, see Anders Nygren, *Agape and Eros*, trans. A. G. Herbert (vol. 1) and Philip S. Watson (vols. 2 and 3) (London: SPCK, 1932–39), 3:286–89. Nygren would undoubtedly classify Teilhard's idea of love as a Christianized *eros*.

60. *HE*, pp. 145–46.

61. *CE*, pp. 91–92.

62. *FM*, p. 204. Of the notion of progress Kant (*Religion within the Limits of Reason Alone*, p. 15) said, "If this belief, however, is meant to apply to moral goodness and badness . . . it has certainly not been deduced from experience; the history of all times cries too loudly against it."

63. *HE*, p. 109; *PM*, p. 110. For further examples of Teilhard's morality of progress, see *HE*, pp. 29, 106; *FM*, pp. 17, 90–91; *AM*, p. 243 n.

Chapter VI   The New Communities and the End of History

1. *Revelation as History*, ed. Wolfhart Pannenberg, trans. David Granskou (New York: Macmillan, 1968), p. 131.

2. *Manif.*, p. 428. See the ten points of the *Manifesto*, p. 429, many of which Marx later realized had already been accomplished in such countries as Switzerland and the U.S.A.

3. Mehring, *Karl Marx*, p. 329.

4. *Letters*, p. 107.

5. For example, the end of conscription (by arming the citizenry), remission of rent payments, democratic election of government officials, wage ceilings, nationalization of church property, abolishment of capital punishment, end of night work for bakers (cf. *Sel. Wks.* I, p. 434).

6. I say with calculation because his private remarks indicated an attitude of disenchantment toward the very myth he was creating (cf. *Corres.*, p. 304). With the rise of the Commune, Marx wrote, exploitation, thievery, and murder ceased; even the cocottes fled to Versailles. "In their stead, the real women of Paris showed again at the surface—heroic, noble, and devoted, like the women of antiquity. Working, thinking, fighting, bleeding Paris—almost forgetful, in its incubation of a new society, of the cannibals at its gates—radiant in the enthusiasm of its historical initiative" (*Sel. Wks.* I, p. 480). The Commune lasted two months.

7. *Corres.*, p. 410. On the Commune's strategic blunders, see *Letters*, p. 123.

8. This is Tillich's accurate judgment in *Der Mensch im Christentums und im*

Marxismus (Stuttgart and Düsseldorf: Ring Verlag, 1953), p. 17.

9. *Grund.*, pp. 141–43; cf. *Capt.* I, p. 35; *Capt.* III, pp. 954–55.

10. *Sel. Wks.* II, pp. 20–21.

11. *Sel. Wks.* I, p. 203.

12. *Capt.* III, pp. 954–55; cf. *Grund.*, p. 142; *Pre-Capt.*, pp. 84–85.

13. Garaudy, *From Anathema to Dialogue*, p. 94; Marcuse, *One-Dimensional Man*, p. 16; *MSS.*, p. 136.

14. *Germ.*, p. 74; cf. on personalism *Germ.*, pp. 28, 68, 70; *Werke*, IV, p. 377; *Grund.*, pp. 17, 142, 151; *Capt.* I, p. 292.

15. *Sel. Wks.* II, p. 330.

16. *Werke, Ergänzungsband*, i, pp. 462–63.

17 *Sel. Wks.* I, p. 441.

18. *MSS.*, p. 189. Proudhon wrote to Marx: "Because we stand in the van of a new movement let us not make ourselves the protagonists of a new intolerance; let us not act like apostles of a new religion, even if it be a religion of logic, a religion of reason" (cited in Martin Buber, *Paths in Utopia*, trans. R.F.C. Hull, London: Routledge and Kegan Paul, 1949, pp. 12–13). The new intolerance was to be salted with tactical concessions to religious liberty, as in Marx's "Critique of the Gotha Program," *Sel. Wks.* II, p. 33.

19. *AE*, p. 402; *FM*, p. 167.

20. Rabut, *Dialogue with Teilhard*, p. 159.

21. *MM*, p. 64.

22. *MM*, pp. 232–33; *AM*, p. 161; cf. *LT*, p. 220; *LLZ*, p. 117; *Building the Earth*, trans. Noel Lindsay (London: Chapman, 1965), pp. 26–27.

23. The year "The Salvation of Mankind" was written; *SC*, pp. 142–43.

24. *BE*, pp. 26–27; *LT*, p. 220.

25. *HE*, p. 133. On eugenics, *PM*, pp. 282–83; *HE*, p. 127; *LTF*, pp. 186–87.

26. *MD*, p. 40.

27. Tillich, *Theology of Culture*, p. 8. Rev. 21:22–23.

28. 2 Tim. 3:1–9; Matt. 24:6–12; and *PM*, pp. 288–89; *MD*, pp. 141–43. Of Teilhard's belief in hell, despite the note of dissonance it conveys to his philosophy of convergence, Rideau writes, "There could be no better evidence that he did not allow his system to run away with him . . ." (p. 188).

29. *SC*, p. 85.

Other Orbis books . . .

THE MEANING OF MISSION

José Comblin

"This very readable book has made me think, and I feel it will be useful for anyone dealing with their Christian role of mission and evangelism." *New Review of Books and Religion*
ISBN 0-88344-304-X CIP   *Cloth $6.95*

THE GOSPEL OF PEACE AND JUSTICE

Catholic Social Teaching Since Pope John

Presented by Joseph Gremillion

"Especially valuable as a resource. The book brings together 22 documents containing the developing social teaching of the church from *Mater et Magistra* to Pope Paul's 1975 *Peace Day Message on Reconciliation*. I watched the intellectual excitement of students who used Gremillion's book in a justice and peace course I taught last summer, as they discovered a body of teaching on the issues they had defined as relevant. To read Gremillion's overview and prospectus, a meaty introductory essay of some 140 pages, is to be guided through the sea of social teaching by a remarkably adept navigator."
National Catholic Reporter
   "An authoritative guide and study aid for concerned Catholics and others." *Library Journal*
ISBN 0-88344-165-9   *Cloth $15.95*
ISBN 0-88344-166-7   *Paper $8.95*

THEOLOGY IN THE AMERICAS

Papers of the 1975 Detroit Conference

Edited by Sergio Torres and John Eagleson

"A pathbreaking book from and about a pathbreaking theological conference, *Theology in the Americas* makes a major contribution to ecumenical theology, Christian social ethics and liberation movements in dialogue." *Fellowship*
ISBN 0-88344-479-8 CIP   *Cloth $12.95*
ISBN 0-88344-476-3   *Paper $5.95*

CHRISTIANS, POLITICS
AND VIOLENT REVOLUTION

J.G. Davies

"Davies argues that violence and revolution are on the agenda the world presents to the Church and that consequently the Church must reflect on such problems. This is a first-rate presentation, with Davies examining the question from every conceivable angle."

National Catholic News Service

ISBN 0-88344-061-X

Paper $4.95

CHRISTIAN POLITICAL THEOLOGY
A MARXIAN GUIDE

Joseph Petulla

"Petulla presents a fresh look at Marxian thought for the benefit of Catholic theologians in the light of the interest in this subject which was spurred by Vatican II, which saw the need for new relationships with men of all political positions." *Journal of Economic Literature*

ISBN 0-88344-060-1

Paper $4.95

THE NEW CREATION:
MARXIST AND CHRISTIAN?

José María González-Ruiz

"A worthy book for lively discussion."

The New Review of Books and Religion

ISBN 0-88344-327-9 CIP

Cloth $6.95

CHRISTIANS AND SOCIALISM

Documentation of the Christians for
Socialism Movement in Latin America

Edited by John Eagleson

"Compelling in its clear presentation of the issue of Christian commitment in a revolutionary world." *The Review of Books and Religion*

ISBN 0-88344-058-X

Paper $4.95

THE CHURCH AND
THIRD WORLD REVOLUTION
Pierre Bigo

"Heavily documented, provocative yet reasonable, this is a testament, demanding but impressive." *Publishers Weekly*

ISBN 0-88344-071-7 CIP   *Cloth $8.95*
ISBN 0-88344-072-5   *Paper $4.95*

WHY IS THE THIRD WORLD POOR?
Piero Gheddo

"An excellent handbook on the Christian understanding of the development process. Gheddo looks at both the internal and external causes of underdevelopment and how Christians can involve themselves in helping the third world." *Provident Book Finder*

ISBN 0-88344-757-6   *Paper $4.95*

POLITICS AND SOCIETY
IN THE THIRD WORLD
Jean-Yves Calvez

"This frank treatment of economic and cultural problems in developing nations suggests the need for constant multiple attacks on the many fronts that produce problems in the human situation."

The Christian Century
ISBN 0-88344-389-9   *Cloth $6.95*

A THEOLOGY OF LIBERATION
Gustavo Gutiérrez

"The movement's most influential text." *Time*

"The most complete presentation thus far available to English readers of the provocative theology emerging from the Latin American Church." *Theological Studies*

"North Americans as well as Latin Americans will find so many challenges and daring insights that they will, I suggest, rate this book one of the best of its kind ever written." *America*

ISBN 0-88344-477-1   *Cloth $7.95*
ISBN 0-88344-478-X   *Paper $4.95*

MARX AND THE BIBLE

José Miranda

"An inescapable book which raises more questions than it answers, which will satisfy few of us, but will not let us rest easily again. It is an attempt to utilize the best tradition of Scripture scholarship to understand the text when it is set in a context of human need and misery."

Walter Brueggemann, in Interpretation

ISBN 0-88344-306-6

ISBN 0-88344-307-4

Cloth $8.95

Paper $4.95

BEING AND THE MESSIAH

The Message of Saint John

José Miranda

"This book could become the catalyst of a new debate on the Fourth Gospel. Johannine scholarship will hotly debate the 'terrifyingly revolutionary thesis that this world of contempt and oppression can be changed into a world of complete selflessness and unrestricted mutual assistance.' Cast in the framework of an analysis of contemporary philosophy, the volume will prove a classic of Latin American theology." *Frederick Herzog, Duke University Divinity School*

ISBN 0-88344-027-X CIP

ISBN 0-88344-028-8

Cloth $8.95

Paper $4.95

THE GOSPEL IN SOLENTINAME

Ernesto Cardenal

"Upon reading this book, I want to do so many things—burn all my other books which at best seem like hay, soggy with mildew. I now know who (not what) is the church and how to celebrate church in the eucharist. The dialogues are intense, profound, radical. *The Gospel in Solentiname* calls us home."

Carroll Stuhlmueller, National Catholic Reporter

ISBN 0-88344-168-3

ISBN 0-88344-170-5

ISBN 0-88344-167-5

Vol. 1 Cloth $6.95

Vol. 1 Paper $4.95

Vol. 2 Cloth $6.95

THE CHURCH AND POWER IN BRAZIL
Charles Antoine

"This is a book which should serve as a basis of discussion and further study by all who are interested in the relationship of the Church to contemporary governments, and all who believe that the Church has a vital role to play in the quest for social justice." *Worldmission*
ISBN 0-88344-062-8 *Paper $4.95*

HISTORY AND
THE THEOLOGY OF LIBERATION
Enrique Dussel

"The book is easy reading. It is a brilliant study of what may well be or should be the future course of theological methodology."
Religious Media Today
ISBN 0-88344-179-9 *Cloth $8.95*
ISBN 0-88344-180-2 *Paper $4.95*

DOM HELDER CAMARA
José de Broucker

"De Broucker, an internationally recognized journalist, develops a portrait, at once intimate, comprehensive and sympathetic, of the Archbishop of Olinda and Recife, Brazil, whose championship of political and economic justice for the hungry, unorganized masses of his country and all Latin America has aroused world attention."
America
ISBN 0-88344-099-7 *Cloth $6.95*

THE DESERT IS FERTILE
Dom Helder Camara

"Camara's brief essays and poems are arresting for their simplicity and depth of vision, and are encouraging because of the realistic yet quietly hopeful tone with which they argue for sustained action toward global justice." *Commonweal*
ISBN 0-88344-078-4 *Cloth $3.95*

THEOLOGY FOR A NOMAD CHURCH

Hugo Assmann

"A new challenge to contemporary theology which attempts to show that the theology of liberation is not just a fad, but a new political dimension which touches every aspect of Christian existence."

Publishers Weekly

ISBN 0-88344-493-3
ISBN 0-88344-494-1

Cloth $7.95
Paper $4.95

FREEDOM MADE FLESH
The Mission of Christ and His Church

Ignacio Ellacuría

"Ellacuría's main thesis is that God's saving message and revelation are historical, that is, that the proclamation of the gospel message must possess the same historical character that revelation and salvation history do and that, for this reason, it must be carried out in history and in a historical way." *Cross and Crown*

ISBN 0-88344-140-3
ISBN 0-88344-141-1

Cloth $8.95
Paper $4.95

THE LIBERATION OF THEOLOGY

Juan Luis Segundo

"It is a remarkable book in terms of its boldness in confronting the shortcomings of the Christian tradition and in terms of the clarity of vision provided by the hermeneutic of liberation. Segundo writes with ease whether dealing with the sociological, theological, or political roots of liberation. His is a significant addition to the recent work of Cone, Alves, Moltmann, and Gutiérrez because it compels the movement to interrogate its own theological foundations. A necessary addition, in one of the more fruitful directions of contemporary theology, it is appropriate for graduate, undergraduate, or clerical readers." *Choice*

"The book makes for exciting reading and should not be missing in any theological library." *Library Journal*

ISBN 0-88344-285-X CIP
ISBN 0-88344-286-8

Cloth $10.95
Paper $6.95